Economics in America

Opposing Viewpoints

Other Books of Related Interest in the Opposing Viewpoints Series:

American Foreign Policy
The American Military
Social Justice
The Welfare State

Additional Books in the Opposing Viewpoints Series:

Abortion
America's Prisons
The Arms Race
Censorship
Central America
Chemical Dependency
Constructing a Life Philosophy
Crime & Criminals
Criminal Justice
Death & Dying
The Death Penalty
The Environmental Crisis
Male/Female Roles
The Middle East
Nuclear War
The Political Spectrum
Problems of Africa
Religion and Human Experience
Science and Religion
Sexual Values
Terrorism
The Vietnam War
War and Human Nature

Economics in America

Opposing Viewpoints

David L. Bender & Bruno Leone, *Series Editors*

Terry O'Neill, Bonnie Szumski,
Susan Bursell, & Julie Zemke,
Book Editors

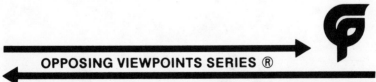

OPPOSING VIEWPOINTS SERIES ®

Greenhaven Press   577 Shoreview Park Road   St. Paul, Minnesota 55126

Library of Congress Cataloging-in-Publication Data

Economics in America.

   (Opposing viewpoints series)
   Bibliography: p.
   Includes index.
   1. United States—Economic policy—1981-
I. O'Neill, Terry, 1944-   . II. Series.
HC106.8.E3   1986   338.973   86-19437
ISBN 0-89908-397-8 (lib. bdg.)
ISBN 0-89908-372-2 (pbk.)

"Congress shall make no law . . . abridging the freedom of speech, or of the press."

First Amendment to the US Constitution

The basic foundation of our democracy is the first amendment guarantee of freedom of expression. The *Opposing Viewpoints Series* is dedicated to the concept of this basic freedom and the idea that it is more important to practice it than to enshrine it.

Contents

Page

Why Consider Opposing Viewpoints?   9

Introduction   13

Chapter 1: What Should Be the Government's Role in Business?

1. Government Involvement Is Essential for a Strong Economy   16
   Gar Alperovitz & Jeff Faux

2. Government Involvement Is Harmful to a Free Economy   23
   George Roche

3. Deregulation Benefits the Economy   30
   Mark Fowler

4. Deregulation Exacts Serious Human Costs   35
   Susan J. Tolchin

5. The Private Sector Is More Efficient than Government   40
   Stephen Moore

6. The Private Sector Is Less Efficient than Government   44
   Gerald W. McEntee

A Critical Thinking Skill: Recognizing Deceptive Arguments   50

Periodical Bibliography   52

Chapter 2: How Serious Is the Budget Deficit?

1. The Deficit Must Be Ended   54
   Lee A. Iacocca

2. The Deficit Is Not a Crisis   58
   Charles R. Morris

3. The Deficit Has Stimulated the Economy   62
   Tom Wicker

4. The Deficit Has Harmed the Economy   65
   Peter G. Peterson

5. Raising Taxes Will Reduce the Deficit   70
   Herbert Stein

6. Raising Taxes Will Not Reduce the Deficit   75
   Bruce Bartlett & Jack Kemp

A Critical Thinking Skill: Distinguishing Between
    Fact & Opinion   80
Periodical Bibliography   82

Chapter 3: What Kind of Taxation Is
Most Appropriate?

1. The Flat Rate Tax Is Fair and Equitable   84
    Philip M. Crane

2. The Flat Rate Tax Will Not Work   89
    Barber B. Conable

3. Taxation to Subsidize the Poor Is Unfair   94
    Howard Baetjer Jr.

4. Taxation Subsidizes the Wealthy, Not the Poor   100
    Mancur Olson

5. Raising Corporate Taxes Will Justly Aid
    the Economy   107
    Robert S. McIntyre

6. Raising Corporate Taxes Will Harm the Economy   112
    Bruce Bartlett

A Critical Thinking Skill: Distinguishing
    Bias from Reason   117
Periodical Bibliography   119

Chapter 4: Is Free Trade Good for
the Economy?

1. The Case for Free Trade   121
    William A. Andres

2. The Case Against Free Trade   130
    Mark Anderson

3. The US Must Restrict Foreign Imports   138
    Joseph M. Gaydos

4. The US Should Not Restrict Foreign Imports   145
    Eric Marti

5. US Trade Is Harmed by Japan's Restrictions   151
    Pete Wilson

6. The Effects of Japan's Restrictions
    Are Exaggerated   159
    Ichiro Hattori

A Critical Thinking Skill:
    Recognizing Stereotypes   168
Periodical Bibliography   170

Chapter 5: Will Farms Survive the Economic Crisis?

1. The Farm Crisis Is Real   172
   Edward M. Kennedy

2. The Farm Crisis Is Exaggerated   177
   T.F. Leonard

3. Government Must Support Farmers   183
   Charles M. Fischbein

4. Government Must Leave Farmers Alone   187
   Don Doig

5. Farm Set-Aside Programs Harm Farmers
   and Taxpayers   191
   James Bovard

6. Farmers Need Set-Aside Programs   197
   Eleanor Zimmerlein

A Critical Thinking Skill: The Ability to Empathize   201

Periodical Bibliography   203

Chapter 6: How Can the US Ease the World Debt Crisis?

1. The US Should Cancel Foreign Debts   205
   Gus Hall

2. Debtor Countries Must Reform Themselves   211
   George B. N. Ayittey

3. The US Must Stop Bad Lending   217
   Patrick J. Buchanan

4. The US Must Encourage Freemarket
   Systems Abroad   226
   Esther Wilson Hannon & Edward L. Hudgins

5. The Debtor Nations Should Put a Moratorium
   on Repayment   233
   Athos Fava

6. The US Should Encourage Innovative Methods
   of Repayment   241
   Robert Wesson & Jon Basil Utley

A Critical Thinking Skill: Evaluating
Sources of Information   248

Periodical Bibliography   250

Glossary   251

List of Organizations to Contact   254

Book Bibliography   258

Index   260

Why Consider Opposing Viewpoints?

"It is better to debate a question without settling it than to settle a question without debating it."

Joseph Joubert (1754-1824)

The Importance of Examining Opposing Viewpoints

The purpose of the Opposing Viewpoints Series, and this book in particular, is to present balanced, and often difficult to find, opposing points of view on complex and sensitive issues.

Probably the best way to become informed is to analyze the positions of those who are regarded as experts and well studied on issues. It is important to consider every variety of opinion in an attempt to determine the truth. Opinions from the mainstream of society should be examined. But also important are opinions that are considered radical, reactionary, or minority as well as those stigmatized by some other uncomplimentary label. An important lesson of history is the eventual acceptance of many unpopular and even despised opinions. The ideas of Socrates, Jesus, and Galileo are good examples of this.

Readers will approach this book with their own opinions on the issues debated within it. However, to have a good grasp of one's own viewpoint, it is necessary to understand the arguments of those with whom one disagrees. It can be said that those who do not completely understand their adversary's point of view do not fully understand their own.

A persuasive case for considering opposing viewpoints has been presented by John Stuart Mill in his work *On Liberty*. When examining controversial issues it may be helpful to reflect on this suggestion:

> The only way in which a human being can make some approach to knowing the whole of a subject, is by hearing what can be said about it by persons of every variety of opinion, and studying all modes in which it can be looked at by every character of mind. No wise man ever acquired his wisdom in any mode but this.

Analyzing Sources of Information

The Opposing Viewpoints Series includes diverse materials taken from magazines, journals, books, and newspapers, as well as statements and position papers from a wide range of individuals, organizations and governments. This broad spectrum of sources helps to develop patterns of thinking which are open to the consideration of a variety of opinions.

Pitfalls to Avoid

A pitfall to avoid in considering opposing points of view is that of regarding one's own opinion as being common sense and the most rational stance and the point of view of others as being only opinion and naturally wrong. It may be that another's opinion is correct and one's own is in error.

Another pitfall to avoid is that of closing one's mind to the opinions of those with whom one disagrees. The best way to approach a dialogue is to make one's primary purpose that of understanding the mind and arguments of the other person and not that of enlightening him or her with one's own solutions. More can be learned by listening than speaking.

It is my hope that after reading this book the reader will have a deeper understanding of the issues debated and will appreciate the complexity of even seemingly simple issues on which good and honest people disagree. This awareness is particularly important in a democratic society such as ours where people enter into public debate to determine the common good. Those with whom one disagrees should not necessarily be regarded as enemies, but perhaps simply as people who suggest different paths to a common goal.

Developing Basic Reading and Thinking Skills

In this book, carefully edited opposing viewpoints are purposely placed back to back to create a running debate; each viewpoint is preceded by a short quotation that best expresses the author's main argument. This format instantly plunges the reader into the midst of a controversial issue and greatly aids that reader in mastering the basic skill of recognizing an author's point of view.

A number of basic skills for critical thinking are practiced in the activities that appear throughout the books in the series. Some of the skills are:

Evaluating Sources of Information The ability to choose from among alternative sources the most reliable and accurate source in relation to a given subject.

Separating Fact from Opinion The ability to make the basic distinction between factual statements (those that can be demonstrated or verified empirically) and statements of opinion (those that are beliefs or attitudes that cannot be proved).

Identifying Stereotypes The ability to identify oversimplified, exaggerated descriptions (favorable or unfavorable) about people and insulting statements about racial, religious or national groups, based upon misinformation or lack of information.

Recognizing Ethnocentrism The ability to recognize attitudes or opinions that express the view that one's own race, culture, or group is inherently superior, or those attitudes that judge another culture or group in terms of one's own.

It is important to consider opposing viewpoints and equally important to be able to critically analyze those viewpoints. The activities in this book are designed to help the reader master these thinking skills. Statements are taken from the book's viewpoints and the reader is asked to analyze them. This technique aids the reader in developing skills that not only can be applied to the viewpoints in this book, but also to situations where opinionated spokespersons comment on controversial issues. Although the activities are helpful to the solitary reader, they are most useful when the reader can benefit from the interaction of group discussion.

Using this book and others in the series should help readers develop basic reading and thinking skills. These skills should improve the reader's ability to understand what they read. Readers should be better able to separate fact from opinion, substance from rhetoric and become better consumers of information in our media-centered culture.

This volume of the Opposing Viewpoints Series does not advocate a particular point of view. Quite the contrary! The very nature of the book leaves it to the reader to formulate the opinions he or she finds most suitable. My purpose as publisher is to see that this is made possible by offering a wide range of viewpoints which are fairly presented.

David L. Bender
Publisher

Introduction

"The ideas of economists and political philosophers, both when they are right and when they are wrong, are more powerful than is commonly understood. Indeed, the world is ruled by little else."

John Maynard Keynes, 1883-1946

Former British Prime Minister Sir Alec Douglas-Home (1963-1964) once stated that "there are two problems in my life. The political ones are insoluble and the economic ones are incomprehensible." A century earlier, one of Douglas-Home's fellow countrymen, writer/philosopher Thomas Carlyle, approximated the Prime Minister's sentiment when he cynically referred to economics as the "dismal science."

From a popular perspective, the "science" of economics has always had its detractors. Terms like micro-macroeconomics, econometrics, and physiocrats, and names like Thomas Malthus, David Riccardo, and Adam Smith, do little to raise the average person's interest level or spur ready comprehension. However, when economics is reduced to such dollars-and-cents language as taxes, recession, and inflation, interest and understanding become imperative to virtually all people.

In the United States, public opinion polls nearly always reveal that monetary issues top society's concerns and complaints; significantly, this occurs in a country that by almost any imaginable yardstick enjoys an enormously high degree of affluence. Americans are also reminded daily by the media that both on a national and international scale, monetary policies, institutions, and even currencies are an integral part of daily life as never before in history. Even local crises frequently set off financial tremors which are felt far beyond their epicenters. In the farm belt, for example, what started as difficulties for farmers soon became difficulties for everyone as farms went bankrupt, food shortages occurred, and grocery prices rose. Whole cities in the late 1970s and early 1980s were dramatically affected by the high interest rates that, among other things, discouraged people from buying new cars and subsequently led to the closing of auto and steel plants; workers were left with only public assistance for income, houses were foreclosed, purchases decreased, and neighborhood stores were forced to close.

13

On the other hand, government economic policies that at first appear to be rather far removed from the life of the average person eventually affect everyone's pocketbook. International trade questions, for example, are settled by political decisions; yet, whether the United States will or will not trade with a particular country, and whether import taxes will or will not be required, determine whether certain goods will be available in stores, whether their prices will be affordable, and whether or not similar American industries will be able to compete successfully without large worker layoffs.

This anthology of opposing viewpoints is concerned with many issues, some of which have been debated since the early days of the American republic. The issues include: What Should Be the Government's Role in Business? How Serious Is the Budget Deficit? What Kind of Taxation Is Most Appropriate? Is Free Trade Good for the Economy? Will Farms Survive the Economic Crisis? and How Can the US Ease the World Debt Crisis? As with all volumes in the Opposing Viewpoints Series, *Economics in America* leaves it to the reader to finally decide who is right. And as with each series volume, the reader will also find that simple answers to the questions posed are not readily found.

What Should Be the Government's Role in Business?

"Only government is capable of assessing the total costs and benefits of economic decisions to the taxpayer and the nation."

Government Involvement Is Essential for a Strong Economy

Gar Alperovitz & Jeff Faux

Gar Alperovitz and Jeff Faux are the authors of *Rebuilding America: A Blueprint for the New Economy* from which this viewpoint is adapted. The writers point out that government involvement in many aspects of the economy has been extremely beneficial. In fact, they claim that much of our history and prosperity would be negatively affected if the government were to follow the independent, individualistic principles many Americans espouse.

As you read, consider the following questions:

1. The authors describe many instances of beneficial government involvement in the economy. List several of these.
2. Many critics of government insist that private companies are much more efficient than government agencies. How do the authors refute this?
3. The major area in which the authors believe the government is most useful is overall economic planning. Why do they think that only the government is capable of doing this?

Gar Alperovitz and Jeff Faux, "Think Again: What We Need Is More Government, Not Less," *The Washington Post National Weekly Edition*, October 22, 1984. Reprinted with the author's permission.

Is government inherently bureaucratic, wasteful, clumsy and burdened by red tape? Do private corporations automatically develop and manage a nation's resources better than public enterprises? Is the free market invariably more efficient than careful planning in guiding and directing a nation's economic destiny?

Unfashionable as it is to say so . . . the answer to all these questions is an emphatic no. In fact, it is almost certain that we will one day look back on the current period of anti-government sentiment in the United States as a brief interlude before a new era of efficient, enlightened and—yes—expanded involvement of federal, state and local government in the economy.

It is pure nostalgia to think that our post-industrial society will be run in the future as if it were a semi-developed, agricultural nation in mid-19th century. There is a worldwide trend toward more government and not even America . . . has been immune to it.

Contrary to common opinion, federal spending as a percentage of Gross National Product has risen, not fallen, during the Reagan administration. In the Jimmy Carter years, federal spending averaged just over 22 percent of GNP; under Reagan it has averaged 24.2 percent.

Government Aiding the Economy

This president, like others before him, has openly used the power of government to manage the economy. He continued the Chrysler bailout. His Agriculture Department handed over $21 billion of surplus commodities to farmers as part of a Payment-in-Kind program. His administration "informally" limited imports of Japanese automobiles and restricted imports of steel, sugar and motorcycles. Not only has the government taken over Continental Illinois National Bank—the nation's eighth largest—but it has virtually guaranteed all large banks that it will not permit them to fail.

The Reagan administration has supported government programs that aid the defense and nuclear power industries. And that is to say nothing of indirect government action, such as the 1981 tax bill that heavily favored big manufacturing industries over small business and the service sector.

The administration's actual record, if not its rhetoric, is part of a trend with a long history. Over the years, the federal government has subsidized regions of the United States with military bases and aerospace projects; an interstate highway system; billion-dollar water projects; rural electrification; ports and waterways. It has promoted American agriculture with price supports for corn, export subsidies for wheat and an elaborate system of allotments, quotas and marketing orders that help growers of tobacco, cotton, sugar, peanuts, oranges, apples and dozens of other commodities.

17

Federal investment in canals and turnpikes, and vast subsidies to railroads, helped "open the West." Government policies that subsidized the development of new labor-saving technologies in agriculture encouraged the mass migration of rural blacks to northern and midwestern cities after World War II.

Public-Private Cooperation Is the Norm

There is nothing unusual about any of this, much as it goes against the grain of American "free enterprise" mythology. In every nation in the world, governments are deeply involved in planning, subsidizing, financing and in some cases operating major sectors of the economy. Such private-public cooperation helps countries compete internationally, avoids wasteful duplication of research efforts, safeguards employment and maintains the stability of communities.

Government Protects Public

Many Americans have forgotten that we set up regulatory agencies in the first place in order to protect the public interest. Industries considered vital to the public—such as transportation, food, finance, communications, and nuclear power—were regulated in order to provide the public a steady flow of safe products in a stable environment. The public outcry over the abuses detailed in Upton Sinclair's *The Jungle,* for example, led to the Food and Drug Act of 1906. Certainly, no one complained that the government should get out of the business of regulating some 50 years later when an FDA medical officer ruled that thalidomide was unfit for the U.S. marketplace (despite the fact that German regulators had approved it).

For all its faults, there are many positive results of government regulation.

Victor Kamber, *USA Today,* July 1984.

The expansion of the Japanese steel industry, which contributed to the devastation of U.S. steel companies, was the result of an economic strategy designed by the Japanese government.

There is no iron law of economics that says private enterprise is innately superior to public enterprise. Big corporations are as vulnerable as big government to the ills of size, bureaucracy and monopoly.

Real conservatives are the first to acknowledge this. The late Henry C. Simons, founder of the Chicago school of economics, came to believe that many corporations (as opposed to individual entrepreneurs) had outlived their usefulness.

Simons recognized the need for restraints on corporate practices. He advocated strong antitrust laws and federal chartering of corporations. He favored public ownership of utilities, railroads and other industries that were not competitive. This highly respected conservative teacher of Milton Friedman declared that "every industry should be either effectively competitive or socialized."

Government-owned, or partially owned, railroad, airline, aircraft, electrical, and automobile companies have been responsible for a good deal of France's industrial innovation and, in the case of aircraft and autos, for a significant part of her manufacturing exports. Government-owned Renault, for example, has been highly successful in competition with private firms. And European governments, working together, built the successful commercial aircraft Airbus.

In Western Europe public enterprises account for 8 to 12 percent of total employment and 15 to 30 percent of total capital investment. Six of the largest 12, and 15 of the largest 50, Western European industrial firms are wholly or substantially owned by governments. For example, West German, Canadian, French, Italian and British governments are major shareholders in their respective oil and gas industries.

Current economic difficulties in Europe have aroused new interest in U.S.-style free enterprise and entrepreneurism. In England, some public enterprises have been sold back to the private sector. However, on balance, the changes in Europe as a whole have been relatively modest. French President Francois Mitterand has brought more banks into the public sector.

Federal Agencies Have Good Record

Despite our anti-government ideology, the record of public agencies in this country is quite different from what the conventional wisdom holds. During World War II the federal government created a variety of efficient businesses—aluminum industries on the West Coast, steel mills and an oil pipeline from Texas to the East Coast, all of which were later purchased by the private sector. The federal government currently operates civilian airports, builds ships in Navy shipyards, manages a third of the nation's land and administers the world's largest pension system, Social Security.

The state of Wisconsin runs the State Life Insurance Fund, created by Republican populist Gov. Robert LaFollette in 1917. State Life is solvent and unsubsidized. Moreover, it sells life insurance for 10 to 40 percent less than its private competitors.

State governments operate liquor stores, hotels, resorts and lotteries. South Dakota makes and sells cement, and Nebraska produces and sells hog cholera serum. Hundreds of localities efficiently run their own water companies.

Comparing the efficiency of public and private enterprises is no easy matter. Public utility companies, for example, often have the disadvantage of serving unprofitable rural areas. On the other hand, they don't pay taxes and can offer investors tax-free bonds. Several studies have found public utilities to be more efficient producers and distributors of electric power, even when their tax advantages are eliminated.

A Twentieth Century Fund study of public authorities in states and cities found that, with some exceptions, "the present system . . . has been generally successful at producing good management and effective operations." The major criticism was that public organizations were too conservative in their operations and tended to reflect the interest and biases of businessmen who dominate their boards.

Government Intervention Improves Lives

The administration's basic assumption—that opportunities for employment and self-support increase when the federal government abdicates its social responsibilities—is rarely questioned. Why? Afraid of the "big government" label, many liberals have failed to insist that only federal intervention can provide impoverished Americans the skills and jobs they need to move off welfare.

Constructive options for reconciling full employment and stable prices can be explored only if we acknowledge the importance of federal action. Refusal to do so will generate more of the aimless wandering now embodied in the "industrial policy" debate, producing catchy slogans but no concrete proposals for revitalizing the economy.

Sar A. Leviton and Clifford M. Johnson, *Minneapolis Star & Tribune,* September 16, 1983.

To be sure, during the recent slowdown in economic growth there is some evidence that the relative productivity of public enterprises in Western Europe declined in the late 1970s. But that seems, in large part, to have resulted from the greater freedom of private managers to lay off workers in recessions. In effect, private companies shifted the costs of unemployment to the public (which paid increased welfare and unemployment costs), while public firms tended to absorb these costs themselves.

This is a point that is too often side-stepped by enthusiastic supporters of the free market and the private sector. While it is all very well to extol the efficiency of private enterprise, it is easy to ignore the costs of this efficiency to taxpayers and communities. In our current, relatively unplanned economy, taxpayers subsidize major corporate investment decisions, which, in turn, often wreak havoc on communities and their tax bases.

Any accountant looking at the overall costs from the taxpayers' point of view of a company's decision to pull up stakes and move would evaluate the "efficiency" of such a move very differently from the company's own bookkeepers.

At present, communities have little power to control the flight of companies and capital. They are caught up in a competition for capital that is ultimately destructive to all. The Sunbelt may be benefiting temporarily from a wave of business investment at the expense of the North and Midwest, but the benefits may only be shortlived. At some point, companies are likely to shut down and move elsewhere to take advantage of cheaper labor, more ample water and other factors, leaving communities to pick up the tab for schools, highways and other services.

Protective Planning

This is where planning comes in. Only a comprehensive approach at both the national and local level can define investment goals that protect communities, jobs and, ultimately, taxpayers.

Since 1978, legislation has been introduced at the local, state, and federal level to require advance notice of plant closings and to aid firms owned by their workers or their communities.

A serious strategy for safeguarding local economic stability would include technical assistance, loans, and loan guarantees to build up community-based enterprises. The federal government has a role to play here. A firm should always be free to move if it so desires; but there is no reason for it to receive tax incentives, grants for training programs and research and development funds from federal, state and local governments if its move throws excessive numbers of people out of work and makes them dependent on public welfare and unemployment funds. In that case, the total costs far outweigh the total benefits.

The closing of a plant by an absentee conglomerate does not necessarily mean that the plant is unprofitable. Rather, it means that the plant is not profitable enough for the liking of the conglomerate. Local owners however, might be willing to settle for a smaller profit, because of the jobs and other economic benefits from keeping the plant running. . . .

Emphasizing Economic Stability

The impact on local communities of unexpected new investment is not always positive, either. In California's "Silicon Valley," the cost of an average house has jumped dramatically, and large numbers of new houses are awaiting basic service hookups. By the year 2000, Houston's population is expected to have grown sixfold from its 1950 level, resulting in congestion, pollution, water shortages, overcrowded schools and hospitals and a huge run-up in real estate values. Because of excessively rapid growth, a city industrial and real estate commission took the almost unheard-of step of recommending that large industrial corporations be encouraged to locate outside the county, since new tax revenue from industry was not adequate to offset the costs of growth.

21

If we are to reduce these costly and inefficient patterns of boom and bust, we must face up to the need for a comprehensive assessment of the cost and benefits of corporate investment decisions. This requires increasing the scope and competence of government planning.

Arguments have been made that a more coherently planned economy would make it harder for this country to compete internationally. In fact, the opposite is the case.

As things now stand, the closing of outmoded factories in declining industries is so threatening to jobs and community welfare that corporations, communities and unions all team together to fight for protection. This only postpones the day of reckoning, perpetuating inefficiency and lack of competitiveness.

But if communities and workers were assured alternative jobs, the impasse could be broken, allowing the modernization to go forward more rapidly.

Benefits of Openly Planned Economy

Planning does not do away with politics; it puts politics out in the open. It forces special-interest groups to stand up and be counted. Cozy alliances between political leaders and economic interests are brought to light. In a more planned economy, there are still deals and compromises, but they can be labeled and evaluated openly.

At present, the expansion of government is carried on behind a smokescreen of free-enterprise rhetoric that confuses the public and makes rational decision-making impossible. A sensible U.S. economic policy would recognize the need to build up a coherent planning capacity at both the national and local level. It would accept the fact that only government is capable of assessing the total costs and benefits of economic decisions to the taxpayer and the nation. It would put community well-being at the center of national planning for full employment. And it would reap the benefits of an economy that mixed public and private enterprises in ways that took advantage of the special contributions of each.

Only such an economic policy allows a satisfactory answer to the question, "What's in it for me?" The answer cannot be that we will beat the Japanese to 40 percent of the world's computer business, but you will lose your job or your business in the process.

"The argument that officials of the State can protect consumers through interventions and regulations was destroyed by Adam Smith more than two centuries ago."

Government Involvement Is Harmful to a Free Economy

George Roche

George Roche, president of Hillsdale College in Hillsdale, Michigan, believes strongly that government should not regulate economic and social matters. This job, he believes, should be left to private individuals and organizations. He writes that government intervention becomes foolish bureaucracy, a costly, wasteful, and anti-social means of unnecessarily controlling citizens.

As you read, consider the following questions:

1. What is meant by the term *bureaucracy?*
2. The author states that the government has only one thing to offer in exchange for the money and obedience it exacts. What is that one thing?
3. List two or three examples of the harmful effects of government intervention as described by Mr. Roche.
4. What do you suppose Mr. Roche believes is "the rightful place" of government in a free society?

Herbert Spencer once noted that on any given day, you could read two stories in the papers about the failures of government programs—and three stories about pleas for *new* government programs to do even more for us!

That was over a hundred years ago, in England, but the point rings truer than ever for us today. The only difference is that now we see more stories about a certain kind of failure, one that seems to us mindless and mean. Such a story might read like this: "The Occupational Safety and Health Administration (OSHA) today ordered the University of Illinois to tear down the handrails alongside walkways on campus, and to install new handrails exactly 42 inches high. According to OSHA, the old handrails are several inches too low to comply with regulations."

The story happens to be true. And when we read it, we know at once here is the federal bureaucracy at work. It may even give us a chuckle—who else but a bureaucrat would be so boneheaded as to insist that handrails must be exactly 42 inches high, and not one inch higher or lower? But it is not so funny when you learn that Illinois had to pay over $500,000 to change those handrails. If it weren't for a petty bureaucratic rule, the money could have been used, say, to hire fifteen full professors, or build a dormitory wing, or add three thousand volumes to the school library.

Perverse and Hurtful Waste

It is precisely this sort of perverse and hurtful waste that increasingly marks the failure of government actions today. *The problem is bureaucracy, and bureaucracy has become a national epidemic.* The federal bureaucracy has more than *tripled* in size in the last ten years. It is *ten times* as large and powerful at it was twenty years ago, at the beginning of the Kennedy-Johnson years. It has swollen a *thousand-fold* in power in the last half century. This titanic expansion of bureaucratic power is shattering the foundations of a free society and menacing the well-being of every citizen. The federal government, designed and intended to be the Servant of the people, now bids to become our Master. . . .

"Bureaucracy," in the abstract, is hardly a new concern. And if the problem were no more than a few harmless bumblers in dusty federal offices, we would have little to worry about. However, a bureaucratic machine so swollen and powerful that it can hold sway over every citizen is indeed a new—and ominous—development in American life. How this situation came to be, what it portends, and what we can do about it, are questions every intelligent American ought to ponder. Soon.

We are all aware that the federal government itself has grown immense in recent times. It is not as well understood, unfortunately, that as government grows, it necessarily becomes more and more bureaucratic and rigid—and authoritarian. The overweening bureaucracy that emerges is less an evil in itself than a reflection of this trend and greater evil: the thrust toward an all-powerful central government.

For fifty years and more, the dominant opinion in or near the seats of power has worked ceaselessly to erect a federal State on the Old World model: paternalistic, autocratic, and utterly alien to the American constitutional ideal. This effort has imposed on us the largest, most costly, most bureaucratic State in all of history, where once we had and long cherished the smallest.

Handmaidens of Power

Every extension of federal power has brought with it new bureaucratic controls and interferences in our lives. This is unavoidable. Bureaus are the handmaidens of political power. They are required by law as well as practical necessity to act as they do, however inflexible, small-minded, and destructive their actions may seem to the rest of us. Such are, and always have been, the consequences of the authoritarian State.

It is in the nature of bureaucracy ever to work "by the book," reducing every aspect of our lives to suffocating rules and lifeless averages. Rulebook methods are the only way State power can be organized. There is no room for intelligent decisions and flexibility. The bureaucratic State, William F. Rickenbacker has written, is " . . . the very opponent and negation of human freedom and individuality. Men strive to excel, the State seeks after averages. Men covet novelty, the State extrapolates from yesterday. Men love to chaffer person to person, the State is a rule book. Men yearn to be free, the State is the sum of liberties lost."

Government Restrains Competition

What is needed is an approach to legislation and regulation which recognizes the public interest is best served in a competitive marketplace, a marketplace where initiative, innovation, and performance are not restrained by discriminatory laws, complicated rules, and unequal regulatory treatment.

Lee E. Gunderson, statement before the Senate Banking, Housing, and Urban Affairs Committee, May 6, 1981.

The bureaucracy has at its disposal one tool only, and that is force: coercive power. This tool has its purposes, but is totally unsuited to the direction of economic or private matters. Most applications of this power in the private sector, unfortunately, cause more harm than good.

Certainly, much of the malaise America has suffered in recent years can be traced directly to the use of bureaucratic power where it does not belong. Our energies as a free people are thwarted by the snarl of red tape and rules. Our schools deteriorate year after year, in exact proportion to the growth of a gigantic educational bureaucracy. Business and industry, chained by literally millions of regulations, are less and less able to provide the jobs and goods we need. The poor, the aged, the disadvantaged, the hurt and handicapped, all supposedly the beneficiaries of government aid, instead become its victims, caught in an endless web of rules and frustrations. Our hopes of bettering our lives, our very dreams, falter under the burdens the bureaucracy imposes.

Half a century's experimentation with do-everything government has proven to be a monstrous, heartbreaking mistake. Instead of "solving" social problems, it has created new and far greater ones. Its ideas and programs go forward on their own momentum despite being repeatedly discredited by practical experience. Its cost is so great as to ennervate the most productive economy the world has ever seen. Its accumulated powers could emerge as totalitarianism in any severe crisis; and a crisis is sure to come if the statist trend continues. In the end, we too could face the fate that has marked every Old World State, every civilization before us: a progressive weakening of society by State exactions, leading to degeneracy, collapse, and death. No people before us who have made the same mistakes, who have chosen to put their faith in the State, have ever escaped this doom. Nor shall we. . . .

Clear Private Goals

It is in the private sphere that we find real purpose, the same so lacking in bureaucracy. Indeed, it is so obvious that we scarcely notice. In our business activities, we know exactly what we are trying to do, which is exactly what the bureaucrat does not know. Business has concrete function. Farming is farming. One makes cars, or sells insurance, or cuts hair: the intent is always clear. Never in unhindered business do we suffer the malady common to bureaucracy that we have no real idea what we are doing. In business, we serve those who would buy our services for their own betterment, and we must do so in a way that is so efficient and effective that we can make a living at it: make a profit. . . .

It is the never-ending search for success, for profit, that gives business enterprise the purpose and direction lacking in a bureau. And it does so in a socially valuable way, for in the unhindered and competitive marketplace, you must serve others efficiently in order to profit. People serving people: this is social cooperation, without any of the negative implications of being forced to do so by State authority. . . .

Government's "Protection Racket"

Let's be clear: protection deals cooked up between politicians and business or labor are not a part of the free market. They are part of the bureaucratic world, and corrupt. The fact is, bureau-

26

cracy has neither goods nor services to sell in the open market. What it does have to "sell" is a line of privilege and protection, backed by State coercion. Often this is lawful—if thoroughly dishonest—as in licensing what people have every right to do anyway, or subsidizing business, or protecting trade unions. But lawful or not, forms of the same protection rackets inevitably proceed in the bureaucratic mode: selling lucrative government contracts for lucrative kickbacks, selling monopolies in labor or business, and literally thousands of other types of corruption.

Less Government—Not More!

In industry after industry, the pervasive effects of governmental interference have so weakened the system's ability to respond to incentives that performance levels have deteriorated to their current abysmal levels. Surely, the solution to the advanced state of depredation of our nation's capacity to deliver is not more of just those policies that brought us down. Those who advocate, in their desperation, more government to solve the problems of our society are demonstrably wrong using the test of history. The solution rests in less—not more—government!

Arthur B. Laffer, "The Solution to Today's Problems: *Less* Government!" Americanism Educational League.

In legitimate business, all exchanges are two-sided, value given for value received. All parties to an exchange enter it voluntarily, and all do so expecting to better their condition by doing so. All parties to an exchange expect to profit from it, otherwise they will not agree to it. In short, everybody comes out ahead, each according to his own scale of values and priorities. This process of free exchange thus facilitates the continual distribution of capital, goods, and labor from those who have less use for them to those who have more. On this fact the modern world is built. Without this, we would have no way to assign the resources and responsibilities needed for economic enterprise. With it, we build a world in which people on welfare can in many regards enjoy a higher standard of living than the kings of old.

One-Way Transactions

Bureaus, on the other hand, derive all their revenues from one-way transactions that are not exchanges at all. Bureaus simply confiscate, through State power, the production of others, without compensation. In such transfers, only one party profits; the other gets soaked. This gives the injured party a perfect incentive *not* to produce. Why bother if you're just going to get ripped off again? The net effect of the transfer, then, is not zero but a net loss of productivity and human wellbeing. Private crime produces the same disincentive—armed robbery on a street corner, for instance—but constitutes such a small percentage of involuntary transfers that its economic damage is minimal. Private crime accounts for no more than 3% of all the one-way transfers, probably less. The rest is bureaucracy and government in general, and the damage is staggering. Government at all levels sucks up something more than 40% of all our productivity through involuntary transfers (as opposed to about 1% from private crime). There is hardly a business in the country that could sustain the loss of 40% of its output without facing bankruptcy in a week. Yet that is the rate of confiscation we, as supposedly free citizens, are forced to bear in order to support the bureaucracy. Small wonder we all struggle and can't get ahead!

The cost of government at all levels today is around a *trillion* dollars a year—a million millions—all of it, of course, confiscated. That works out to about $4,500 per person, or $18,000 a year for a family of four. The smaller part of this—much the smaller part—goes for national defense and other State functions most of us regard as legitimate. But most pays for bureaucracy. Without this bureaucratic exaction, families would be keeping $12,000, $15,000, $18,000 more of their income than they do now. Is bureaucracy worth that much to you? Are you willing to have it go on doing what it is doing, at such a cost to you? If you were offered, say, a $15,000 per year pay increase in exchange for not having a bureaucrat on hand in Washington to "solve" your problems for you, would you take it? . . .

Anti-Market Regulations

The argument that officials of the State can protect consumers through interventions and regulations was destroyed by Adam Smith more than two centuries ago, and has never been tenable in economic theory. All such measures are anti-market, and all, by their nature, tend to create monopoly for some and disadvantage for others. That is why corrupt businesses and industries seek to be regulated in the first place, and scream bloody murder at the threat of deregulation, a phenomenon we have seen often in the past few years. *Of course* they hate deregulation: it will cost them their bureaucratically protected monopoly and force them to face the disciplines of the market: competition and the need to serve customers efficiently. Nobody wept more bitterly about deregulating the oil industry than the "consumer advocates"; many and loud were their warnings that this would raise fuel prices for consumers. And it did for a few months, as the market sorted itself out. Then the price of oil started dropping like a stone. Within a year the so-called "energy crisis" that was so frightening to some—mainly people who detest the market—turned into a worldwide oil glut that is breaking the power of OPEC. The market works. Bureaucratic controls don't.

The real question, then, is one you never hear from the "consumer advocates": who or what will protect us from bureaucracy? There are no economic checks or disciplines whatsoever on bureaucratic activities. Utterly insulated from economic risk or loss, bureaus keep right on growing, no matter how badly or wastefully they perform; no matter that they have been obsolete for a decade or a century in what they do. Not only do we pay their bills in taxes, we pay in increased consumer prices in every economic activity they regulate. Bureaucratic controls invariably destroy market efficiency, so increase the cost of goods. The net effect is that we get more bureaucracy and less to eat for our dollar. Some claim that this is "protection" for the consumer, but you'd spend a lot less buying the Brooklyn Bridge every week. . . .

Free Enterprise and Bureaucracy Irreconcilable

Free enterprise and bureaucracy are worlds apart, irreconcilable, hostile, forever sundered. The character of each is fully shaped by its purpose, the one economic, the other political; the one social, the other antisocial and exploitative if uncontrolled.

Surely the ways of the one and the other should be clear enough by now so that we can assign each to its rightful place.

"Generally, where government control over people's lives and commerce is lessened, the common man is better off."

Deregulation Benefits the Economy

Mark Fowler

Mark Fowler is chairman of the Federal Communications Commission. Despite his position as a government official, he advocates less government regulation in order to restore incentives to economic growth. He believes that economic regulation is particularly costly and wasteful. In the following viewpoint, he argues that deregulation, the removal of government regulations, benefits both corporations and the public.

As you read, consider the following questions:

1. How does Mr. Fowler believe that excessive regulation has harmed the economy?
2. What are some of the benefits Mr. Fowler lists that have resulted from deregulation of specific industries?

Mark Fowler, "Bringing Back the Incentives," *The Washington Times*, January 8, 1986. Reprinted with permission.

Tax reform stays in the news.

I am struck with the similarity between the rationales for tax reform and for my specialty, deregulation. At bottom, both rely on restoring incentives to create opportunity and foster excellence.

In economic policy, one issue dominates: what is the proper role of government? Some government is necessary, but its proper role is limited. When it exceeds its proper bounds, it impedes the efficient workings of our voluntary economy. At worst, it jeopardizes our liberty.

This central issue has not changed since 1776, when Adam Smith wrote the *Wealth of Nations*. But it has taken different forms. Post-World War II debates over the merits of central planning and socialism are today disputes over industrial planning, comparable-worth wage standards, and other regulations. The impulse to substitute government intervention for the workings of the market has burdened our economy with the enormous inefficiencies and remains a potent force in our political life.

Counterrevolutionary Movements

While this urge may never die, it can be contained by seizing the offensive. In this larger struggle, tax reform and deregulation are really counterrevolutionary movements. Like most political issues, they will be won or lost on the battleground of ideas.

Too often tax and regulation policy debates get mired in a rhetoric of conflict, usually between "consumers" and "business." But the fact is, individuals consume services both directly and indirectly. We consume telecommunications services directly when we make or receive telephone calls. We consume them indirectly when we purchase goods and services whose production involves the use of telecommunications. There, businesses act as consumers' agents in purchasing and trying to minimize the costs of these services.

By looking at it this way, we destroy the illusion that cost can somehow be shifted from "consumers" to "business." It is possible to charge consumers below-cost prices for telephone service, but only by charging them higher prices for other goods and services they consume. Such schemes are not costless to society.

Mispricing Distorts Free Market

Put differently, it's not just a matter of taking out of one pocket and putting back into another. When a resource like telecommunications is mispriced, it distorts the whole process of voluntary exchange. There is a shift toward using other resources whose social costs are greater. In telecommunications, many large users are building their own facilities to reach long-distance carriers solely to avoid the artificially high prices they face to connect to them through local telephone company facilities. This uneconomic bypass of the public telephone network is a concrete manifestation of regulatory distortion. It also raises rates for the remaining small-business and residential customers.

If inefficient government intervention and the resulting price distortions are eliminated, on the other hand, productive exchange is expanded. Since the 1981 cuts in marginal rates, the most affluent taxpayers have paid in a larger share of total federal income tax receipts. Lower marginal rates have led them to move some of their investments from tax shelters to more profitable ventures. At the same time that other taxpayers face a reduced tax burden, society gets a greater return on this group's investment because market forces have a freer hand in directing it.

Regulation Harms Efficiency

Regulation reduces the role of entrepreneurship and hard-headed business decision making; it substitutes for these virtues the arts of public relations and bureaucratic administration. The corporate officers of electric utilities [for example] are not businesspeople in the normal sense. How could they be? They operate in an environment where direct competition is illegal, product prices are set, and rates of return are guaranteed. Under regulation, those successful as utility heads have, of necessity, become adroit at placating regulators and packaging decisions for public consumption. We should not be surprised, for example, that when utility managers are encouraged with government subsidies to build nuclear plants, they respond even if some projects make little economic sense in the long run. Nor should these managers be judged harshly when they are asked to meet conflicting regulatory goals and operate under conditions of risk directly induced by the regulatory process.

John C. Moorhouse, *Electric Power: Deregulation and the Public Interest*, 1986.

With regulatory reform, the results are already beyond expectation. As the falling dollar and foreign competition have spurred U.S. manufacturers to improve productivity, so deregulation provides the impetus for the service sector. As *Fortune* magazine put it, "What the Japanese were to Detroit, deregulation has been to finance and transportation."

Consumer Benefits

Price competition has given consumers an airline industry with lower average prices, more price and quality options, reduced labor costs, and more efficient use of planes and airports. Changes in work rules for one airline alone led to productivity gains of $47 million since 1982. On average, airfares have fallen 24 percent since 1978. The shift to hub and spoke route configurations (the heart of cost savings) is perhaps the most visible manifestation of how deregulation has changed the way airlines do business. Deregulation has also helped boost productivity in banking. And impressive productivity gains have come in trucking and railroads.

In FCC [Federal Communications Commission]-regulated industries, efficiency gains have been striking. Broadcast and telephone companies have new flexibility and business freedom. Most agree that the FCC's actions relaxing ownership and other restrictions have played a primary role in the striking rise in broadcast-station prices. The typical broadcasting company's value has risen 40 percent from December to June, compared with a 12 percent rise in Standard & Poor's Industrial 500 index.

In the telephone industry, AT&T and the regional companies have pared labor and other costs in some cases by more than 10 percent *since* divestiture. They are also installing new technology and introducing new services at faster rates. AT&T's long- distance competitors are adding billions of dollars of state-of-the-art transmission and switching plants.

Equally important, long-distance prices of AT&T and many of its competitors have fallen almost 12 percent in the past 17 months as a result of the FCC's reform of long-distance pricing. An annual loss estimated at more than $1.5 billion, caused by inefficient pricing of telephone services, is finally being reduced. And because efficiency losses grow disproportionately as price distortions increase, the greatest efficiency gains from moving long-distance rates to cost will come in the initial stages of reform.

Consumers benefit as long-distance prices better reflect their costs. People will call more and talk longer. Companies will turn to a fuller exploration of the technological efficiencies made possible by microwave, fiber optics, coaxial cable, and satellites. New services may become economic. Greater use of computers can be expected.

Commitment to Deregulation

These improvements directly result from our commitment to open entry and deregulation. While important work is left to be done, our success has been registered in the stock market. Since divestiture, and as of the end of June [1984], stock prices of telephone companies (AT&T and the regional companies) have done more than twice as well as the Standard & Poor's Industrial 500 index.

These tangible benefits demonstrate that generally, where government control over people's lives and commerce is lessened, the common man is better off. This suggests that a revision of Washington procedure is long overdue. That is, rather than requiring businessmen to plead the case for no government regulation, the government must first demonstrate a compelling state interest before it may interfere.

As we think about regulatory policy, we must never forget the role of private incentives in providing opportunity and fostering excellence. We possess bewildering amounts of data, but the truth is that we are surrounded by a jungle of ignorance.

Here or there, now and then, insightful, persevering, or lucky people come onto places where the cutting is easier and are able to advance the boundaries of knowledge. We are all made better off by the few Indiana Joneses who dare and do. Simply avoiding risks and slowing changes, all too often government's response, retards growth and postpones prosperity.

We all know there is no such thing as a free lunch. When policymakers forget this admonition, the public suffers. But the caveat to this rule is equally important. For the voluntary transactions made possible by deregulation and various other reforms not only benefit the companies involved, they also lead to lower prices and better services for the public—a lot more lunch for the same money.

"Cost cutting became a higher priority than such social goals as mine safety or chemical waste cleanup."

Deregulation Exacts Serious Human Costs

Susan J. Tolchin

Susan J. Tolchin, a professor at George Washington University in Washington, DC, is co-author of *Dismantling America*. In the following viewpoint, she writes that the movement toward deregulation, removing government regulation of various industries, has led to serious problems, particularly ones of safety. She also contends that deregulation, contrary to the promises of its advocates, has resulted in higher prices for many goods and services.

As you read, consider the following questions:

1. List three examples of the harmful effects of deregulation that Ms. Tolchin describes.
2. Does Ms. Tolchin acknowledge any benefits at all of deregulation?
3. What does the author say is "the real question"? How do you think she would answer that question? How would *you* answer it?

Susan J. Tolchin, "Deregulation Bandwagon Leaves Behind Real Social Human Cost," *St. Paul Sunday Pioneer Press and Dispatch,* September 30, 1984. Reprinted with the author's permission.

Now that the rush to deregulate is ebbing, it is time for some damage assessment.

It is becoming apparent to some members of Congress that under the rubric of deregulation, a sweeping restructuring of national priorities has occurred. In the urge to grasp the economic benefits of deregulation, very real social and human costs were overlooked.

We were once a nation committed to clean air and water, a safe work place and consumer protection. We were also committed to a kind of national transportation policy and universal telephone service, and to the notion that banks—like airlines and telephones—were akin to public utilities.

Since Deregulation

•Since airline deregulation, Bakersfield, California—population 105,000—has seen 13 different airlines come and go—many of them into bankruptcy. In the meantime, Bakersfield went into a tailspin.

"They just killed us," Stephen P. Schmitt, aviation director in charge of Bakersfield's airport, said. "Passenger boardings dropped from 148,000 per year to 48,000. We've lost business that could have come to Bakersfield and didn't. Business has left Bakersfield. That's what deregulation gave us, and they still haven't put Humpty Dumpty back together again."

•Americans are paying bank fees today that are double what they paid in 1979, according to a study by the Consumer Federation of America.

"The fees have become a virtual blizzard," says Rep. Fernand St. Germain, D-R.I., chairman of the House committee on banking, finance and urban affairs. "Fees for deposits, fees for low-balance savings accounts with the 'low balance' arbitrarily defined by the bank, fees for transfer of funds, fees for closing accounts. In some cases, the fees virtually wipe out the interest on small accounts, negating congressional efforts to give small savers a break."

•In Tennessee, the telephone company proposed a 120 percent increase in rates. Rep. Albert Gore Jr., D-Tenn., organized telephone councils to help his constituents cope with the problems of deregulation.

In a series of six hearings Gore held across the state, farmers, senior citizens, the poor, hospitals, universities, rural telephone cooperatives and small telephone companies testified that they would suffer under the new rates, made necessary—or possible— by the breakup of AT&T.

The move to deregulate reflected a bipartisan consensus. It was led by many of Congress' leading liberals and conservatives and by officials in the Ford, Carter and Reagan administrations. It was a response to what was sometimes rightly considered the ossification of the regulatory agencies, which were often inefficient, arrogant and captive of the industries they supposedly regulated. Deregulation proponents hoped to encourage competition, stimulate economic growth, eliminate waste and reduce inflation.

Theory Brings Higher Prices

According to the theory behind deregulation, airline fares and routes, for example, would be determined by the marketplace, not by a government agency. The resulting competition led to much cheaper fares for passengers flying on popular routes.

Released from government-imposed ceilings on interest rates, banks offered some of their customers substantially higher returns on their money, as well as a wider variety of services. The marketplace was also opened to companies previously barred by AT&T's virtual monopoly, forcing long-distance rates down.

© 1984, The Philadelphia Inquirer/Washington Post Writers Group

Acting on the blueprint designed—but not fully implemented—by the Carter White House, the Reagan administration made the Office of Management and Budget the nation's regulatory czar. OMB now has the power to approve all major regulations within the context of a cost-benefit standard. Thus, an agency responsible for fiscal austerity determines social priorities for issues like safety, health and the environment.

The results were predictable: Cost cutting became a higher priority than such social goals as mine safety or chemical waste

37

cleanup. Regulations began disappearing down what became known as the "black hole at OMB," often following secret visits from the industry representatives, according to congressional testimony.

Costly Tradeoff

In the first flush of enthusiasm for cheap fares to Disney World, many ignored the costly tradeoffs. The negative consequences of deregulation are still given short shrift by its proponents, who focused more on costs than on benefits, especially when those benefits were intangibles: life, health, community stability, regional prosperity.

The winners in deregulation include those with more than $500 in bank deposits, who earn higher interest rates and receive more services; frequent fliers between populous cities, and habitual users of long-distance telephone lines. But those with less money, who rarely fly or just need a telephone to call the corner druggist will be disadvantaged.

In the broadest sense, deregulation has created a restructuring of national priorities. Airline deregulation is, for example, an assault on a national transportation policy that sought to assure easy, reasonable, reliable access to all sections of the nation.

Many towns and small cities, as well as businesses, are suffering from the uncertainty and upheaval resulting from the immediate aftermath of deregulation. Deregulators contend, however, that there is insufficient public demand for flights into small communities, and that it is misguided public policy to maintain these services.

Sen. Mark Andrews, R-N.D., requested a study by the Congressional Research Service (CRS) on fare increases to test administration claims that air fares have increased at a rate lower than the inflation rate. The CRS showed that, of 30 pairs of cities selected at random, 17 experienced increases in all fare classes—after being adjusted for inflation—since the advent of deregulation. In 10 of the pairs, either the coach or the discount fare increased by more than 50 percent when adjusted for inflation.

Similar to the promises of airline deregulation, telephone divestiture and deregulation was promoted as a pro-consumer measure, and also undermined another national priority: universal telephone service. Like most industrialized nations, the United States long regarded a telephone in every home as important not only to the individual user, but to the prosperity of the business community. True, it was more difficult to install and maintain telephone lines in rural communities, but such a telephone system helped a raft of businesses and institutions.

Finally, who can deny the role of banks in the circulatory system of American business? But this, too, is being undermined by some of the unanticipated outcomes of banking deregulation. Forty-eight banks failed last year, the most since 1942, and the number already is higher this year.

On the other side of the counter, customers with small accounts are having the window shut in their faces. Under banking deregulation, "the move to affluent markets, and away from the blue-collar, the elderly and the less well-to-do, is being accomplished through an elaborate fee system that effectively prices the 'undesirables' out of the market," charged St. Germain.

To redress the inequities of banking deregulation, St. Germain

---

Squeezing the Poor

In its early days, America's regulated telephone system encouraged the widest possible consumption of telephone service, promoting access even to poor and rural households. Now, under deregulation, the companies are squeezing these poor and rural customers for their last pennies—and nickels, dimes, quarters, and dollars.

Editorial, *The Progressive*, December 1983.

---

has proposed a two-track government policy. Banks that exploit deregulation to help the affluent at the expense of the poor would have to get along without federal assistance—such as insurance bailouts. The Federal Deposit Insurance Corporation and other federal assistance would also be restricted to those banks that help their communities, he suggests.

What Is Ideal Relationship?

The debate over deregulation is not a debate between those who believe in government and those who love and hate the Federal Register. It transcends the debate over whether a free market can really exist in an advanced industrial society, and the debate between economists and social planners. The real question is how far should government go to protect society, and when should it allow the free market to prevail?

The regulation of airlines, banks and the telephone service reflected an earlier view that these industries were more than merely entrepreneurial—they were central to the nation's business and commerce. But unleashing these industries from the constraints of regulation has left certain segments of the public unprotected. Not surprisingly, the burden has fallen on those least able to protect themselves.

"Private contractors tend to be more efficient than their public sector counterparts . . . because they face different incentives."

The Private Sector Is More Efficient than Government

Stephen Moore

Stephen Moore, a policy analyst for the Thomas A. Roe Institute for Economic Policy Studies at The Heritage Foundation, believes that the move toward using private organizations and companies to perform tasks traditionally carried out by government is long overdue. In the following viewpoint, he writes that the profit motive makes private contractors more efficient than governmental agencies.

As you read, consider the following questions:

1. What are some of the areas that the author believes are, appropriately, being turned over to the private sector?
2. What does Mr. Moore say competition contributes to efficiency?
3. What proof does Mr. Moore provide to show that privatization is indeed more efficient?

Stephen Moore, "How to Privatize Federal Services by 'Contracting Out,'" The Heritage Foundation *Backgrounder,* March 13, 1986. Reprinted with permission.

Privatization has come of age. The Reagan Administration's FY 1987 budget argued that considerable budget savings can be achieved without cutting services but by transferring government functions to the private sector—in short, by privatization. A major privatization device is "contracting out," an inelegant term to describe what happens when the government hires private firms to provide government services under contract. A number of highly specialized goods and services for some time have been provided by private contractors. Notable examples include delivery of sophisticated communications satellites and military weapons procurement. But the greatest potential for budget savings would come from the federal government turning to private firms to supply such routine services as data processing, janitorial services, and maintenance work. These are generally known as "commercial services" because they are activities that are routinely provided in the private sector by commercial firms. . . .

When the federal government contracts out an activity which is commercial in nature, it retains its funding responsibility, but relies on private sector competition to assure that the good or service is delivered at the lowest possible cost and at high quality. The federal government currently employs nearly one million workers who perform 11,000 separate commercial activities. This workforce includes electricians, dentists, janitors, plumbers, caterers, laboratory technicians, and even veterinarians.

Since 1981 at least a dozen studies have investigated the potential savings from contracting with private vendors for such services. Such contracting out now is routine in thousands of cities and is being carried out on a limited basis on the federal level. The findings of eight representative studies are shown in Table 1.

Different Incentives Inspire Efficiency

Private contractors tend to be more efficient than their public sector counterparts—not because federal employees are less able, but because they face different incentives. Since private firms operate under competitive conditions, they have a powerful incentive to seek innovative approaches to reduce the cost of providing their service. If they do not keep cost down and quality up, they soon will lose contracts to their rivals. No such incentive exists in the public sector. The lack of competition removes the pressure to be more productive. In fact, there are perverse incentives, for if a public sector agency becomes more efficient at providing a service, then that agency is likely to see its budget cut—to reflect the savings—for the next year.

Injecting competition into the procurement process even generates greater efficiency within the bureaucracy. Example: an analysis of cost comparisons in the Department of Defense reveals that the cost of services provided by federal employees fell by 17 percent when they were forced to compete with private firms.

This alone has saved the Department over $100 million since 1982.

If contracting out were expanded on the federal level, the Congressional Budget Office envisions a $1.2 billion reduction in government costs. The Office of Management and Budget's latest projection puts the figure at $3 billion.

Improved Service Quality

The most outspoken opponent of contracting out predictably has been the American Federation of State, County and Municipal Employees. The union charges that while contractors may indeed provide services at lower cost, they "frequently cut corners by hiring inexperienced, transient personnel at low wages, by ignoring contract requirements, or by providing inadequate supervision." This complaint is refuted by performance evaluations of contracted activities which reveal that, if anything, service quality is enhanced by hiring private firms.

Table 1
Cost Savings Estimates From Contracting Out
Studies Conducted Since 1981

Source of Study	Type of Service	% Savings from Contracting Out
Ecodata, under contract with HUD		
" "	Municipal janitorial services	73
" "	Municipal refuse collection	42
" "	Municipal overlay construction	96
American Public Works Association	Highway and street maintenance	16
Department of Defense	Department services contracted between 1980 and 1982	22
Department of Defense	Revised 1985 estimate, all DOD contracted services	29
U.S. Air Force	Review of 132 contracted functions	33
Institute of Transportation Studies, University of California, Irvine	Municipal contracting of urban mass transit	25-50
U.S. General Accounting Office	Federal cleaning costs	50
Office of Management and Budget	Agencywide review of 60,000 positions contracted	24

A 1984 study of contracted municipal services by Ecodata, Inc., found no diminution in service quality. In fact, it concluded that "for many of the services, the individual cities with the lowest costs of service delivery also achieved among the highest levels of quality." Further corroboration of service quality is found in the California Tax Foundation 1981 survey of 81 local governments. By a margin of two to one, cities indicated that service had improved from contracting over those that complained of poorer service.

There findings were to be expected. Private contractors typically are forced to meet rigid performance specifications, and the quality of services they provide is closely scrutinized. With public delivery, by contrast, such accountability is low or nonexistent.

A 1983 Joint Economic Committee of Congress (JEC) study of federal procurement finds that offering federal contracts to the private sector greatly stimulates business expansion. Equipment and other capital purchased by a private firm to fulfill the terms of a federal contract are likely to be later adopted for other commercial ventures. By contrast, the government, because of its limited flexibility, often has capital sitting idle upon project completion. Technological spin-offs to other commercial markets from government funded research and development were particularly important, the study notes.

Contracting out also permits the federal government to marshall the specialized talents of private companies on a temporary basis, rather than keeping such expertise permanently within the government. Agencies acknowledge that this option offers the government greater flexibility in responding to changing priorities. . . .

The goal of government procurement, set down by the 1972 Commission on Federal Procurement, is to obtain "products and services of the needed quantity at the lowest reasonable price available." But thanks to congressionally imposed restrictions on contracting out, and the "civil disobedience" characterizing bureaucratic responses to contracting initiatives, the taxpayer has been denied the full benefits of contracting out under Ronald Reagan. In 1986 there are more federal workers performing commercial activities than ever before, and the competitive procurement process is more regulated and restricted than it has ever been. . . .

The Gramm-Rudman-Hollings [deficit reduction plan] timetable for federal deficit reduction means that Congress and the White House must seize every opportunity to cut unnecessary spending. Since contracting out cuts spending while preserving the level of services to beneficiaries—and in many cases improves the quality of service delivery—there is every reason why lawmakers should step up the pace of contracting out. Failure to do so will indicate that Washington is still not serious about cutting the deficit with the minimum of service disruption.

"The overwhelming evidence is that contracting out is not the easy answer for the tough fiscal problems faced by state and local governments."

The Private Sector Is Less Efficient than Government

Gerald W. McEntee

President of the American Federaton of State, County and Municipal Employees (AFSCME), Gerald W. McEntee is an outspoken opponent of privatization and particularly that aspect of it which involves the use of private companies to perform traditionally government-provided tasks. In the following viewpoint, Mr. McEntee writes that privatization of public services results in higher costs, poorer services, corruption, and lack of accountability.

As you read, consider the following questions:

1. What are some of the "hidden costs" that Mr. McEntee says are often forgotten when the costs of public vs. private services are being compared?
2. Mr. McEntee says that "true competition," one of the benefits touted by the supporters of privatization, is most often lacking in the "bids" of private companies to perform public services. On what does he base this contention?

Gerald W. McEntee, "City Services: Can Free Enterprise Outperform the Public Sector?" *Business and Society Review,* Fall 1985. Reprinted with permission.

Contracting out public services—using private companies to perform the work of state and local governments—has increased dramatically in recent years. "Privatization" has been promoted as the panacea for budget problems. However, the overwhelming evidence is that contracting out is *not* the easy answer for the tough fiscal problems faced by state and local governments today.

The American Federation of State, County, and Municipal Employees (AFSCME) has studied the issue of contracting out for many years. The on-the-job experience of AFSCME's 1 million members across the country clearly shows that using private firms to deliver public services has serious shortcomings.

Historically, the U.S. government provides many public services directly, but there has always been some degree of contracting out, particularly at the federal level. In the early years of this century, cities and towns around the country turned to private companies to run local streetcar systems, to collect garbage, to provide fire protection, and to perform other basic public services, often because their communities lacked the needed public resources.

Gross Abuses

But there were problems: Contractors frequently overcharged municipalities; under-the-table payoffs by contractors were common; contractor-provided services were notorious for their poor quality. It was also the era of big city political bosses, and municipal contracts became a favored way of lining pockets and rewarding political cronies.

"Because of gross abuses," Ralph W. Widner, staff vice-president of the Urban Land Institute, has noted, "the reform movement of the 1920s tried to professionalize the delivery of quality public services by making them part of the municipal government." Prodded by reformers, many municipalities decreased their dependence on contractors and delivered more services using the public work force.

Now, state and local governments have been returning to the use of private contractors. In 1982, Widner noted, "The pendulum is swinging back the other way. It will continue to swing until there is another round of abuses and scandals and then [will] swing back the other way."

Experience with contracting out at the state and local levels has demonstrated severe weaknesses in the practice of using private firms to deliver public services. For example:

Higher Costs

Rather than saving money for state and local governments, contracting out often results in higher costs—especially when the true costs of contracting are actually considered. Private companies exist to make a profit; the necessity of a profit drives up the costs, if not immediately, then eventually.

Frequently, a contract, originally awarded at an attractive rate, becomes more and more expensive. This common practice among contractors is called "buying in" or "lowballing." In order to obtain the contract and thus get a foot in the door, a firm offers a very low price to perform a particular service. As contract performance continues, however, the city or state finds itself dependent on the particular contractor to such an extent that it cannot change contractors or take back the service.

This situation often occurs in long-term contracts for services, such as trash collection, which require expensive, well-maintained equipment. After contracting out such a service, a municipality often sells its equipment, leaving it no alternative except to use a contractor. Thus, the contractor who has obtained the first contract with a "lowball" bid can now raise prices on subsequent contracts because the government may no longer have the equipment or the work force to provide the service.

Privatization and Greed

One of the most severe threats facing both public workers and public services is "privatization" and contracting-out. . . .

Communities that use the public services get ripped off. The companies that take over quickly move to maximize profits by cutting services, lowering quality and making services less accessible. . . .

Greed is the name of the game and the public till is tapped by "consultants" and "management firms."

Bill Davis, *Daily World,* June 19, 1986.

Additionally, when the costs of contracting are considered, some states and municipalities forget the "hidden" costs such as contract preparation, the administration and monitoring of the contractor's performance, and the use of public facilities and materials.

Poorer Services

Contracting out often results in poorer services for citizens. Contractors, looking for ways to reduce their costs and maximize their profits, frequently "cut corners" by hiring inexperienced, transient personnel at low wages, by ignoring contract requirements, or by providing inadequate supervision.

The inability of governments to formulate adequate contract specifications also leads to decreased quality and quantity of services. State and local governments often discover to their chagrin that it is extremely difficult to write a contract that ensures that government gets what it wants for the agreed-on price. Or, they learn that work tasks performed as a matter of course by public employees turn out not to be covered under the agreement with a contractor.

Public managers directing a public work force have a large degree of flexibility to respond to unforeseen circumstances; on the other hand, a contractor has the clear right to refuse to do anything—even the smallest task—that isn't in the contract. Even experienced contract writers find it extremely difficult to design a document for complex services that covers all unforeseen circumstances and emergencies. When a contract's performance specifications are too narrow or contain loopholes, the inevitable result is a decrease in the quality of services for the public.

Corrupt Activities

The age-old problem of corruption in contracting out has not improved over time. Contracting is all too often associated with bribery, kickbacks, and collusive bidding. Also, contracts have frequently become a tool of political patronage to reward supporters of successful candidates—just as in the days of the spoils system, when public jobs were doled out to winning candidates' backers.

True competition in contracting is more often the exception than the rule in many state and local governmental jurisdictions. Contracts for trash collection, social services, and architectural, engineering, and consulting services are often awarded under no-bid or negotiated-bid conditions. Where bidding ostensibly occurs, there is often collusion, as the ongoing paving and electrical contracting scandals demonstrate. In addition, contracts often are "wired" by contracting officials (i.e., written so that only one favored or politically connected firm can possibly meet the specifications).

Lack of Public Control

Contracting out results in less accountability by the government to its citizens. When citizens complain about a contracted service, government can often do little more than complain in turn to the contractor or enter into costly contract renegotiations or termination proceedings.

At a time that many citizens feel government is too removed from the people it serves, contracting out pushes the level of accountability and responsiveness one more giant step away. In addition, a dual system of government is created—one with workers who are subject to strict personnel regulations and pay and benefit schedules, all of them public; another with workers who are subject only to the rules set by their private employers.

With competent public management, there would be no need even to consider contracting out in many of the instances in which it is now used. Contracting out is frequently used to mask the inadequacies of public officials who can't manage their own departments properly. Any state or local governmental agency with skilled managers should be able to effect the same kinds of economies and efficiencies that good private managers achieve—and without the added problems that contracting out brings.

If there is dissatisfaction with the performance of a given in-house service, public managers should not automatically assume that contracting out is the answer to the problem. At a minimum, public officials must be willing to explore the alternatives to contracting out; that is a basic management responsibility. Much can be done in-house to improve the cost and quality of the delivery of services.

For example, in New York City, a new concept of school feeding, The Energy Factory [a program designed and implemented by public employees], addressed the problems of low turnout for lunches and high levels of waste. The Energy Factory approach offers children food they are familiar with and allows them to choose from a menu. Every meal exceeds federal nutrition standards, and the cost of the program is within the regular food service budget. Also, in New York City, it was found that custodial and printing work which was costing the city $1.1 million a year for contracts could be performed by city employees for $525,000 per year, about a 50 percent savings.

No Need to Consider Privatization

With competent public management, there would be no need even to consider contracting out in many of the instances in which it is now used. Paul D. Staudohar, professor of business and economics at California State University—Hayward, has written: "There is no innate reason why private employees should perform better than their public-sector counterparts. . . . Waste and inefficiency are found in all levels of service—private and public."

Even some organizations which generally favor contracting out have found numerous pitfalls in the policy of relying on the private sector for public services.

American Federation of State, County and Municipal Employees, *Passing the Bucks: The Contracting Out of Public Services,* 1984.

In Rochester, New York, public administrators determined that improved public management, combined with a productivity-minded public employees work force, could provide city trash collection services 20 to 30 percent cheaper than private contractors.

And, in Rhode Island, an agreement between the state and the employees of the Ladd Center for the Retarded provided that community-based facilities would be primarily staffed by state employees. This approach ensured that patients would continue to receive experienced care by public employees and that quality of services would be maintained.

Responsible government requires improving the quality of public management and public service, not the selling off of government. Public officials all too often have used contracting out to prop up weak management. In every case of failure, in every case where the quality and efficiency of a public service have deteriorated and the cost has increased, where control over public services has diminished, where corruption has occurred, the public endures the consequences and the public pays the bills.

Public service, provided directly by government, is a distinguished hallmark of a civilized society. It is also an American tradition that deserves the best protection and safeguards we can give it.

Recognizing Deceptive Arguments

People who feel strongly about an issue use many techniques to persuade others to agree with them. Some of these techniques appeal to the intellect, some to the emotions. Many of them distract the reader or listener from the real issues.

When evaluating an argument, it is important to recognize the deceptive, or distracting, appeals being used. Here are a few common ones:

a. *bandwagon* — the idea that "everybody" does this or believes this

b. *scare tactics* — the threat that if you don't do this or don't believe this, something terrible will happen.

c. *strawperson* — distorting or exaggerating an opponent's ideas to make one's own seem stronger.

d. *personal attack* — putting down an opponent *personally* instead of rationally debating his or her ideas

e. *hyperbole* — extravagantly exaggerating one's own claims or the weaknesses of opponents

f. *testimonial* — quoting or paraphrasing an authority or celebrity to support one's own viewpoint

Below are listed several statements, many of them taken from the viewpoints in this chapter. *Beside each one, mark the letter of the type of deceptive appeal being used. If a statement is not any of the listed appeals, write N.*

50

1. A new trade policy may mean that we will beat the Japanese to 40 percent of the world's computer business, but you will lose your job in the process.

2. Who else but a bureaucrat would be so boneheaded as to insist that handrails be exactly 42 inches high, and not one inch higher or lower.

3. There are no economic checks or disciplines whatever on bureaucratic activities.

4. We consume telecommunication services directly when we make or receive telephone calls.

5. Free enterprise and bureaucracy are worlds apart, irreconcilable, hostile, forever sundered.

6. As *Fortune* magazine puts it, "What the Japanese were to Detroit, deregulation has been to finance and transportation."

7. Half a century's experimentation with do-everything government has proven to be a monstrous, heart-breaking mistake.

8. In the broadest sense, deregulation has created a restructuring of national priorities.

9. Contracting public services to private companies is not the answer; in every case where the quality and efficiency of a public service has deteriorated and the cost has increased, where control over public service has diminished, where corruption has occurred, the public endures the consequences and the public pays the bills.

10. When we examine the issue of privatization carefully, we all know that it is an essential direction for the country to take.

11. A Twentieth Century Fund study found that the present system of government-operated utilities has been successful in producing good management and effective operations.

12. While it is all very well to praise the efficiency of private enterprise, it is easy to ignore the tremendous financial and social costs of this efficiency to taxpayers.

13. The federal bureaucracy has swollen a *thousand-fold* in the last half century; this titanic expansion of bureaucratic power is shattering the foundations of a free society and menacing the well-being of every citizen.

Periodical Bibliography

The following list of periodical articles deals with the subject matter of this chapter.

Stephen Barone
"How Stupid Can They Get?" *Reason*, April 1986.

Stuart M. Butler
"Privatization: The Antidote to Budget-Cutting Failures," *USA Today*, July 1984.

Kathleen Day
"Re-Regulating the Savings and Loans," *The Washington Post National Weekly Edition*, May 26, 1986.

Michael King
"Taking the Brakes Off Transportation," *Black Enterprise*, June 1984.

Robert Kuttner
"Ma Bell's Broken Home," *The New Republic*, March 17, 1982.

Robert Kuttner
"The Private Market Can't Always Solve Public Problems," *Business Week*, March 10, 1986.

Robert E. Linton
"Through the Financial Looking Glass," *USA Today*, May 1984.

Ken Livingston
"All Revved Up and No Place to Go," *Reason*, March 1986.

Tibor R. Machan
"The Ethics of Privatization," *The Freeman*, July 1986.

Tom Morganthau
"For Sale: Uncle Sam," *Newsweek*, December 30, 1985.

Marvin N. Olavsky
"Hornswoggled!" *Reason*, February 1986.

E.C. Pasour Jr.
"Why Regulators Can't Regulate Effectively," *The Freeman*, June 1986.

Lee Smith
"Reagan's Budget: Selling Off the Government," *Fortune*, March 3, 1986.

Michael Specter
"Soft Landing," *The New Republic*, April 28, 1986.

Donald R. Wells and L.S. Scruggs
"Toward Free Banking," *The Freeman*, July 1986.

2 CHAPTER

How Serious Is the Budget Deficit?

"If Americans really understood how deep in the hole they are . . . they would not only accept sacrifice, they'd demand it."

The Deficit Must Be Ended

Lee A. Iacocca

Lee A. Iacocca, the chairman of Chrysler Corporation, gained notoriety when he pulled his nearly bankrupt company out of the worst slump the auto industry has ever known. In the following viewpoint, Iacocca compares that situation to the budget crisis facing the federal government. He believes that it should pay back its debts as responsibly as did the Chrysler Corporation. Pointing out that large deficits would be a burden on future generations, Mr. Iacocca insists they must be reduced as quickly as possible.

As you read, consider the following questions:

1. How does Mr. Iacocca illustrate the severity of the federal deficit?
2. Why does he think tax reform is a decoy?
3. According to the author, who is responsible for reducing the federal deficit?

Lee A. Iacocca, "Sacrifice and Pay Back the Billions Now," *Los Angeles Times*, November 24, 1985. © 1986, Los Angeles Times Syndicate. Reprinted with permission.

When I was growing up in the 1940s, we used to have a lot of expressions just like the kids do today. We were always preoccupied with numbers. A fast car would "go like 60." Everybody wanted to "live to be a hundred." And a "million" of anything was awesome.

All I knew was that a million was close to infinity. But now, 40 years later, "billion" (that's a thousand million), has crept into my vocabulary. No, I don't go around saying "Baby, you look like a billion," but I did borrow $1.2 billion when Chrysler was dying (and paid it back); I spent a billion to bring out our new mini-vans, and I just signed a billion-dollar labor contract. But just as I'm getting the hang of what "a billion" means, "trillion" starts cropping up. (That's a thousand billion!)

Except for astronomers, hardly anyone ever uses the word "trillion." Even our own federal government didn't comprehend it until 1981 when, after 206 years, it found itself $1 trillion in debt. And with that debt doubling in just four years to $2 trillion, people are starting to ask, "Hey, what is this?" In four more years, when that same debt reaches $3 trillion, those same people are going to get downright mean about it.

Individual Burden

Let me try to explain this mess for you. Let's imagine that our government follows its own truth-in-lending laws and levels with us. Every year with our tax forms we would get a statement telling us where we stand on our debt. Right now it would read like this for the average family of four:

"Dear Mr. and Mrs. Taxpayer:

"Your share of the national debt is now $34,737.32. In the past 12 months your share has increased by $4,233.56. Your share of the interest bill this year is $2,174.73.

"Have a nice day."

If Americans saw the debt personalized like that, it might start a revolution. And maybe we need one.

The interest alone on the debt is now running about $150 billion a year. Remember, that doesn't pave a single road, hire a single cop, educate a single kid or feed a single poor family.

Just five years ago at Chrysler, we had a similar problem. Our debt was so high, I found myself paying more than $400 million a year in interest alone. That meant I was more than $1 million in the hole every single day before I even got to work.

A Financial Mess

I know how Chrysler got into such a financial mess. Some bad luck. Some bad decisions. Some people in the wrong jobs. And some screwed-up priorities. But I'll be damned if I know how the most powerful country on Earth got into such a financial mess. And most of it in just the last five years—during a period of "recovery!"

If things weren't bad enough, Washington in its infinite wisdom has now decided that tax reform is more important than the deficit.

Talk about fooling the people with a decoy. They tout the new tax-reform bill as saving the average family about $400 per year. That helps it play in Peoria. But in that same year, that same Peoria family's share of the national debt goes up by $4,000, or 10 times more than the tax break. So their account gets credited for $400 and debited for $4,000.

They must think we're all pretty stupid out here in the boondocks. But we know how to balance a checkbook. We know how to live on a budget. And we sure as hell know what happens when somebody in the family goes nuts with the credit card.

Pass the Plastic

Washington has gone from "tax and spend" to something a lot worse—"borrow and spend." Now it's pass the plastic and send the bills to the kids. So maybe we should hear from the kids on this subject. Maybe we should restrict the vote to those under 30 years old, because they're the ones getting stuck with the bills.

Three years ago, I suggested that we start balancing the books by cutting the deficit—then only $120 billion—in half. My plan was super-simple: Cut $30 billion in expenses and add $30 billion in revenues. (That's a tax increase, folks.) To keep it fair and bipartisan, you attack the two most sacred of all the sacred cows in Washington. You cut 5% out of defense ($15 billion) and match it dollar for dollar with a $15-billion cut in domestic programs. Then you nail the revenue side with 15 cents a gallon on gas (that's worth $15 billion) and a $5 per barrel tax on imported oil (another $15 billion).

My "four fifteens" would still work today, but now it would take $100 billion to cut the deficit in half, so I guess we would need "four twenty-fives."

I was surprised (and honored) when the President called me in to discuss this plan. But I was quickly disappointed when his advisers told me that such a plan could never work. They never challenged the economic sense of it, just the politics.

Asking for Sacrifice

My idea's major political flaw was that it asked for sacrifice. It was the gas-tax part that really gagged the pollsters. They said it was the most unpopular tax you could lay on the American people. And that was with a gas tax of 4 cents a gallon (today it's all the way up to 9 cents) compared to $1 to $2 in most other nations of the world.

Politicians get elected by giving us goodies, not by taking them away. As Walter Mondale learned the hard way, asking for sacrifice is political suicide. So we can't get too mad at the politicians for letting the deficits run wild. Suicide is a lot to ask of anybody.

And that leaves nobody to blame but ourselves. The people in Washington live by polls. They don't lead public opinion, they follow it. Democracy works from the bottom up. So the answer is to change the polls. The day the pollsters report that a majority of Americans are willing to sacrifice in order to turn our budget scandal around, you'll see it fixed.

Pay It Back

I'm convinced that if Americans really understood how deep in the hole they are, and just what they are doing to their kids' futures, they would not only accept sacrifice, they'd demand it.

When I paid off our loan guarantees, I said: "We borrow money the old-fashioned way; we pay it back." I think the same goes for us as a nation. We borrowed it and we ought to start paying it back. And I mean now!

> *"The deficit is not a crisis. Cutting it too enthusiastically, in fact, could even bring on a recession."*

The Deficit Is Not a Crisis

Charles R. Morris

Not all economists and politicians have been alarmed about the increasing federal deficits. According to Charles R. Morris, author of the following viewpoint, the deficit will not bring about higher inflation or interest rates, nor will it cause a recession. Though Mr. Morris acknowledges that large deficits are not ideal, there are, he says, "worse possible worlds." Charles R. Morris is the author of *A Time of Passion: America 1960-1980* and *The Cost of Good Intentions*, an analysis of the New York fiscal crisis. He is working on a book about the arms race.

As you read, consider the following questions:

1. Why does the author compare putting in a good word for the deficit to speaking up for heresy in medieval Rome?
2. According to the author, what are some explanations for what he calls "the peculiar ruddiness" of the American economy?
3. Mr. Morris cautions against cutting the deficit too enthusiastically because drastic cuts could cause a recession. Do you agree? Why or why not?

Charles R. Morris, "Why a Large Deficit Poses No Real Crisis," *Los Angeles Times*, January 5, 1986. Reprinted with the author's permission.

Putting in a good word for the federal deficit is like speaking up for heresy in medieval Rome. Like ancient heretics, the deficits have been officially anathematized and consigned to the eternal flames, this time by the . . . Gramm-Rudman deficit-reduction law, mandating specific dollar amounts of cuts, rather than by papal decree.

Our benighted medieval forebears, of course, blamed heresies for crop failures, plagues, bad weather and Mongol invasions. Our modern age condemns deficits for more scientific reasons: Everyone knows that deficits cause inflation, high interest rates and tight credit conditions, and will inevitably bring on a recession. Well, sort of. Or at least if we're willing to take the pronouncements of our economic science with a good dollop of faith.

Deficit and Inflation

Consider the effect of the deficit on inflation rates. In 1979, the federal deficit was about $74 billion. In 1985, it [was] . . . about $211 billion. Inflation in 1979 was running at an annual rate in excess of 13%. In 1985, it [was] . . . about 3.6%. If anything, inflation ought to stay flat or drop slightly. . . . Oil prices are falling; natural gas prices are falling; tin, copper and most other metals are at their lowest levels in years. There is a glut of farm products, factory production is still only about 80% of capacity and wage settlements continue to be very restrained.

What about interest rates? Between 1979 and 1981, before the big run-up in the federal deficit, the prime bank lending rate hovered near 20%; now it's less than half that, and the consensus economic forecast is for lower interest rates. . . . Even Henry Kaufman, Salomon Bros.' resident economic guru, who always predicts higher interest rates, prognosticates lower rates this year.

Is credit getting tighter because federal borrowing is crowding out the credit markets? Hardly. The federal government mounted its biggest refinancing campaign in history in the fourth quarter [of 1985] and long-term bond rates actually dropped because there was so much demand for the government's paper. The amount of capital raised for companies on Wall Street in 1985 broke an all-time record, and investment bankers are forecasting another record year.

No Danger of Recession

Is a recession near? The only danger signal on the horizon is that, for the first time in three years, the consensus economic forecast predicts *no* recession. . . . Up until now, most economists have been consistently gloomy—and consistently wrong. For the last three years the United States and Japan have been the fastest growing economies in the world and there is no end in sight. Witness the long-delayed boom in the stock market.

The American economy is by no means perfect. The dollar is

still too strong, for instance, making foreign imports cheaper than they should be. The persistent U.S. trade deficit means that foreigners, notoriously the Japanese but also Germans and Latin Americans, are showering America with high-quality goods at cut-rate prices, raising the American standard of living.

There are worse possible worlds. Consider the plight of poor Britian. Some two decades or so ago, the country lost its nerve, or its willingness to produce, and began to run persistent trade and central government deficits. Investors fled from sterling and the country settled into a kind of fatalistic seediness, growing poorer year by year, with stiff upper lips. Much better to have the Japanese sending over high-quality cars and stereo sets.

Increased Corporate Cash Flows

There are explanations for the peculiar ruddiness of the American economy in the face of huge deficits that go beyond the workings of a benign providence. One is that the Reagan 1981 tax changes, by allowing companies very generous investment tax shelters, vastly increased corporate cash flows. The cash flows don't show up in corporate profits since they're hidden in the depreciation lines.

Deficit Myths

The Federal budget deficit is a genuine problem, but the problem has been exaggerated by two myths: first, that it will abort the expansion by crowding out private borrowers, and, second, that the Federal debt will impose an intolerable burden on our children.

Robert Ortner, *The New York Times*, October 19, 1984.

For at least the first few years of the economic rebound, the boom was very much an investment-led one; and companies' rich cash flows from lower taxes allowed them to increase investment without markedly increasing debt. But the money had to come from somewhere. In effect, the company debt that would have ordinarily been required to finance the rapid investment showed up on the government's books as a deficit resulting from lost tax revenues. Whether that is good or bad is anyone's guess, but it exaggerated the size of the federal deficit and probably made its economic impact appear greater than it was.

Breaking Records

The net inflow of foreign investment funds, estimated at some $130 billion in 1985, is also breaking records. With most of Europe emerging from a prolonged slump, and much of the rest of the world unstable, the United States is an attractive place to invest. . . . As long as foreigners stand ready to buy U.S. securities, the government can keep running deficits, interest rates will keep dropping and there will be plenty of credit for business.

The price, of course, is that foreigners will own a bigger piece of America. Currently, foreigners own about 5% of government securities and perhaps 1% of business and real property assets. The numbers are hardly overwhelming, and whether the trend is good or bad may depend on whether you are a bank executive just fired by new overseas partners or an unemployed worker in Tennessee who is going to get a job at a new Japanese automobile factory.

America and Japan

But the biggest reason immunizing America from the traditional bad effects of big deficits—and in many ways, the most important new economic reality—is the growing interdependence of the American and Japanese economies. Together the two countries account for about 30% of world output: America takes a third of its imports from Japan, or half of Japan's exports; the Japanese buy a quarter of America's exports.

America gives the Japanese a free military umbrella, furnishes most of its food and raw material imports and provides an investment market for the huge and growing surplus of Japanese funds. The Japanese work hard, produce excellent manufactured products, massively underconsume and save a large proportion of their incomes. Without a U.S. consumer market, Japan would have a serious recession, maybe a crash; without the Japanese savings to finance American borrowings, all the scare stories about big deficits might come true.

This is not the best of all possible worlds. Surely, America's future would be more secure if Americans were as efficient, productive and thrifty as the Japanese, and if America's boom had been accompanied by balanced budgets and trade surpluses.

Not a Crisis

But is is far from the worst of all worlds. Certainly, if the whole Japanese nation suddenly launched on a national spree, the supply of savings America needs for its expensive tastes might dry up. That is not going to happen soon, however.

The current federal deficits are too large and should be reduced, if only to quiet the political din. And one day the Japanese probably will lose some of their thrifty habits. But the deficit is not a crisis. Cutting it too enthusiastically, in fact, could even bring on a recession. The real crisis may be in the economics profession. Insisting that the sky is falling may deprive it of the last vestiges of credibility it still retains.

"To move toward a balanced official budget . . . is to move in exactly the wrong direction."

The Deficit Has Stimulated the Economy

Tom Wicker

Deficits, according the the economic system of thought called supply-side economics, can be effectively used to improve the economy. In the following viewpoint, Tom Wicker, columnist for the *New York Times,* agrees with this position. He believes the large federal deficit has stimulated the economy and brought America out of a recession. He cautions against reducing the deficit drastically or suddenly, claiming such action could have a drastic impact.

As you read, consider the following questions:

1. What, according to the author, would be the *disadvantages* of continued large federal deficits?
2. What does he fear more than these disadvantages?
3. Why does Mr. Wicker believe returning to a restrictive policy would be a mistake?

Tom Wicker, "Repeating the Past," *The New York Times,* May 30, 1986. Copyright © 1986 by The New York Times Company. Reprinted by permission.

Since Ronald Reagan took office in 1981, the gross public debt has more than doubled, from $930 billion to $1.9 trillion, reflecting huge annual Federal deficits that reached $212 billion in fiscal 1985.

The conventional view is that this has been a disaster; the [1985] Gramm-Rudman-Hollings Deficit Reduction Act—a monumental abdication of Congress's power of the purse—is based on that assumption.

But without those deficits and their stimulating effect, the deep recession of 1981-82 would have been far worse. Unemployment would have gone well above the 10.7 percent actually recorded, and the brisk recovery of 1983 and 1984 would have been impossible.

In his new book, "How Real Is the Federal Deficit?" Robert Eisner of Northwestern University explains what happens. Presidents Carter and then Reagan followed tight fiscal policies, and the Federal Reserve pursued tight monetary policy, from 1977 to 1981, because they perceived the *official* Federal deficits of the period to provide too much stimulus to the economy. In fact, by Mr. Eisner's calculations of the effects of inflation and interest rates, those official deficits actually were "adjusted surpluses" that had a depressing economic effect and produced the 1981-82 downturn.

The Deficit Fueled Recovery

But in 1982, when the effects of increased military spending and the tax cuts of 1981 began to be felt, a real Federal deficit fueled recovery. From a surplus amounting to 1.45 percent of gross national product in 1981, the adjusted high-employment budget swung to a deficit of 2.01 percent of G.N.P. in 1982—a total change of 3.46 percentage points, one of the largest swings to expansion on record.

But those big real deficits are continuing. Before any action under Gramm-Rudman, Congressional Budget Office projections of the official high-employment budget (calculated on the basis of 5.1 percent unemployment) showed the deficit rising to $225 billion by 1990. Even Mr. Eisner's adjustments for price and interest effects would leave a real deficit of $116 billion that year.

Mr. Eisner agrees with critics of such deficits that if they continue they will involve "costs to the American people," in that the economy would be less productive and "more of our products and earnings would be going to foreign owners of our productive assets and government securities." But, he asks, "what are the costs of alternatives?"

To reduce Social Security benefits would break "a social contract" and be perceived as unfair to one particular group. Big non-military spending cuts are not only politically difficult, but, Mr. Eisner argues, might be in some cases "a reckless reduction in investment in the human and public capital on which our future well-being depends"—health, education and research, for good examples. Reductions in military spending and/or "a general increase in taxes" appear preferable—except, of course, to President Reagan and to a lot of Americans opposed to both.

Mr. Eisner's view is that if continuing deficit stimulus takes the economy close to full capacity, deficits of the present size "would contribute to inflation and a costly, restrictive monetary policy." But these costs might well be outweighed by the costs of deficit-reducing action—particularly the drastic and unnecessary budget cuts that would be forced by Gramm-Rudman-Hollings.

As originally proposed, that act would reduce the official deficit in $36 billion annual bites from $180 billion in 1986 to about zero in five years. If Congress actually allowed this to happen, Mr. Eisner's figures show that the high-employment budget adjusted for price and interest effects would produce, by fiscal 1990, a real Federal *surplus* of $114.4 billion—more than 2 percent of G.N.P.

The consequences of such a restrictive policy, Mr. Eisner points out, would be "sobering"—which is an understatement. The rate of growth of real G.N.P. would fall to 2 percent by 1990, if the Federal Reserve maintained a relatively easy monetary policy, and to 1 percent if it didn't. Unemployment would rise 1 or 2 percent from 1987 to 1990—and Mr. Eisner thinks these projections probably are too optimistic. By its reductions in aggregate demand and purchasing power, such a course would bring on the worst recession since the 1930's.

Large Deficits Are the Right Medicine

As the Reagan Administration and business leaders flounder around for a way out of this [economic] mess, their natural inclination is to follow the path . . . [of] substantial budget cuts and tax increases.

It is precisely the wrong medicine. . . .

No one wants to say it aloud these days, but what is needed is a large deficit in the Federal budget. Significant Government spending would create jobs and stimulate growth. Given the current decline of consumer spending, it is the only way out.

The Progressive, March 1983.

Thus, we may be in the process of making the same mistake made in the late 70's—turning to a restrictive policy on the basis of a *perceived* deficit that is by no means as threatening as conventional economic wisdom would have us believe. With unemployment still at about 7 percent and real economic growth well below its potential, to move toward a balanced official budget—as Gramm-Rudman-Hollings requires—is to move in exactly the wrong direction.

"The only healthy course is to . . . move promptly to reduce the deficit."

The Deficit Has Harmed the Economy

Peter G. Peterson

Peter G. Peterson, an investment banker, is chairman of the Council of Foreign Relations, a research organization located in New York, and chairman of the Institute for International Relations. In the following viewpoint he expresses concern over what he terms a "gambling mood" toward the federal deficit. While other economists may wait for the deficits to diminish of their own accord, Mr. Peterson believes large deficits have hurt the economy and will continue to do so unless aggressive steps are taken to reduce them.

As you read, consider the following questions:

1. According to the author, what indications show the economy is not as strong as some estimates claim?
2. Why is Mr. Peterson worried about "the gambling mood" regarding the deficit?
3. The author makes predictions about directions the economy might take. How useful are these predictions? Do they effectively prove that large deficits are as harmful as Mr. Peterson suggests? Why or why not?

To borrow former Senator Howard Baker's words, we are now taking a "riverboat gamble" with the economy by our increasingly relaxed attitude toward the Federal budget.

[In 1985] the widespread conviction that we faced deadly $200 billion deficits as "far as the eye could see" produced the Gramm-Rudman-Hollings law mandating cuts in spending. Now, according to official estimates splashed across our front pages, today's red ink torrent will dry up to a "mere" $104 billion trickle in five years under "current policy"—that is, even without the politically painful moves on spending or taxes required by Gramm-Rudman-Hollings. The message is that we can relax on the deficit.

A Risky Bet

Such is the bet we are taking. Yet it is a bet born more of hope than a sober figuring of the odds.

For one thing, we have heard it before. In 1981, supply-side forecasts said there weren't going to be any deficits after 1984; we were going to "grow our way out" and enjoy large trade surpluses as well. In 1982, despite deficit clouds on the horizon, President Reagan declared that "a balanced budget is not that far distant." In 1984, the Treasury Department questioned whether deficits even mattered. By 1985, they had become public enemy No. 1. Yet now we seem to have taken a fresh dose of economic valium rediscovering how pleasant it is to wish the deficits away.

Make no mistake about it: we are in a gambling mood. Everything seems to be going our way. With heady bursts of real growth over the past three years, some now predict expansion "as far as the eye can see," almost as if we had repealed the business cycle. Where energy experts were once predicting perpetual hikes in oil prices, the stock market now seems to be treating oil's cheap price as permanent. Against the backdrop of falling inflation and interest rates, the dollar is down, foretelling a boost in exports. Meanwhile, foreigners keep sending their money here, patiently financing almost 60 percent of our budget deficits.

Euphoria vs. Reality

Having ingested these statistical cocktails, the stock market has been on a roll. It now seems no less eager to swallow the news that our Federal deficit has miraculously become self-correcting. Yet this euphoria on the trading floor is not matched by board room realities. Indeed, what we may be looking at is the greatest decoupling in recent memory of the "financial" economy from the "real" economy: euphoric markets on the one hand, nervous managers on the other.

Moreover, we are soon due for some inflationary pressure as the falling dollar pushes up our import costs faster than we cut back purchases from abroad. If this is accompanied by an unexpectedly large budget deficit or a slowing economy, the fickle

confidence of those who have been funding our deficits could turn and turn fast.

There was a possible harbinger of this in the bond market, which . . . caught a case of the jitters when it appeared that Japanese investors—suffering heavy exchange losses and facing declining yields—might be losing their appetite for dollar instruments. What if this trend were to grow into a general flight from the dollar? Imports would become even more expensive, boosting inflation. Foreign capital would begin to disappear, touching off ferocious competition among borrowers. This in itself would tend to drive up interest rates, but as the dollar continued to fall, the Federal Reserve Board might well have to kick them higher by tightening up to "protect" the currency—perhaps bringing on a recession, aggravating third-world debt problems and provoking a financial crisis.

Playing Make Believe

Suppose, however, that confidence holds. The dollar descends gently. Demand for imports declines, dampening protectionist sentiment. The trade deficit drops, albeit more slowly. But so, too, does the foreign capital inflow that finances it.

Suppose also that our budget deficit remains at or above current levels. In that event, our Government's voracious appetite for credit—equal to a stunning 77 percent of net private savings last year—would increasingly have to be satisfied from domestic sources. We would face the specter from which the inflows of foreign capital have delivered us over the last several years—intensifying competition for funds, rising interest rates, dwindling investment: in short, old-fashioned "crowding out." This would knock the wind out of housing, the stock and bond markets and growth prospects generally, placing borrowers, the banking system and third world exporters in an ever-tighter squeeze.

In short, whether the dollar and unsustainable trade deficits decline precipitously or smoothly, the United States will have to make do with smaller flows of foreign savings in the future. If the Federal need for credit—which will be satisfied at any price—stays high or climbs, it will consume domestic savings urgently needed for productive investment and will drive up real interest rates. Simply put, the worse the combination of a dollar that falls too far too fast, and a deficit that stays too high too long, the more we cheat the future.

Reduce the Deficit Promptly

The only healthy course is to complete the dollar's correction (another 10 to 15 percent drop) and, at the same time, move promptly to reduce the deficit. That way, demand for and supply of savings will decline in tandem.

Since we're betting on a disappearing act to produce this healthy result, it is only prudent to examine what's behind this miracle-to-be. For openers, the Congressional Budget Office figure assumes zero growth in defense authority over the next five years. Is that plausible—let alone desirable? How about interest rates? The Office of Management and Budget bets that Treasury bills will yield a mere 4 percent in 1991, while 10-year issues will yield only 4.5 percent. (The Congressional Budget Office figures are 5.5 percent and 6.3 percent, respectively.) Neither projection allows for a recession, blithely adding five more years of growth onto the last three. The Congressional Budget Office predicts an average 3.4 percent real growth rate; O.M.B., 3.8 percent. If all this comes to pass, 1991 deficits will "only" be $104 billion.

But what if real growth keeps up at a slightly lower rate—say, a healthy 3 percent; and what if the Treasury faces a 7 percent financing rate, and what if we expand the defense budget from this year's level at a real rate of 2 percent? While these assumptions scarcely fit the definition of pessimism, they would generate a 1991 deficit of about $200 billion. For every percentage point rise in interest rates, this deficit would climb by almost $25 billion. Further, let us suppose it turns out that we have not repealed the business cycle after all, and end up with a recession similar to that of 1973-75. In that case, deficits could climb above $300 billion, three times worse than the rosy estimates now emanating from Washington.

Act Now

These possibilities leave me with only one conclusion: we must act decisively on the budget front and we must act now. We should take advantage of growth, oil prices, low inflation and the mood of optimism to face hard choices; such action will be virtually impossible during any downturn. If a recession hits next year and we have done nothing, the interest costs alone by 1988 could consume nearly 60 percent of private savings.

For some time, I, along with five former Treasury secretaries and over 500 leading Americans from both parties who have joined together in a group called the Bipartisan Budget Appeal, have pressed for a fair program of deficit reduction. The program would first place top priority on cutting spending generally and in particular slowing the rate of increase in the virtually untouched non-means-tested entitlement programs (including Social Security and Federal pensions) going to middle and upper-income citizens, programs that now amount to over $372 billion and have been compounding at a 12 percent rate for the last 15 years; second, reduce the rate of increase in defense spending; third, link spending cuts to new revenues from consumption-based taxes (Could there be a better time for a gasoline tax?).

By 1981, it had taken America 200 years to amass a national debt of a trillion dollars. Since then, as a result of our riverboat gamble that record growth would end deficits, we have seen this debt double to $2 trillion. America had metamorphosed from the world's largest creditor to the world's largest debtor. Meteoric interest costs, the fastest growing part of the Federal budget, already consume a stunning four of every 10 individual income tax dollars. I doubt that our children and grandchildren will appreciate perpetually servicing that debt plus however much our deficits add to the total. Washington's wisdom says the deficits, like winter, will just go away. Shall we bet again?

"The country moved from a flush of enthusiasm for tax reduction to a sad recognition that taxes were too low."

Raising Taxes Will Reduce the Deficit

Herbert Stein

Senior Fellow at the American Enterprise Institute and editor of its publication *AEI Economist,* Herbert Stein is also A. Willis Robertson Professor of Economics at the University of Virginia. He has written for *The Wall Street Journal, Fortune,* and *The Economy Today.* In the following viewpoint, excerpted from his book *Presidential Economics: The Making of Economic Policy from Roosevelt to Reagan and Beyond,* Professor Stein argues that taxes *must* be raised if the excessive deficit is to be reduced.

As you read, consider the following questions:

1. Professor Stein writes that "we talk as if deficits were terribly important." Why, then, according to him, have we not made any significant reduction in the federal deficit?
2. Professor Stein seems to believe that nearly everybody has come around to the belief that raising taxes is essential. What does he say has brought about this view?
3. Professor Stein writes that most of the new tax revenue should come from the middle class. Why?

Nothing better reveals the vacuum in economic policy than the gap between the nearly universal statements of aversion to budget deficits and the prospect of exceptionally large deficits for as far ahead as the eye can see. No one any longer talks about balancing the budget. There is a tacit agreement that the things that would have to be done to eliminate the deficit cannot be done—which means only that the necessary action is considered worse than the deficit.

But if zero has been abandoned as a goal for the size of the deficit no other goal has received any general support. Everyone in the political process wants to be known as supporting a lower deficit than his rivals. . . . All the participants are willing to do something to reduce the prospective deficits, but each is willing to do only things that he was willing to do anyway, without regard to the size of the deficit. The President is willing to cut social programs he wanted to cut even when the deficits did not loom so large. Many "liberals" are prepared to cut the defense program, or to raise taxes on the "rich" in order to reduce the deficit—never having felt much need for a large defense program or much concern about the after-tax incomes of the upper-income minority.

Lots of Talk, Little Action

The fact is that talk about reducing the budget deficit has become largely a ritual. Everyone believes that there are other people out there who are greatly worried about budget deficits and it is therefore necessary to show that one shares that worry. But the reasons for the worry are not cogent or agreed-upon and do not lead to any clear idea about the proper size of deficit, if it is not zero, or to much action.

There are people who believe that deficits don't really matter. They believe that the size of government expenditures matters. Government spending subtracts from the output available for private use. They are concerned about that subtraction—mainly to keep it as low as possible. But whether that subtraction is financed by taxation or by borrowing seems to them of no great importance. This attitude leads to a certain anomaly. People who hold this view are usually reluctant to avow it when expenditure decisions are being considered. Wanting to hold expenditures down, they would like all decision-makers to believe that they should not spend money unless they raise taxes to pay for it. But the decision-makers are not likely to accept that discipline unless they see some reason why they should raise taxes, and they will not see that unless they think that the difference between taxing and borrowing matters.

Our present situation is that we talk as if deficits were terribly important, we act as if they didn't matter very much, and we really don't know what the nature and size of their effects are. It is not easy to be positive in laying down principles for deciding on policy toward deficits. All one can do is to try prudently to adapt policy to a rather cautious and moderate view of what the effects are. . . .

One of the basic premises of Reagan economics was that politicians liked to raise taxes, or at least had no great aversion to raising taxes. The standard political philosophy was thought to be "tax and tax, spend and spend." Because the politicians had no proper appreciation of the evils of taxes they were willing to raise taxes to pay for increases of government expenditures that were clearly excessive. If this propensity to tax was resisted and indeed if, with strong presidential leadership, taxes could be reduced, excessive expenditures would also be reduced and other good things would happen. . . .

Raise Taxes

Heller: There's no way that the deficit can be cut to a manageable size without raising taxes. A deficit-reduction package must include three elements: A cutback in the defense buildup, a slowing of the rising cost of medicare and other entitlements, and tax increases.

US News: Why can't the deficit problem be solved simply by cutting spending, now more than 900 billion dollars a year?

Heller: Impossible. Food stamps, welfare and other social programs for the poor have been cut to the bone already. They probably deserve more, not less, money. Cutting back middle-class entitlement programs can't do the job, either. And even if you hold the defense buildup to as little as 3 percent real growth annually, you still would have to phase in 100 billion dollars of tax increases to balance the budget by 1989.

Interview with Walter Heller, *US News & World Report,* August 20, 1984.

When the President proposed a big tax reduction in 1981, although Congress resisted some parts of the reduction it readily accepted the idea. But within a year the President was joining those, a majority in the Congress, who believed that taxes were too low. . . .

An Undertaxed Society

Between 1981 and 1983 the country moved from a flush of enthusiasm for tax reduction to a sad recognition that taxes were too low—that we were, as George F. Will put it, an undertaxed society. The basic reason for this change was experience with the effort to cut government expenditures. Until Reagan became President it was always possible to believe that a determined budget-cutter in the White House could find vast amounts of money in expenditure programs that could be eliminated—and that Congress would be forced to eliminate them if some of the revenue was removed. But we have seen that "even" President

Reagan could not propose a budget that cut expenditures enough to hold deficits down without more taxes than were left after the 1981 tax cut. This may have been in part for political reasons. That is, there may have been bigger cuts that he would have liked to make if the Congress and the country would have accepted them. But undoubtedly he and his colleagues, once in office, discovered that the needed or justifiable expenditures were larger than they thought. And the political reason is not to be disregarded either, because it is an indication of the public's wishes, which should not be disregarded.

No one likes tax increases. What was recognized by 1983 was that the consequences of failure to raise taxes—which were to forgo certain expenditures or to accept a larger deficit—were worse than the consequences of a tax increase. But this recognition did not assure the result. As indicated earlier, although almost everyone thought the prospective deficits were too large there was not any compelling agreement on the proper size of deficit. This raised the strong possibility that when it came right down to the hard decision the President and Congress would settle for a token tax increase and token deficit reduction. There would always be a question whether now was the right time for a tax increase, however much the long-run need was recognized.

Moreover, the nature of the tax increase is critical—whether individual income taxes, corporate taxes, selective excises or general consumption taxes. There will be much disagreement about that, which may prevent achievement of a tax increase of adequate size. The nature of the tax increase will also influence its effects. Any tax increase will have adverse economic effects—if considered in isolation from the beneficial effects of reducing the budget deficit. But some tax increases will have more adverse effect per dollar of revenue than others.

A Tax Increase Now Needed

The conditions that give rise to the need for more revenue suggest what is the nature of the appropriate tax increase. A tax increase is now needed because it is necessary to devote a larger share of the national output to defense and to private investment and undesirable to reduce the share devoted to the consumption of the very poor. That means basically that it is necessary to reduce the share of the national output devoted to the consumption of middle-income people, the consumption of the rich absorbing only a tiny part of the national output. . . .

The relative merits of [tax-raising] approaches are less important than the need to get acceptance of the idea that somehow the taxes on the middle-income American must be increased and that this must be done without increasing the tax burden on the very rich or the very poor. This becomes clear once one abandons the notion that growth of the economy, perhaps under the

73

stimulus of supply-side tax cuts, will provide for all our wants. Once that is accepted, priorities must be established. Our priorities, I am suggesting, should be the defense of the country, the promotion of economic growth and support of the living standards of the very poor. If that is the case we must look to the consumption of the middle-income American as the source from which we tend to these priorities. That does not mean a decline in middle-income living standards. It does mean a decline in middle-income consumption in the rising national income will have to decline, so that the absolute standard of living rises more slowly than it otherwise might for a while. . . .

One can easily be skeptical of the possibility of achieving an increase in the taxation of middle-class people, especially if the increase is not extended to the upper-income people, since the middle-income people are the large majority of the voters. But such skepticism would not be entirely justified. The public, including the middle class, has shown a capacity to learn some things about the tax policy that serve the national interest and to accept the implications of them. The 1981 tax cut was an indication of that. True, almost everyone got something out of that act. But still the public accepted with equanimity some tax changes that in other times would have been strongly resisted as handouts to the rich. . . . Perhaps that was an isolated occasion, but politicians and leaders of opinion should not act on the assumption that the citizens are incapable of farsighted and public-spirited action.

Everyone Must Sacrifice

I do not want to suggest that it is only the middle class that must sacrifice. The tens of billions probably needed to reduce the deficit can only come from the middle class, because that is where the money is. To try to get any significant amount out of upper-income people would be futile and counterproductive. There has been some lessening in the resentment and envy toward the rich and powerful that animated tax legislation in the past, as well as greater recognition of the economic folly of the taxation those feelings inspired. But the upper-income people, corporate heads and their representatives have an obligation not to exploit the situation by using their influence to defend tax preferences that are unjustified in equity or economics. Percentage depletion and provision of excess loss reserves by financial institutions are examples. If we enter a period of more stable prices it may even be necessary to think again about that perennial blister, the taxation of capital gains. For a long time the closing of such loopholes was resisted on the ground that the high rates of taxation made them necessary if the economy was to function. Now that the highest rates of individual income taxation, and the effective rate of corporate profits taxation, have been substantially reduced it is time to reconsider the loopholes.

"Raising taxes will not cure the deficit."

Raising Taxes Will Not Reduce the Deficit

Bruce Bartlett & Jack Kemp

Bruce Bartlett, author of Part I of the following viewpoint, is John M. Olin Fellow at the Heritage Foundation. Part II is taken from an interview with New York Republican Senator Jack Kemp in *US News & World Report*. Mr. Bartlett and Senator Kemp both believe that the national deficit cannot be reduced by raising taxes. Instead, they argue that government spending must be drastically cut.

As you read, consider the following questions:

1. Mr. Bartlett lists three "myths about the state of the economy." Briefly state them in your own words.
2. Why does Mr. Bartlett believe that it may not be necessary to do *anything* to reduce the deficit? Does Senator Kemp agree with this view?

Bruce Bartlett, "A Tax Hike Is No Cure for the Deficit," The Heritage Foundation *Backgrounder*, March 3, 1986. Reprinted with permission.

Jack Kemp, "Raise Taxes to Cut the Federal Deficit?" Reprinted from *U.S. News & World Report* issue of August 20, 1984. Copyright, 1984, U.S. News & World Report.

I

Raising taxes will not cure the deficit, for the deficit is not caused by insufficient taxes, but by excessive spending. In the past ten years, in fact, federal tax revenues have almost tripled, despite the reduction in tax rates. The trouble is that federal spending has grown even faster than revenues. . . .

Rather than giving consideration to tax gimmicks as a means of reducing the deficit, Congress should be pressing ahead with the only solution to the red ink—cutting federal spending.

Economic Myths

Those who advocate tax increases to solve the deficit problem base their argument on a series of myths about the state of the economy.

Myth 1: The deficit derives from Americans being "undertaxed."

Many tax increase proponents claim that the deficit was caused by Ronald Reagan's tax "cuts" of 1981. But the fact is that revenues have remained relatively constant as a share of gross national product, despite the 1981 tax cut. Spending, however, has exploded. . . . Deficit reduction efforts, moreover, thus far have concentrated disproportionately on raising taxes, rather than cutting spending. . . .

Myth 2: A tax increase will not affect economic growth.

Those who advocate tax increases to deal with deficits tend to assume that the economy can benefit from lower deficits without suffering from the tax hike itself. They assume that it is possible to have it both ways: higher growth and lower unemployment resulting from previous tax cuts, along with the alleged benefits from lower deficits, such as lower interest rates, resulting from a new tax increase.

A related error is to assume that taxes will be increased with the least possible economic damage. Yet, given the political makeup of Congress, it is more likely that new taxes would take the form of increased taxes on capital—hitting saving and investment rather than consumption. If taxes on capital were raised, saving could fall by as much or more than the amount of the tax. The result: rising interest rates, even as deficits fell.

Myth 3: Congress will use the new revenues to cut the deficit, not spend them.

It is wishful thinking to assume that new revenues, however raised, will be applied to deficit reduction, rather than fueling additional spending. More likely, any deficit reduction due to increased revenues simply will alleviate the pressure to control spending. If the deficit is ever brought under control by raising taxes, spending is almost certain to take off again—unless checked by a balanced budget/spending limitation amendment to the Constitution.

Because the U.S. economy is extremely complex, actions dealing with one problem may create others. High interest rates are still an irritant, but have declined sharply despite large budget deficits. Interest rates on three-month Treasury bills, for example, have fallen by half since 1981, from 14 percent to a current level of about 7 percent. How much further do advocates of tax increases think rates would fall if the budget were balanced? In 1969, the last year the U.S. had a balanced budget, Treasury bill rates averaged 6.7 percent—only slightly lower than they are today.

If it is unlikely that lower deficits will push interest rates down further, what benefits can be expected? Some argue that the deficit raises the exchange value of the dollar and thereby penalizes exports. But if interest rates are now about what they were when the budget was balanced—and lower than in many competing countries—what continues to draw foreign funds into dollar-dominated assets? If foreign investment in dollar assets is a problem, and it almost surely is not, balancing the budget is not going to solve it.

Cut Expenditures

Those people who are properly worried about the deficit unfortunately offer an unacceptable solution: increasing taxes. Curing deficits by raising taxes is equivalent to curing someone's bronchitis by shooting him. The "cure" is far worse than the disease.

For one reason, as many critics have pointed out, raising taxes simply gives the government more money, and so the politicians and bureaucrats are likely to react by raising expenditures still further. Parkinson said it all in his famous "Law": "Expenditures rise to meet income." If the government is willing to have, say, a 20 percent deficit, it will handle high revenues by raising spending still more to maintain the same proportion of deficit. . . .

No, the only sound cure for deficits is a simple but virtually unmentioned one: cut the federal budget. How and where? Anywhere and everywhere.

Murray N. Rothbard, *On Principle*, May 28, 1984.

It has also been argued that the federal deficit causes inflation. But this is an argument with little evidence. In the past four years, in fact, inflation has subsided as the deficit has mounted.

It is even questionable whether any action is needed to curb the deficits. They appear to be coming under control under current policies. If the Administration estimates are correct, the budget deficit will fall to 1.9 percent of gross national product by fiscal 1988; this would be the lowest level since 1979. Independent projections reach similar conclusions. The Congressional Budget Office's (CBO) most recent forecast, for example, shows the deficit falling by $20 billion a year without congressional action.

The case for tax increases to balance the budget thus is extremely weak.

II

Q Representative Kemp, why do you oppose tax increases to reduce the huge federal deficit?

A The deficit is now declining rapidly as revenues generated by the strong recovery grow at 12 percent a year while spending rises only 4 to 4½ percent. The deficit will continue to decline as the recovery proceeds and pressure is put on Congress to cut spending.

Q So the deficit can be reduced by the combination of economic growth and spending cuts—

A Yes. A tax increase would be counterproductive. It would impede the recovery and expand the deficit, not reduce it.

Q What kinds of spending cuts do you favor?

A I would cut corporate-welfare spending, such as the Export-Import Bank and the synfuels program. By abolishing the synfuels program, for example, we could save 14 billion dollars of subsidies for major oil companies to convert coal and shale into synthetic fuel at very high prices. But the big savings will come from keeping the recovery strong so that people are working and don't have to draw on federal benefit programs. Look at the budgets of state and local governments. They now have a surplus of about 55 billion dollars because of the strong recovery.

Q What level of federal deficit is acceptable?

A It's not the dollar size of the deficit that counts. What's important is the relationship of the deficit to the total economy. The federal deficit now amounts to about 4.5 percent of the 3.7-trillion-dollar economy. We should aim to reduce that ratio to below 1.5 percent by 1986, or 1987 at the latest.

Reform Taxes Without Ill Effects

Q And we don't need to punish ourselves by raising taxes to achieve that goal?

A That's right. But we do need tax reform. By adopting a modified flat tax, we could raise more revenues by taxing the underground economy and by enabling the overall economy to perform more efficiently. We also could protect lower-income families from paying more tax and make certain that no one pays more than a 25 percent tax rate again.

Q Do you favor slowing the rising cost of defense?

A We have already. Democrats and Republicans alike say we need to spend more for defense. They differ over how much more. Both the Senate and House totals are below the President's request. I support the higher Senate amount. I share the President's belief that if the choice is between rebuilding our nation's defense capability and accepting a deficit, he would accept a deficit.

Q With inflation as low as it is, should the Federal Reserve help trim the deficit by lowering interest rates?

A With inflation dropping and the dollar rising against foreign currencies and the price of gold declining, that suggests that money is too tight and the Fed should ease. It's not the economy that's overheated. It's the Fed.

Distinguishing Between Fact and Opinion

This activity is designed to help develop the basic reading and thinking skill of distinguishing between fact and opinion. Consider the following statement as an example: "The federal deficit was one trillion dollars in 1985." This statement is a fact which could be proved by looking at the federal balance sheet. But consider this statement: "The federal deficit will destroy America's economy." Such a statement is clearly an expressed opinion. Anyone who favors large deficits would disagree; anyone who fears large deficits would agree.

When investigating controversial issues it is important to be able to distinguish between statements which are stated as fact and those which are clearly statements of opinion.

The following statements are taken from the viewpoints in this chapter. Consider each statement carefully. *Mark O for any statement you feel is an opinion or an interpretation of facts. Mark F for any statement you believe is a fact. Mark N for any statement you believe is too controversial to decide.*

If you are doing this activity as a member of a class or group, compare your answers with those of other class or group members. Be able to defend your answers. You may discover that others will come to different conclusions than you. Listening to the reasons others present for their answers may give you valuable insights in distinguishing between fact and opinion.

If you are reading this book alone, ask others if they agree with your answers. You will find this interaction very valuable.

> O = opinion
> F = fact
> N = too controversial to decide

1. The interest on the federal deficit is running about $150 billion a year.
2. Tax reform is far more important than the deficit.
3. In 1979, the federal deficit was about $74 billion.
4. Henry Kaufman, Salomon Brothers' resident economic guru, predicts lower interest rates this year.
5. Up until now, most economists have been consistently gloomy—and consistently wrong.
6. For the last three years, the United States and Japan have had the fastest growing economies in the world.
7. The dollar is still too strong, making foreign imports cheaper than they should be.
8. The United States is an attractive place to invest.
9. America takes half of Japan's exports; the Japanese buy a quarter of America's exports.
10. America's future would be more secure if Americans were as efficient, productive, and thrifty as the Japanese.
11. The current federal deficits are too large and should be reduced.
12. The conventional view is that large federal deficits have been a disaster.
13. According to economist Robert Eisner, continued large deficits would contribute to inflation.
14. The Gramm-Rudman-Hollings Act proposes to reduce the deficit to zero in five years.
15. To move toward a balanced budget is to move in exactly the wrong direction.
16. We are taking a gamble with the economy by our increasingly relaxed attitude toward the federal budget.
17. The Congressional Budget Office and the Office of Management and Budget have predicted different growth rates for the next five years.
18. If a recession hits and we have done nothing about the federal deficit, the interest costs alone could consume 60 percent of savings.
19. We talk as if deficits were terribly important, we act as if they didn't matter much, and we really don't know what their effects are.

Periodical Bibliography

The following list of periodical articles deals with the subject matter of this chapter.

Robert J. Bresler — "The Deficit Dilemma: A Question of National Character," *USA Today*, May 1986.

James Dale Davidson — "Budget Talk with Tom and Ralph," *Reason*, June 1986.

Peter V. Domenici — "The Ghosts of Deficit Forever," *The Washington Post*, January 21, 1986.

Jeff Van Drunen — "The Debt: Catastrophic Urgency, Little Concern," *The Freeman*, October 1984.

Milton Friedman — "Why Deficits Are Bad," *Newsweek*, January 2, 1984.

J. Peter Grace — "Government Waste—A Danger to Our Freedoms?" *USA Today*, May 1986.

Thomas M. Humbert — "Understanding the Federal Budget," *The Heritage Foundation Backgrounder*, January 27, 1984.

Jack Kemp — "My Plan to Balance the Budget," *Policy Review*, Spring 1986.

Richard D. Lamm — "Four Governors: Disaster Is Lurking in the Budget Deficits," *The Washington Post National Weekly Edition*, January 30, 1984.

Los Angeles Times — "Is the National Debt Really a Serious Threat to US Economy?" November 10, 1985.

John Palmer and Stephanie Gould — "Should We Worry About the Deficit?" *The Washington Monthly*, May 1986.

Ronald Reagan — "Spending Is the Problem, Not Taxes," Speech in *The New York Times*, February 6, 1986.

Alice M. Rivlin — "Why and How to Cut the Deficit," *The Brookings Review*, Summer 1984.

Peter Samuel — "Battling the Budget Bulge—Gracefully," *Reason*, May 1984.

The Washington Times — "Budget Deficits: What to Do?" February 14, 1984.

What Kind of Taxation Is Most Appropriate?

"Not only would the flat rate be fair to all Americans, but I am convinced it would result in a greater collection of revenue."

The Flat Rate Tax Is Fair and Equitable

Philip M. Crane

Philip M. Crane is a Republican representative from Illinois. A member of the House Ways and Means Committee and former chairman of the Republican Study Committee, Mr. Crane was the first member of Congress to introduce a proposal for a flat rate tax. In the following viewpoint, he argues that the flat rate tax would foster the basic principles upon which the tax system was founded: equity, efficiency, and simplicity.

As you read, consider the following questions:

1. How would the flat rate tax tap revenues from the "underground economy," according to the author?
2. The author believes that lower and middle income people will not pay more taxes. Why is this?
3. How does the author believe that a flat tax would simplify taxation?

Philip M. Crane, "A Flat Rate Tax on Income—A Fair Tax," *USA Today*, September 1984. Copyright by The Society for the Advancement of Education. Reprinted with permission.

The need for a vast overhaul of our complicated Federal tax code is obvious, and there is now reason to believe a major restructuring could be completed in the next Congress. The most pressing need is for a simplification of the present intricate income tax, and the answer to the problem is to substitute a flat rate tax for the progressive rates which now claim as much as 50% of taxable income. . . .

Not only would the flat rate be fair to all Americans, but I am convinced it would result in a greater collection of revenue. For one reason, Americans who now evade the income tax because they consider it to be confiscatory and/or unfair would be willing to contribute to the cost of government if they felt the new system evenly distributed the burden of Federal expense.

A flat rate tax would certainly tap some of the "underground economy," which is now pegged at almost $300,000,000,000. This figure translates to almost $100,000,000,000 in uncollected taxes. The greater part of this is represented by unreported income of individuals. Just short of a quarter-of-a-trillion dollars is hidden from the Internal Revenue Service by these Americans. The areas of tax-dodging include wages, dividends, interest, rents, pensions, and capital gains.

There is, however, no reason to believe that those engaged in such illegal activities as drug peddling, gambling, and prostitution would begin paying taxes even with a flat rate tax, so that income would remain unreported.

Ignoring Inflation

The current income tax is insensitive to inflation, which pushes taxpayers into higher income brackets due to the graduated rate structure. Married couples and families are also penalized as a result of graduated income taxes, The complexity of the tax creates onerous problems of compliance, administration, and enforcement, frustrating all parties participating in the payment and collection of income taxes.

The complexity is best illustrated by the fact that there are over 2,000 pages of Internal Revenue Code. There are 10,000 pages of IRS regulations to explain the code—inadequately. One can expect six IRS offices to render six different interpretations. The Office of Management and Budget states that one-half of all Federal paperwork is related to income tax. Over 40% of all taxpayers pay someone to prepare their income tax forms—to the tune of more than $50,000,000,000. It is estimated that American taxpayers spend 650,000,000 hours to complete their tax forms.

A Simple Tax

A proportional tax on all individuals at one low flat rate would provide a return to the basic principles upon which our income tax system was founded: equity, efficiency, and simplicity. By repealing all personal tax preferences, including deductions, exclusions, and credits, as well as increasing the personal exemption to insulate the poor from any tax liability, we could have a simple tax—one which could easily be complied with, administered, and enforced, and one which would eliminate the need for tax shelters.

A Simpler, More Equitable System

Why not a true flat rate tax on total earnings in place of the present complex, inequitable, and inefficient income tax? . . . The advantages are substantial. The major objection that has forestalled debate on this type of tax reform has been that it will impose huge costs on middle- and low-income households. . . . The efficiency gains are sizable enough to offset a large part of these costs. Moreover, once it is recognized that transfer programs are a better way to insure adequate income for the truly impoverished, the possibility of a meaningful improvement in our tax system becomes real. We can have a simpler, more easily understood, more equitable, and more efficient tax system.

Edgar K. Browning and Jacquelene M. Browning, *The Cato Journal,* Fall 1985.

Perhaps the doubling of the current $1,000 personal deduction is not sufficient. We could certainly consider increasing the personal deduction further if that is necessary to provide adequate protection to low-income Americans.

Since becoming interested in the flat rate concept, I have consulted with the Treasury Secretaries of three administrations on the topic. As far back as 1975, during the Ford Administration, I asked then-Secretary of the Treasury William Simon for a study on the subject. In reply, he informed me that a flat rate of 14% would result in the collection of the same amount of money brought in under the complicated code.

When Jimmy Carter was president, Secretary of the Treasury Michael Blumenthal reported that a flat rate tax of only 10.4% was needed to match the amount collected under the current system.

In 1982, in response to a letter to Secretary Donald Regan, the Treasury Department informed me that a study conducted by that agency revealed that a 13% flat rate tax in 1983 would produce the identical sum gathered from personal income tax payments in 1981.

I'm flexible on just what the flat rate should be and would be willing to amend my legislation to read 13% if that is the figure needed to obtain the same amount of income tax revenue as now collected.

A number of criticisms have been leveled against my proposal.

A major fallacy which all of the opponents of my legislation seem to embrace is that lower- and middle-income Americans will pay more. That simply isn't true.

The lower-income group will be protected by the doubling of the personal exemption. As noted earlier, an even higher figure could be used if it is determined this additional protection was necessary.

Middle-income taxpayers are already carrying the burden of the current progressive tax system. The IRS Preliminary Statistics of Income Report for 1978 revealed that 60% of the total income tax was paid by Americans whose adjusted gross income was between $15,000 and $50,000, although they comprised only 45% of all taxable returns.

The progressive marginal rates are most burdensome to those in the middle class who find themselves unable to increase their incomes without incurring higher and higher rates of taxation. Inflationary bracket creep forces the middle-income groups into higher income tax brackets, causing them to transfer a larger portion of their real income to the government. A flat rate would generally tax the middle-income groups at a lower marginal rate. Their tax burden would be stabilized, and bracket creep and the marriage penalty would be eliminated.

We certainly dispute those who contend a progressive tax system is one which is fair to all taxpayers. Our current progressive tax is anything but fair to everyone.

Eliminate Tax Shelters

The tax burden of the American taxpayer today appears to depend on the expertise of his tax adviser, not his income. For example, in 1979, while 20,000 families with adjusted gross incomes of more than $100,000 paid income taxes on more than 40% of that income, another 20,000 families in the same high-income area paid taxes on less than 15% of the adjusted gross. Furthermore, the higher the income, the more opportunities for tax avoidance become available. The need for tax shelters would be eliminated by my bill.

Actually, our progressive tax system breeds unfairness. Every exemption, deduction, and exclusion injected into the progressive rate structure creates an upside-down effect. The higher the marginal rate of the taxpayer, the more valuable the deduction of exemption from taxes. For example, a $10,000 tax-exempt bond redemption avoids $5,000 in taxes for the 50% bracket taxpayer, but only $2,000 for one in the 20% bracket. Repealing these preferences would end a major cause of inequity in the tax code.

The Most Generous People

A great deal of vocal opposition has been voiced by those who fear the elimination of certain deductions. Those agencies which must rely upon charitable contributions are particularly concerned. They see a drying-up of many sources of income if a flat rate tax is put on the books.

I can not accept the theory that Americans will stop giving to the needy if they are denied a tax deduction in return. Americans are the most generous people in the world. Great contributions were made during the 19th century and in this century before the income tax deduction became a possible factor in our giving. Rest assured, this country's charity is not tied to its tax form.

The housing industry fears the dropping of the interest and tax deductions on homes might be devastating. Leaders in this field fail to recognize that Americans will have more money available for their housing needs—and other needs as well—if they are given a fair tax code.

We can not dispute that tax lawyers and accountants will see their incomes drop from tax consultant efforts, but this is hardly a reason to deny the entire taxpayer population from being treated equally.

Since I first introduced my flat rate bill, other legislators have come forth with proposals. One of these which has received some attention is really not a flat rate tax plan at all, since it climbs from a low of a 14% rate to a maximum of 28%. In addition, many deductions are retained.

Americans have been paying Federal income taxes for seven decades. The time has arrived when the law which governs those payments must be reshaped—reduced to a less complicated form which will be fair to all citizens.

"It is hard to make a simple tax fair in a complex economy like ours."

The Flat Rate Tax Will Not Work

Barber B. Conable

Barber B. Conable, professor of political science and public policy analysis at the University of Rochester, retired from Congress in 1984 after ten terms as a representative from upstate New York. He was the ranking Republican on the House Ways and Means Committee and a leading advocate of tax reform. In the following viewpoint, Mr. Conable argues that while a flat rate tax sounds desirable, it is highly unlikely that it would ever work. He believes the US government could never accept a reform this drastic.

As you read, consider the following questions:

1. What reasons does the author give to support his conclusion that present tax system flaws are exaggerated?
2. Who does the author believe would benefit most from a flat rate tax?
3. Who does the author believe would benefit the least from a flat rate tax?

Almost everyone can find some reason to like the idea of a flat tax. Economists tell us that broadening the tax base and reducing tax rates would be desirable, and that if all income were taxed without exclusion, credit, or deduction, a 14% rate would raise as much money as our current unpopular and complicated system.

That sounds wonderful to everyone: the rich like it because it will reduce their taxes, the poor because they suspect the rich now pay no taxes, the conservatives because our current progressive system "punishes" success, and the liberals because deductions and other tax preferences are the instruments of the devil. A flat tax certainly sounds good—until you study some of the realities that make it difficult to get there from here.

The first reality working against the enactment of a flat tax is that the flaws of the present system are greatly overstated. Treasury figures show that as a rule of thumb the top 10% of the taxpayers pay nearly 50% of the aggregate income taxes. That's the profile of a progressive system, and most Americans still believe a tax based on a person's ability to pay is fairer than one (however broadly based) with some other central criterion.

Complicated But Unavoidable

The system is complicated, to be sure, but for unavoidable reasons. First, it is hard to make a simple tax fair in a complex economy like ours. And Congress responds to perceived inequities one at a time, rarely working with the original master plan in mind. The cry for equity from troubled economic interests is the greatest enemy of simplicity. Second, legislative disagreement is resolved by compromise, which blurs philosophical outlines and complicates rules. Last, any law as long on the books and as sensitive to public opinion as our Internal Revenue Code is going to be amended over and over again. Assuming a new, simple tax law could sweep away the whole thing, the evolutionary, comlexifying process would resume in Congress immediately.

In short, for all its flaws, the current Internal Revenue Code is a historical document that seeks to collect more from the rich than the poor, that has tried to reflect the complexity of the economic arrangements people make in a modern society, and that is frequently changed because people think it can be made fairer by legislative refinement.

Few People Itemize Deductions

A second reality working against enactment of a flat tax is the surprisingly limited number of people who have a stake in such a change. Sixty-four percent of our current taxpayers do not itemize their deductions, and so would not gain anything in terms of simplicity.

As to fairness, that's in the eye of the beholder. The tendency of a flat tax is to reduce taxes significantly for the wealthy, making up for lost revenue by raising taxes slightly for everyone else. Since the average American sees a need for tax reform because he believes that he is paying too much while others pay too little, a change that raises taxes for the majority isn't going to be viewed as reform. The lucky few whose taxes would go down and those whose returns would be simplified because they now itemize their deductions are not the people politicians worry about most.

"Henry, meet Huxley Parrish. . . . You two have something in common. . . . The proposed Senate bill would put you in the same bracket!"

Reprinted by permission: Tribune Media Services.

A third reality making enactment of a flat tax tough is the importance of the interests that believe they benefit from the current system. They are by no means unworthy, nor are they politically unorganized or impotent. For instance, local and state governments benefit from local and state tax deductions, homeowners and consumers from interest deductions, and churches and other charities from charitable contribution deductions. Tax-exempt municipal bonds create jobs and low-cost housing. Fringe benefits, now largely untaxed, provide valuable services and finance retirement, and have become one of our most important sources of savings. Those who take risks to create economic advancement and jobs are encouraged by special treatment of their capital gains.

A last reality discouraging enactment of a flat tax now is the extent to which tax changes have been entangled in the public consciousness with our grave fiscal problems. If the federal deficit is our biggest economic threat, what is the point of passing a "revenue neutral" tax reform measure? But if the whole effort is seen by the average American as a smoke screen for a tax increase, and the issue of political honesty is raised, that becomes a burden even an ultimately popular reform cannot carry.

A theory is abroad in the land that if the tax system were made fairer (that is, if other people were required to pay a bigger share of the burden), everyone would be willing to pay higher taxes to reduce the deficit. In fact, every tax reform bill passed by Congress from 1969 to 1982 included a significant tax reduction to sell the package politically, even though the structural changes were generally seen as making the total system fairer.

Compromised Proposals

Actually, prospects for a simple flat tax have already been compromised right off the public agenda. Messrs. Bradley and Gephardt, the first formal flat tax advocates (the Fair tax plan), quickly and repeatedly accommodated the realities I have mentioned above by graduating their tax rate from 14% to 30%, creating exclusions for poor people and retaining partial deductions of charitable contributions, real estate taxes, and mortgage interest, the three most popular tax preferences. Messrs. Kemp and Kasten (the Fair and Simple plan) varied the formula somewhat, with a 25% maximum rate, retention of tax exempt bonds, and indexing of capital gains.

The Regan Treasury recommendation . . . moves "in the direction" of a flat tax, although it doesn't represent as fundamental a reform as Fair or Fair and Simple. Secretary Regan proposes a maximum individual tax rate of 35%, eliminates fewer tax preferences, cuts the number of tax brackets back to three, and achieves revenue neutrality by transferring a higher tax burden to business through repeal of the 1981 Tax Act's accelerated depreciation and investment tax credit.

A Long Way From Enactment

It is a sophisticated proposal and must be taken seriously, but it is a long way from enactment and seems to be more fervently supported by the President's enemies than by his friends. Doubtless the anti-Reagan enthusiasts will want to pick and choose among Secretary Regan's proposals rather than swallow the package whole, and Regan will wind up opposing some of his own fragments. Certainly the business community is nervous about massive changes in the tax rules affecting capital formation. Such nervousness works against the risk-taking on which the dynamic of our economic system depends.

What's likely to emerge, then, for all this talk of flat taxes and their compromised offspring? Here are some of my expectations:

• No massive tax change. We'll continue testing the assumptions of our current code, and there will be more wistful talk of basebroadening and simplification, but incrementalism will be more popular than radical change.

• Expect an effort to keep fiscal solutions separate from tax reform. This could result in a temporary individual surtax on virtually all income brackets, the termination of which could become the lever to buy whatever tax reform is ultimately achieved.

• Expect some White House reassurance to the business community that capital formation is still a high priority for the next four years, and that changes in business taxation will be fully discussed and, if made, will be phased in over long transition periods. . . .

If all this sounds craven—a mountain rumbling and a mouse coming forth—remember that representative government, because it is accessible and accountable, is not likely to be highly adventurous. Are you sure you'd like it if it were?

> "Even where one does have an obligation to care for certain others, the government may not justly enforce this obligation by taxation."

Taxation to Subsidize the Poor Is Unfair

Howard Baetjer Jr.

Howard Baetjer Jr. is on the staff of the Foundation for Economic Education (FEE), an organization that promotes laissez-faire capitalism. It opposes governmental interference in economic affairs beyond the minimum necessary for maintaining peace and property rights. Mr. Baetjer's efforts at FEE center on introducing "the philosophy of freedom" to students. In the following viewpoint, he argues that the government has no right to tax individuals in order to help the poor. That should be an individual's, not a government's, concern, he argues. He further believes that people have a right to be selfish and morally bereft if they like, and the government has an obligation to protect that right.

As you read, consider the following questions:

1. What, according to the author, is "transfer taxation"?
2. Why don't the rich have an obligation to help the poor, according to the author?
3. After reading this viewpoint and the following viewpoint by Mr. Olson, do you believe that government has an obligation to help the poor by taxing the rich? Why or why not?

Howard Baetjer Jr., "Of Obligation and Transfer Taxation," *The Freeman*, November 1984.

In today's redistributionist society, government promises a more equitable distribution of wealth than the market's actual allocation. It does so by transfer taxation: taxing everyone and subsidizing some. Of the several arguments for this transfer taxation, one of the most common runs as follows: *those who are well-off have an obligation to care for those who are not well-off; therefore the government may justly tax the former to support the latter.*

This argument is false: its premise is a partial truth from which the conclusion does not follow in any case. A well-off individual may or may not have a moral obligation to care for those who are not well-off. But even where he does, it is not the government's business, because this positive kind of obligation derives from the values and standards of that individual, not from others' rights. It is the government's business to defend rights, nothing more. Where rights are not involved, it is solely the individual's business to make use of his own property in accordance with his own values and standards. Indeed, as far as *rights* are concerned, the individual even has a right to act at odds with his values and standards, to be mean and selfish, so long as he respects others' rights. The proponents of liberty must understand and affirm this if they are to answer fully this argument for transfer taxation.

False Conclusions

"The government may justly tax the former to support the latter." Consider this conclusion to see where the argument is leading. What is logically implied in the notion that the government may take the property of the well-off to support the worse-off? One implication is that the worse-off have a right to the property of the well-off, a right which justifies the transfer. Some make this point explicitly, speaking of "welfare rights," or contending that the right to life itself includes the right to such property of others as is needed to support life. But if property is owned by A in the first place, then B can have no right to it—to own something is precisely to have a right to it. Another implication is that the majority in power has just authority to threaten A with force to make him give up his property, which they then turn over to B—taxation, remember, is ultimately backed up by the policeman's gun. But this authority negates both the rights of minorities against tyrannical majorities, and the right to pursue happiness—to use one's talents and property in pursuit of one's own ends.

This argument's conclusion that some may justly be taxed to support others thus collapses before fundamental principles. One is tempted to let the argument rest there: with a conclusion so far out of line with basic rights, the reasoning to it simply must be invalid. But this rebuttal is not enough. The reasoning is so persuasive that we must deal with it, too. Many who are troubled by transfer taxation believe also that people *should* give to those in need, that it is wrong for them not to. Government responds to other wrongs, they reason; surely it should respond to this one. Let us now see where this reasoning breaks down.

The Confusion: Should or Must?

The crucial error in the argument is a confusion of two meanings of *obligation*—meanings which are evident in the ways we use the word *should*. One usage pertains to fundamental obligations deriving from other people's rights; in this sense it is synonymous with "must." A man should pay his debts—because the people from whom he has borrowed have a right to their property. He should allow others to assemble, worship, work and trade as they please—because others have a fundamental right to act free of restraint (so long as they act peacefully). He should not murder—because others have a right to life. When we say a person "should" do this sort of thing, we refer to obligations that derive from basic rights. Notice that in each example here, what is immediately at stake pertains not to the individual obliged, but to the others: *others'* property, *others'* liberty, *others'* lives. The individual is obliged because he is dealing with things to which others have a right.

Save Taxes By Eliminating Welfare

The best thing that we can do for the disabled, the needy and deserving is to privatize welfare, to eliminate government assistance and welfare programs. The savings in taxes will help the private business sector expand and increase employment. Working people will have much more left in their paychecks because of reduced taxes and will, thus, be better able to work on assistance programs of their own choosing.

David Bergland, *What About the Poor?* 1984.

A second usage of *should* pertains to what is desirable or preferable. In this sense it is synonymous with "would do better to." One "should" eat healthful food—because that is preferable to eating tainted food. One should change the oil in his car periodically—because that will help preserve the car. One should be pleasant in dealings with others—because such treatment will make life more agreeable. When we say a person "should" do this sort of thing, we refer to "obligations" that derive from what is best. Notice that in each of these cases, what is immediately at stake pertains to him, not others: *his* health, *his* car, *his* behavior. He is "obliged" not because of anybody's rights, but because of what is sensible, what is best under the circumstances. . . .

But if what is involved is the individual's own, then he has only the "obligation" to do what is preferable. Consider the case at issue in this argument for transfer taxation, for example: care for those who are worse off than some well-off individual. What precisely is "care," in this context? It is not the psychological feeling of wishing others well, but the physical realization of that feeling: the money, food, clothing or shelter provided: it is whatever the well-off individual gives or might give to help the worse-off person. And whose is it? Ah, yes—here is the question. Until it actually has been given (if the notion of property rights is to have meaning), it is the property of the giver. He alone has a right to these things that might, if he decides to give them, become "care" for someone else. The individual is thus "obliged" to do with these things whatever is preferable, whatever is best among the many uses to which he might put them.

A Matter of Preference

With this distinction between kinds of obligation in mind, let us consider again the premise of the present argument. Does one who is well-off have an obligation to care for those who are not well-off? When one does, clearly, the obligation is of the second kind—a matter of what is preferable among available choices. But this idea raises additional questions: Preferable to whom? According to what standard?

The answer to these questions is inherent in each individual's inescapable responsibility for his own actions: each individual is bound to make his decisions according to his own values, his own sense of right and wrong, good and bad, better and best. About situations involving others' rights, this decision is relatively simple: the primary value of respecting rights is inherent in man's nature, and anyone thinking clearly will recognize this. But where one's own property is concerned, one does not have the primary value of rights as a guide, and he must therefore weigh the importance of lesser values. Would it be more valuable, in his honest judgment, to devote a certain amount of his time and property to caring for a certain group of people less well-off than he? Or would it be preferable to devote that time and property to the future security of his family, or to recreation, or to increasing his job skills, or to cancer research, or to a struggling symphony orchestra? He must choose; he cannot do all. What should he do? No one can answer this but the individual himself. With his property, it is his responsibility to decide. Where he is responsible, his proper basis for decision is his own standards, his own values. If he acts contrary to these, he betrays himself. What he is obliged to do is what is preferable according to his own values. . . .

Understanding Personal Values

Well, then, does a well-off person have an obligation to support those who are not well-off? That depends on his own (honest, actual) pattern of values. If, in a given situation, he sees others' need

97

and believes he should do something to relieve it, then he has a moral obligation to do so. But this obligation derives from his own standards. It does not derive from the standards of the government, or "society," or any other individual. If, on the other hand, he sees that need but believes he should devote his time and money elsewhere, then he has a moral obligation to do that instead.

Any obligation for an individual to care for the less well-off is secondary. It exists to the extent that the individual values such care above all the other purposes to which he might devote his time and attention. Anyone who values more highly some other purpose (such as, for example, securing the future well-being of one's family) does not have any such obligation.

Invalid Logic

The premise of this transfer-taxation argument is thus a partial truth, an over-generalization. *Some* of those who are well-off have an obligation to care for some of those who are not well-off, but some do not; obligations vary from individual to individual and situation to situation. No sound argument can be based on a partial truth, of course, but also the logic here is invalid: even where the premised conditions are true, the conclusion does not follow. Even where one does have an obligation to care for certain others, the government may not justly enforce this obligation by taxation.

Taxing for the Needy

The mainstream view today is that the political process should be used to provide for human needs. Most persons think it's proper for someone else, through taxes, to pay for services rendered to the "needy.". . .

Now we have the concept of government as a provider, dispensing to favored beneficiaries monies seized through taxation. Thus is a limited government quickly transformed into an unlimited State, the plunderer of property and proprietor of lives that it was supposed to protect. Such a change in role leads to a massive growth in the size of government as well as a higher burden of taxation to sustain it.

Robert G. Anderson, *Notes from FEE*, January 1986.

In the first place, of course, no one but the individual himself can know his actual standards and values for the use of his own property, and hence what sort of obligation he has to care for others, if any. And how could the government enforce obligations that it could not identify? In the second place, since government has no power over the individual will, mind and spirit, transfer taxation does not really make an individual *give* to, or *care for* others. In transfer taxation the *government* gives . . . what it has taken by force. Caring has nothing to do with the matter. Thus the alleged obligation to care or give, is unenforceable by its nature. . . .

It is well for others to try to *persuade* someone when they think he is selfishly rationalizing away an obligation he actually does feel towards others. But no group, whether the majority, the "society," the ruling junta or the government, may rightly force someone to act against his wishes in what is fundamentally his affair.

In passing, let us affirm the implication of this: that individuals have a right to *ignore* their personal, moral obligations to those who are worse off. Indeed, they have a right even to be selfish, mean-spirited, ungenerous and miserly, as long as they do not intrude on others' rights. They *should* not behave this way, of course—they and everyone else will lose by doing so—but they have that right. And the rest of us, in private and through government, are obliged to respect that right.

Conclusion: A Fallacy

In the final analysis, what can be said for the contention that *"those who are well-off have an obligation to care for those who are not well-off; therefore the government may justly tax the former to support the latter"?* Nothing. It is fallacious throughout. The well-off may or may not have such an obligation, but even where they do, it is a personal obligation entirely beyond the proper scope of government. The premise is a partial truth, unrelated to the conclusion, which in any case proposes a bald violation of fundamental rights. There is no ethical justification for transfer taxation. On the contrary, transfer taxation itself is at odds with ethical principles. Care for those who need care is a matter of individual values and individual responsibility.

"A nation that redistributes income to its poor buys a civilized and humane society, and it buys this with a miniscule share of the national income."

Taxation Subsidizes the Wealthy, Not the Poor

Mancur Olson

Mancur Olson teaches economics at the University of Maryland and is the author of *The Rise and Decline of Nations.* In the following viewpoint, Mr. Olson writes about the tendency of conservatives to blame America's economic problems on government subsidies of the poor in the form of tax-supported welfare. The real trouble, Mr. Olson argues, is with the massive tax subsidies received by huge corporations and special interest groups.

As you read, consider the following questions:

1. Where does most redistribution of income occur, according to the author?
2. What does the author believe is wrong with tax loopholes?
3. According to the author, what happens to a society that does redistribute income?

Mancur Olson, "What We Lose When the Rich Go on the Dole: Tax Deductible Llamas Hurt the Economy More than Welfare Cadillacs," *The Washington Monthly,* January 1984. Reprinted with permission from *The Washington Monthly.* Copyright by THE WASHINGTON MONTHLY CO., 1711 Connecticut Avenue, NW, Washington, DC 20009. (202) 462-0128.

Liberals and conservatives have long bickered over the question of whether welfare is good or bad for the economy. Liberals have rallied to the defense of New Deal and Great Society programs aimed at providing things as diverse as Social Security checks, food stamps, housing subsidies, and medical care for the poor and the elderly. Their argument has been that these expenditures are a stimulus to depressed sectors of the economy and invigorate those members of society who might otherwise despair of ever contributing productively to the system.

Conservatives, on the other hand, have called for a retreat from the generous welfare policies of the past. They argue that the huge growth in government social programs since the thirties has been a drag on our economy, swallowing up more and more money to redistribute income and encouraging the poor to look upon government benefits as a substitute for the kind of hard work that creates prosperity.

Neither side is at a loss for arguments to support its theory. Conservatives point to the miserable performance of the British economy in recent years and attribute this to the legacy of its Labor governments. Conservatives also argue that during the 19th century, a period of unprecedented economic advance, the world came closer to laissez-faire and free trade than at any other time. Finally, there is the example of the last decade, when the welfare state has become larger than it ever has been, while economic performance has turned sour. . . .

No Noticeable Difference

Conservatives and liberals find themselves fighting to a similar draw when they debate whether welfare states can provide their poorer members with a higher standard of living than more conservative, laissez-faire states can. Liberals argue that the poor, left to fend for themselves, will flounder; conservatives argue that the rising tide will lift all boats. Again, there is no consistent correlation between the ideology of either the left or the right and reality. A traveler will see no great differences in the standard of living of the poor when he or she travels from Switzerland, where the role of government and the welfare state is fairly small, to Sweden, where it is relatively large. Nor can one observe a difference in the standard of living among the poor in traveling from Japan to Great Britain, even though Britain's welfare state is larger than Japan's.

If the size of government and the extent of its effort to maintain a welfare state bear little relation to the prosperity either of a nation or of its poor, what does mainly determine whether an economy thrives, or whether the situation of the poor improves? It is, in large part, whether a society avoids redistribution to favored groups in its middle and upper classes. Unfortunately, governments often collect money from the society as a whole and pay it out to groups that are far from poor. This not only fails to help the poor, but is destructive to the economy as well.

To Each According to His Clout

It is welfare for those who are not poor that largely explains why economic growth is slowing down. The culprit is not so much left-wing or right-wing ideology as the acquisitiveness of special interests at the expense of the collective interest of the nation. By lobbying the government or combining and colluding in the marketplace to influence prices and wages, these organizations—professional associations of physicians and lawyers, labor unions, trade associations, farm organizations, and oligopolistic collusions—bring greater harm to the economy at large than benefits to themselves.

The Wealthy Should Pay

When we talk about tax reform, what does the average person think of? He is upset at a neighbor that makes $90,000, or a person in a nicer area than he lives who makes $200,000 a year and pays no taxes. He thinks that is unfair. That is what he thinks about tax reform.

When he reads of 250 corporations in America, the giants of industry, who because of their shrewdness and their cleverness and their ability to interpret the law pay no taxes, it hurts him. He thinks that he has been taken in, and rightly so. . . .

Is it right? Is it right that corporations of America should pay no taxes, that the wealthy of America should find loopholes? The answer is no.

Thomas P. O'Neill Jr., on the floor of the US House of Representatives, December 11, 1985.

Most organizations for lobbying or cartelization have no incentive to make the society in which they exist more efficient or prosperous; the members of the organization will get only a minute fraction of the society's gains from greater efficiency. Normally these organizations can best serve their members by seeking a larger slice of the economic pie rather than enlarging it. If, as is the case in countries like the United States and Great Britain, the organizations are small in relation to the whole society, they rationally will persist in distributional struggle even if the loss to society is much greater than the amount won by the special-interest group. For example, the lawyers gain larger fees by blocking no-fault insurance, but the rest of us lose much more than they gain when our society becomes more complex and litigious as a result. An organization that represents 1 percent of the income earning capacity of the country will bear on average only 1 percent of any losses in social efficiency, but will obtain the whole amount redistributed to its membership. So its clients will gain from any redistribution unless the excess burden is a hundred times or more greater than the amount redistributed. A society dense with organizations for collective action is thus like a china shop filled with wrestlers battling over the china, and breaking far more than they carry away.

History Proves Little Difference

There are three reasons why ideological differences between laissez-faire governments and welfare-state governments ultimately have little bearing on whether an economy prospers. First, they overlook the force of cartelization, by which firms and individuals in the marketplace can maintain noncompetitive prices or wages, obstruct the free flow of resources, and slow down the innovation that brings more rapid economic growth. History shows that this process can occur in either a laissez-faire economy or a welfare-state economy.

The second reason the traditional argument about the limits of government or democracy does not explain the variation in economic performance across countries is that it neglects the way the governments really work. Socialist and free-market theorists alike presume that governments distribute benefits rationally, for good or ill. But the rationality of government action is undermined to a great extent by the lobbying process. For example, Congress maintains price supports for the dairy industry, even though this has meant higher milk prices for consumers and so many farmers producing milk that the government has just started a program to pay farmers *not* to produce milk. Why does the government get tangled up this way? Because it is reacting in large part to the lobbying efforts of the dairy industry, rather than serving the interest of the nation at large.

The third reason why the traditional slogans of left and right have failed to be of much help focuses specifically on the issue of welfare. Simply put, the traditional ideologies of left and right make the mistake of focusing on the extent to which government policies redistribute from the rich and middle class to the poor, instead of on the overall picture of redistribution, of which payments from the rich and middle class to the poor are only a small part.

The Tail of the Elephant

When we focus on government policies that are designed to aid low-income people, we are looking at the tail of the elephant—at only a tiny part of what governments actually do. Most redistribution is not from upper- and middle-income people to low-income people; it's from middle-income people to other middle-income people, or from the whole society to particular groups of rich peo-

"It was a nice tax system, while it lasted."

Bob Englehart, *The Hartford Courant*, reprinted with permission.

ple, or from one group to another where the groups are distinguished not by one being poor and one being rich but only by the fact that some groups are organized and some are not.

This is not an accident. There is no society in which the poorest are well organized. If you look at contributions to candidates for the House of Representatives or the Senate, you do not find organizations of welfare mothers or other recipients of public assistance for the poor giving major campaign contributions. Nor do you find well-organized or well-financed lobbies working for the poor in other societies. It is big firms, upper-income people, the professionals, and blue-collar workers with jobs who are organized. And it is to these groups for the most part that the government redistributes income. In any society, there is always some compassion and sympathy and hence some aid to the poorest people. But that is only a small part of what the government does.

Because the middle and upper classes have a greater capacity than the poor to lobby on their own behalf, traditional ideology ends up playing less of a role in the health of an economy than the degree to which redistribution is restricted to its theoretical goal—taking from the well-off to help the poor. If much of the money that ostensibly is used to provide a comfortable cushion for those at the bottom is actually diverted to the middle and upper classes, the nation not only fails to achieve its humanitarian objectives, but injures its economy as well.

Even if redistribution to the poor equaled redistribution to the non-poor, whatever loss to the economy that came from the poor deciding to sit back and enjoy a free ride, as the conservatives put it, would be far less than the loss that came from the rich and middle class who would have gone on the dole. This is because the poor are, on average, less productive than the non-poor. They are more likely to be handicapped, or lack marketable skills, or to be aged or abandoned mothers. There are exceptions, but for the most part, people who are very productive and whose productive skills are prized in the society are not poor. It thus follows that subsidies to the poor, although they tend to have some adverse effect on incentives (as conservatives rightly claim), usually reduce production by less than do subsidies to the non-poor.

Loopholes and Ranks

Indeed, the higher one goes up the income scale, the greater the damage done by the inefficient use of time and resources. Institutional arrangements or policies that misallocate the labor of healthy males in their prime working years—such as featherbedding and restrictive work rules—are very damaging to the efficiency of a society, yet are commonplace. The professional associations and public policies that largely control the practice of law and of medicine are even more costly to society, because it is the efforts of some of the most highly educated and energetic people in the society that are being misdirected. Yet few areas of modern society are so rife with cartels, anticompetitive rules, and other redistributions as are the law and medicine. Tax loopholes not only induce people to become tax accountants and lawyers, and thus divert some of the most able and aggressive out of more socially productive pursuits, but also twist much of the productive capacity of the whole society into tax-favored activities that contribute little to prosperity. Yet such loopholes are becoming more numerous. Tariffs, tax concessions, and bailouts to major corporations divert or enfeeble some of the most productive enterprises in the whole economy, yet such tariffs are becoming more common each year.

Sacrificing the Economy

A nation that redistributes income to its poor buys a civilized and humane society, and it buys this with a miniscule share of the national income. The greatest loss it must endure is a modest reduction in the supply of cleaning women. A country that subsidizes workers in their prime working years sacrifices not a dust-free living room but the very muscle of the economy. The society that permits its professions to cartelize and control public policy loses amounts for each professional that make welfare payments seem trivial. And a people that gives tariffs or tax loopholes or bailouts to major corporations, whose great scale could normally have been attained only through exceptional productivity, is accumulating deposits of fat in the arteries that lead to its heart.

"The taxation of capital and business income in the United States is deeply flawed."

Raising Corporate Taxes Will Justly Aid the Economy

Robert S. McIntyre

Robert S. McIntyre is director of federal tax policy at Citizens for Tax Justice, a private consumer advocacy organization that investigates federal tax law. In the following viewpoint, Mr. McIntyre criticizes the often-cited supply-side tax theory. According to the theory, the more tax breaks the government gives private corporations, the more these corporations will reinvest in equipment, personnel, and research. McIntyre argues that in practice, the opposite is true: The more corporate tax breaks, the less investment. Given this fact, he believes that there is no justification to reduce corporate taxes, and that consumers should insist on reforms that force corporations to pay their fair share.

As you read, consider the following questions:

1. The author compares two major corporations, GE and Whirlpool. What conclusions does he draw from this comparison?
2. What does the author believe really influences corporate investment?

Robert S. McIntyre, "Voodoo Incentives," *The New Republic,* February 25, 1985. Reprinted by permission of THE NEW REPUBLIC, © 1985, The New Republic, Inc.

A year ago I bought a Whirlpool washing machine and a General Electric dryer. I have no regrets about the washer, but the dryer has been a bit of a disappointment. It's more flimsy than the washer, and the belt is already starting to squeal. What's worse, having bought the G.E. machine makes me feel unpatriotic. Whirlpool, I have since learned, has been doing its utmost to reduce the federal budget deficit by paying what is apparently the highest federal income tax rate among major corporations, and it has contributed to the country's long-term economic health by increasing its investment in new plant and equipment. General Electric, on the other hand, has been the nation's champion tax refund recipient while at the same time cutting back on its investment.

To be precise, from 1981 through 1983 Whirlpool earned $650 million in pretax profits in the United States and sent $297 million of that to the U.S. Treasury, for a tax rate of 45.6 percent—just about exactly the 46 percent the corporate tax code nominally prescribes. High taxes notwithstanding, Whirlpool managed to increase its capital spending by seven percent. In contrast, General Electric earned $6.5 billion in domestic profits, but paid no income taxes. Taking advantage of the many "investment tax incentives" provided by the 1981 tax cut, G.E. actually got the Treasury to supplement its earnings with $283 million in tax rebates. The company compounded the indignity by cutting its purchases of new plant and equipment by 15 percent between 1981 and 1983. In short, General Electric has been taking the taxpayer to the cleaners.

Incentives Failed

Although the Whirlpool-G.E. comparison is striking, it is not atypical. Indeed, it neatly illustrates the ironic results of the first three years of the Reagan administration's "supply-side" tax program. A random sampling of 250 of the country's largest and most profitable companies that we recently completed at Citizens for Tax Justice demonstrates that the companies that enjoyed the most tax "incentives" cut their investment the most. Companies with at least one no-tax year between 1981 and 1983 reduced investment by 15.7 percent. Firms that paid a total of no taxes or actually received net tax rebates over the three years cut investment by 19.3 percent. An even more select group—companies that did not pay taxes in any of the three years—slashed investment by 29.6 percent. In sharp contrast, the 50 companies with the highest tax rates over the three years—the firms that by supply-side thinking had the least incentive to invest—increased their capital investment by a total of 4.3 percent, despite paying 33.1 percent of their profits in taxes.

How can this inverse correlation between "incentives" and investment be explained? Perhaps, you might think, the nontaxed companies that cut investment simply weren't doing very well.

But all of the corporations we examined were highly profitable. In fact, the after-tax profits of the companies paying no taxes between 1981 and 1983 were almost exactly equal to the after-tax earnings of the 50 highest taxed firms. . . . But even if the resurgence in investment in 1984 is included, the record is still dismal. . . . Real business investment in plant and equipment rose by only 3.5 percent—far less than the 28.6 percent increase in real plant and equipment in the previous four years.

Taxes Don't Have Much Effect

The best explanation is that companies invest only when they need new plant and equipment to produce products they can sell to consumers. When consumers don't spend money, plants are idled and new investment drops. Taxes—or lack thereof—don't seem to have much to do with it.

Even as the ink was drying on the Reagan tax bill in August 1981, the business managers responsible for investment decisions (as opposed to the corporate lobbyists, whose job is solely to secure lower taxes) began explaining why the massive new tax breaks really wouldn't increase their investment plans after all. The chairman of one major U.S. corporation told *The New York Times* that "with or without the tax bill we would have done what we did

ALL I ASK IS A FAIR PROFIT AND A REASONABLE CHANCE FOR AN UNFAIR PROFIT.

in 1981 and what we plan to do in 1982. One can spend money on men and materials only at a given rate. Beyond that it becomes foolish."

Demand-Side Explanations

The annual reports of the companies we surveyed confirm that investment decisions are determined by "demand-side" market forces rather than by "supply-side" theories. W.R. Grace & Co., for example, despite $684.1 million in profits between 1981 and 1983, actually made $12.5 million off the tax system by selling its excess tax breaks. At the same time, it reduced new investment by 15.8 percent in 1982 and by another 37 percent in 1983. In its 1983 annual report, the company explained that investment was cut "in response to the reduced demand" for its products. (Incidentally, the chairman of W.R. Grace is J. Peter Grace, namesake of the commission on government waste. He thus enjoys a unique dual role: in his free time, he's a critic of "wasteful" federal spending; during business hours, he's the recipient of it.)

Many other firms also offered such "demand-side" explanations for their investment cutbacks. Tenneco cited "the weakness in natural gas demand" to explain its 31.8 percent investment drop between 1981 and 1983, despite its use of tax "incentives" to pay no taxes on $2.7 billion in profits and claim an extra $189 million in tax rebates. Colt Industries, which lobbied intensively for the "incentives" in the 1981 Reagan tax bill, saw its capital spending peak in 1980. By 1983, Colt had reduced its investment spending by 39 percent from 1980, explaining to shareholders that "the slow recovery in capital spending by American industry continued to affect our capital goods businesses."

Although tax breaks do not seem to stimulate corporate investment, they do increase after-tax profits. And the added corporate cash flow they generate comes with no strings attached. It can be used to increase dividends, expand cash reserves, fund mergers or acquisitions, raise executive pay, or beef up advertising budgets. The companies we studied increased dividends by 17 percent over the three years, even as their investment fell by 15.5 percent. Many low-tax corporations, including G.E., Phillips Petroleum, Fluor Corp., and Union Pacific, bragged about their additions to cash reserves. And a large number of firms reported substantial use of funds to acquire other companies—not surprising given the record-breaking $209 billion wave of mergers over the 1981-83 period (with 1984 another $100-billion-plus record).

"A Hollow Clink"

The evidence that the Reagan administration's original loophole-based economic strategy was misdirected has been accumulating since it was enacted. As early as September 1981, Treasury Secre-

110

tary Donald Regan was complaining about the lack of business response to the supposed incentives. "It's like dropping a coin down a well," he told a group of Midwestern businessmen. "All I'm hearing is a hollow clink." By mid-1982, most of the self-styled "supply-siders" had left the Treasury in disgrace, their economic prognostications shattered by the deepest recession since the 1930s. As the boom in tax shelters continued to make a mockery of "supply-side" promises, others remaining at Treasury became increasingly outspoken in their distaste for loopholes. Assistant treasury secretary John Chapoton surprised a Texas audience by calling for repeal of the Reagan administration's own "Accelerated Cost Recovery System"—the corporate tax code's single biggest loophole.

The tax reform plan proposed by the Treasury was the final repudiation of the "incentives" approach. The Treasury proposal would eliminate almost all the loopholes that currently clutter the corporate tax laws. It would cut the corporate tax rate from 46 to 33 percent—and would still raise $160 billion in additional corporate income taxes by 1990. "The taxation of capital and business income in the United States is deeply flawed," the Treasury proposal declares. "It is best characterized as irrational. . . . The tax law provides subsidies to particular forms of investment that are unfair and that seriously distort choices in the use of the Nation's scarce capital." If there is any sense of accountability in Washington, no corporate lobbyist—no matter how persuasive, no matter how many campaign contributions he or she may control—should be able to prevent the repeal of the host of corporate tax "incentives" that, based on the overwhelming evidence, have failed.

111

"Any tax change . . . which affects . . . the ability of U.S. firms to compete internationally can have consequences far greater than the dollar value of the taxes involved."

Raising Corporate Taxes Will Harm the Economy

Bruce Bartlett

Bruce Bartlett is John M. Olin Fellow of the Heritage Foundation, a private research institute dedicated to individual and economic freedom and a limited government. In the following viewpoint, Mr. Bartlett argues that current corporate tax breaks not only foster re-investment in the economy, but give corporations the edge necessary to compete in the international market. Tax reform proposals that raise corporate taxes will leave US corporations vulnerable to international competition.

As you read, consider the following questions:

1. Why does the author believe it is essential for government to encourage corporate research and development?
2. Why does the author argue that corporations should be able to write off 100% of their equipment purchases?
3. What will happen if tax reforms to increase corporate taxes become a reality, according to the author?

Bruce Bartlett, "The House Tax Bill: Penalizing U.S. Competitiveness," The Heritage Foundation *Backgrounder,* January 27, 1986. Reprinted with permission.

The U.S. economy is now very international. Imports and exports amount to 15 percent of Gross National Product—roughly double that in the early 1970s. The flow of foreign capital into the U.S., moreover, is close to $100 billion per year; this has important implications for interest rates and exchange rates. Any tax change, therefore, which affects the investment climate in the U.S. or the ability of U.S. firms to compete internationally can have consequences far greater than the dollar value of the taxes involved. . . .

Most economists agree that research and development (R&D) expenditures play a key role in competitiveness and productivity growth. As Table 1 indicates, the U.S. has been running a large trade surplus in R&D-intensive products and a deficit in non-R&D-intensive products. It is essential for the U.S. to maintain technological leadership, especially when there is concern over the trade deficit.

Table 1
U.S. Trade Balance in R&D-Intensive and
Non-R&D-Intensive Manufactured Product Groups, 1970-80
(in billions of dollars)

Year	R&D-Intensive	Non-R&D-Intensive
1980	52.4	− 33.5
1979	39.3	− 34.8
1978	29.6	− 35.4
1977	27.1	− 23.5
1976	29.0	− 16.5
1975	29.3	− 9.5
1970	11.7	− 8.3

Source: National Science Board

In the late 1970s, when it became apparent that the U.S. technological lead was slipping, it was widely blamed on a slowdown in U.S. R&D expenditures, coupled with a major increase in R&D spending by America's international competitors. Between 1964 and 1978, for example, U.S. R&D expenditures as a share of GNP fell by 25 percent, while R&D expenditures increased in Japan by 32 percent and in West Germany by 47 percent.

Congress responded in 1981 by wisely instituting a 25 percent tax credit for boosts in R&D spending. The credit applies only to the extent that a company's qualified research and development expenditures in a given year exceed the average for the previous three years. The House tax reform bill, however, reduces the credit to 20 percent and restricts its use. No reason is given for the change. Reagan's tax reform proposal would retain the R&D tax credit at the 25 percent rate and extend it for another three years, subject to some redefinition of qualified research.

Too Soon To Judge

There is, to be sure, debate on the merits of the R&D tax credit. One problem in resolving the debate is that the credit has existed only three years. Because the credit is incremental in nature, the major benefits are to be expected in the future, not immediately. Nevertheless, the available empirical evidence indicates that the R&D tax credit did increase R&D expenditures.

Consumers Pay Corporate Taxes

Should there even be a corporate income tax? Isn't this tax simply passed on to the ultimate consumer? Nobody really knows. As economist David Bradford points out, "Only one thing is for sure. Business does not pay." The possible real victims are shareholders, as legal owners of the corporations; consumers, as purchasers of tax-inflated goods or services; and/or employees, as receivers of tax-reduced wages and salaries. This, of course, is a political advantage in the tax. Since no one is certain who pays, there is little organized opposition to the tax. To the tax-leviers it is a victimless crime.

Susan Lee, *Forbes*, August 13, 1984.

The best reform would be to make the R&D tax credit permanent. Explains the Congressional Budget Office: "It is generally recognized that research benefits the nation more than it benefits any individual company, and that private firms tend to devote less resources to research and development than the public interest would warrant; this is particulary true for the high-technology industries." Moreover, as long as firms believe the tax credit is temporary they are unlikely to respond fully to it. . . .

Cost of Capital

The cost of capital—capital being the plant, equipment, structures, and financing needed to create goods and services—is a key element in international competitiveness. If the cost of capital is higher in the U.S. than in other countries, the U.S. has a harder time competing in capital-intensive products. Capital also is critical to productivity growth. Nations that are able to provide their workers with newer, more efficient plant and equipment, in the long run, will enjoy higher productivity and will be better able to compete internationally. . . .

Lagging U.S. capital formation and productivity were key reasons why, in 1981, Congress sharply cut the tax burden on fixed capital by allowing accelerated depreciation. By all accounts, this 1981 strategy worked. Investment spending during the current economic expansion has been significantly higher than the average for postwar recoveries and expansions.

The Theory of Depreciation

The 1981 tax cut shortened depreciation schedules. Depreciation is the wearing out of plant and equipment. Firms are allowed to deduct from their gross income a percentage of this depreciation annually to allow them to build a reserve for replacing their plant and equipment when it wears out. The shorter the schedule, the faster the reserve accumulates. In theory, depreciation rates should correspond to the actual rate at which plant and equipment wear out. Some critics argue that the 1981 depreciation schedules are shorter than real economic depreciation rates. Thus, it is said, firms have had their capital investment subsidized by the tax code.

It is true that some capital investment is subsidized, especially when depreciation allowances are combined with the investment tax credit (ITC), which gives firms a 10 percent credit against taxes owed for investments in machinery and equipment. But from the standpoint of international competitiveness, what matters is that U.S. depreciation rates must compete with those of other nations. Depreciation schedules are an important factor used by multinational companies to calculate the after-tax rate of return on their potential investment. If the U.S. after-tax rate of return is lower than elsewhere, the U.S. risks losing that investment.

In a recent survey, the international accounting firm of Arthur Andersen & Co. found that the present value of U.S. depreciation rates is not particularly generous by world standards. . . .

The present value rates mean that, adjusted for the interest and the inflation rates, firms are able ultimately to deduct more or less than the full cost of a piece of equipment. A theoretically ideal capital cost recovery system would allow firms to deduct exactly 100 percent of the present value of equipment; no more, no less. Yet, . . . only under the extremely optimistic assumption of zero inflation does the current depreciation system lead to a U.S. rate of at least 100 percent. Under both the Administration's depreciation proposals and the House bill, firms ultimately would deduct less than the full present value of their investment. This means they would have less capital to replace or modernize their aging plant and equipment. This translates directly into lower productivity and fewer jobs.

Both Reagan and the House would eliminate the investment tax credit, first introduced in 1962 by John F. Kennedy, lengthen depreciation rates, and cut corporate tax rates. These changes, it is claimed, will encourage firms to invest without regard to tax considerations. The different tax treatment of various forms of investment is thought to induce considerable distortion in investment decisions, costing the nation billions of dollars in efficiency. But while evening out tax rates on different forms of investment and between different industries is laudable, this should not be accomplished at the expense of an overall increase in taxation on capital. The U.S. already double-taxes saving and investment. This disincentive to invest would be made worse under both the House bill and the Reagan proposal. . . .

US Taxes More than Competitors

The U.S. taxes capital more heavily than most industrialized countries, and far more than Japan, its most successful competitor. It makes little sense to increase taxation on capital still further. Some economic forecasting firms are predicting a sharp slowdown in economic growth and a rise in unemployment if the House bill passes. The culprit, warn these forecasters, will be the increased cost of capital.

Many analysts have argued that the economic stagnation of the 1970s was linked to the 1969 increase in capital gains taxes, since this tax hits most heavily the most dynamic, innovative sector of the economy. In 1978 Congress slashed the capital gains tax from a maximum of 49 percent to 28 percent. The result: a massive outpouring of venture capital, risk taking, and innovation that, among other things, sped the development of Silicon Valley and the computer revolution. At the same time, revenues from the capital gains tax increased. . . .

A rise in the capital gains tax would impair U.S. competitiveness. The higher tax would hit high technology, the area most stimulated by previous capital gains tax cuts and the area in which the U.S. is most competitive.

Congress should compare U.S. treatment of capital gains with that of this nation's toughest international competitors. This would reveal that even the current 20 percent capital gains tax in the U.S. is high by international standards. . . . If the serious flaws of the House bill are not corrected, this tax "reform" could hamper seriously the U.S. ability to counter the brutal global economic competition that it faces.

Distinguishing Bias from Reason

The subject of taxation often generates great emotional response in people. When dealing with such a highly controversial subject, many will allow their feelings to dominate their powers of reason. Thus, one of the most important critical thinking skills is the ability to distinguish between opinions based upon emotion or bias and conclusions based upon a rational consideration of the facts.

The following statements are based on the viewpoints in this chapter. Consider each statement carefully. *Mark R for any statement you believe is based on reason or a rational consideration of the facts. Mark B for any statement you believe is based on bias, prejudice, or emotion. Mark I for any statement you think is impossible to judge.*

If you are doing this activity as a member of a class or group, compare your answers with those of other class or group members. Be able to explain your answers. You may discover that others will come to different conclusions than you. Listening to the reasons others present for their answers may give you valuable insights in distinguishing between bias and reason.

If you are reading this book alone, ask others if they agree with your answers. You will find this interaction very valuable.

R = *a statement based upon reason*
B = *a statement based on bias*
I = *a statement impossible to judge*

1. The need for a vast overhaul of our complicated federal tax code is obvious.

2. Given recent Congressional voting trends, there is reason to believe a major tax code restructuring could be completed in Congress.

3. A flat rate tax is the only reasonable solution to America's tax problems.

4. Based on 1986 income-per-capita figures, the flat tax would result in greater federal revenue than a progressive tax.

5. If the government would stop giving money to those who are not really poor, the rest of us would have far fewer taxes to pay.

6. Though government has the *ability* to give to those in need, it does not necessarily follow that it *must* give to those in need.

7. If Americans understood how unfair a progressive tax is, they would certainly prefer a flat tax.

8. Our present tax system has never been as bad as some economists make it sound.

9. A flat rate tax sounds appealing, but an examination of current statistics and economists' predictions show that it would probably overburden the poor and middle classes.

10. The lower class will always complain about any tax system that benefits the upper class.

11. A flat rate tax would indeed lower 50 percent of Americans' tax rates, but there is every indication that it would decrease federal revenue.

12. No true American would tolerate a flat rate tax.

13. It is the government's business to defend rights, not redistribute income.

14. It is impossible to predict exactly what a flat rate tax would do to the American economy, in spite of well thought out predictions.

15. If property is owned by A, then B can have no right to it, for to own something is precisely to have a right to it.

16. Taxation is theft.

17. Welfare states do not always guarantee elimination of property; nor do laissez-faire governments guarantee high standards of living.

Periodical Bibliography

The following list of periodical articles deals with the subject matter of this chapter.

Nancy Amidei	"Dealing a Fair Tax Reform," *Commonweal,* October 4, 1985.
Bruce Bartlett	"Read It and Weep," *National Review,* April 20, 1984.
Edgar K. Browning and Jacquelene M. Browning	"Why Not a True Flat Tax Rate?" *Cato Journal,* Fall 1985.
Timothy Condon	"Putting Junior to Work," *Reason,* November 1985.
Congressional Digest	"The Tax Reform Controversy," February 1986.
A.J. Davies	Letter, *Reason,* May 1986.
Gregory Fossedal	"Corporate Welfare Out of Control," *The New Republic,* February 25, 1985.
George Gilder	"The Triumph of Politics," *National Review,* June 6, 1986.
Michael Harrington	"The Snare of Poverty," *Los Angeles Times,* June 1, 1986.
David Heim	"Greed and Envy," *The New Republic,* February 27, 1984.
David Kahan	"Give Poor Families Tax Relief," *The New York Times,* February 15, 1986.
Wassily Leontif	"What It Takes to Preserve Social Equity," *The New York Times,* February 1, 1985.
Robert S. McIntyre	"Essentials of Tax Reform," *The Washington Monthly,* July-August 1986.
The New American	Special Issue: "Taxing America," April 21, 1986.
Paul Craig Roberts	"The Seduction of Supply-Siders," *National Review,* June 6, 1986.
Hans F. Sennholz	"Taxes and Unemployment," *The Freeman,* July 1986.
U.S. News & World Report	"Time to Increase Taxes?" December 30, 1985/January 6, 1986.

Is Free Trade Good for the Economy?

Economics in America

"An open system of international trade is the very foundation for a healthy economy."

The Case for Free Trade

William A. Andres

The most essential trade issue is that of free trade. Advocates of free trade argue that government should stay out of international trade and let the free market determine the supply and demand of goods. Dissenters argue that the US must trade with many countries which regularly practice trade restrictions and that America's open policy places US industry at a disadvantage in the international marketplace. In the following viewpoint, William A. Andres, chairman of the executive committee of the Dayton Hudson Foundation, makes a case for the former. He argues that trade protection of any form harms the American Consumer.

As you read, consider the following questions:

1. What is the "hidden pricetag" of trade protection, according to the author?
2. Why does the author argue that competition is the best way to determine the supply of goods?
3. How does trade protection hurt the consumer, according to the author?

William A. Andres, from a speech delivered to the American Association of Exporters and Importers in New York City on May 23, 1985.

Quite frankly, the more involved I have become in the trade issue, the more aware I have become of just how uphill our battle is to preserve an open trading system. A trading system that means so much to all of us!

In recent years, protectionist measures have cropped up almost like "brush fires" in such areas as: imported footwear, steel, copper, uranium, machine tools, tuna, and especially textile and apparel.

As we watched the forces of protection gain victory after victory, retailers came to an important realization: Despite our numbers and our economic clout, retailers and consumers alike are being almost totally ignored on the trade issue. That's why a growing number of retailers are making trade a priority issue. Our reasons can be summed up in a half dozen major points, which I'd like to share with you now.

First, trade restrictions are terribly costly. Customers who shop our stores are spending billions of dollars too much for imported goods because of a complex and often arbitrary system of government restrictions on international trade. The costs are *hidden*, in that they don't show up on the pricetag, but they are there just the same.

How high is the "hidden pricetag?" Well, if we adjust for inflation the figures in a study released in 1983 by the Center for the Study of American Business at Washington University, here's what we find: Last year, American consumers paid foreign governments and foreign manufacturers, conservatively, more than $4.4 billion for textile and apparel quotas alone. That's $4 billion that left this country just to pay for the right to buy imported goods. A real windfall for the economies of those countries, and it makes no sense for Americans whatsoever!

In addition, American consumers paid almost $19 billion because of textile and apparel tariffs, which are a *tax* we pay our own government on the value of apparel entering this country.

That brings the total "hidden tax" on imported textile and apparel to more than $23 billion last year; $23 billion that couldn't be invested in goods and services to fuel this economy and keep it growing. Obviously, the hidden pricetag for protectionism is high, and it is getting higher all the time.

Imports Increase the Standard of Living

Second point. Value-oriented goods, including imports, are critical to a high standard of living in this country. They help American consumers, especially low and middle-income consumers, stretch their family budgets.

I am convinced that the steady rise in the level of imports coming into this country has been a very significant factor in America's progress in bringing down inflation — which, as we know, was the number one economic problem in this country a few years

WE'VE GOT TO KEEP THOSE BLASTED FOREIGN IMPORTS OUT OF THE COUNTRY!

PROTECTIONISM WILL JUST TRIGGER RETALIATION BY OTHER COUNTRIES...

AND ALL YOU'LL END UP DOING IS MAKING MORE UNEMPLOYMENT

BUT IT'LL BE MADE IN AMERICA!

By Wasserman

ago. Import restrictions strike hardest at those people in our society who can least afford it — our low and middle income families. And it drains the very lifeblood of a healthy economy, which is discretionary income.

When the consumer has money to spend, retail sales go up. When they don't, the reverse is true. And, as we all know very well, when retail sales are up, the economy is up. When they're down, so is the economy. The truth is, the best "job insurance" for all of us — retailers, suppliers, importers and exporters alike — is a consumer with plenty of discretionary income.

Third point. Import restrictions are a totally inefficient and costly way to "protect" American jobs. Obviously, the perception that American jobs are being lost due to foreign competition is what gives protectionism its momentum. That is the major reason why the Textile and Apparel Enforcement Act now has 236 co-sponsors in the House of Representatives and 43 co-sponsors in the U.S. Senate! That proposed legislation would cut textile and apparel imports immediately, cap future growth in imports, set up a complex new import licensing system and guarantee, through legislation, a specific and growing *share* of the market for domestically-produced textiles and apparel. All these features intended are to "protect" the jobs of American textile and apparel workers. But they will have the net effect of raising prices, and drastically reducing the customer's selection of goods.

In response, I want to make it clear, up front, that retailers are just as concerned about the jobs issue as anybody. Workers are our neighbors, our friends, our families, and most of all, our customers. If they're out of a job, they can't shop in our stores, so it stands to reason that we care about this issue.

Protectionism's Hidden Pricetag

But the truth is, when you weigh the "hidden pricetag" of protectionism against the jobs supposedly saved, the cost-per-job "saved" is indefensible! Several studies have been done on the cost-benefit ration of trade restrictions. Here's what they show: Consumers pay an estimated $110,000 a year in higher prices to save a $24,000-a-year job in the steel industry; they pay $77,000 a year to save an $8,000-a-year job in the footwear industry, and between $35,000 and $80,000 a year for a $10,000-a-year job in the textile industry.

For *that* kind of money, the American people could buy an awful lot of retraining and transition assistance for affected workers, and still have the benefit of lower prices! For instance, let's suppose that we eliminate textile and apparel quotas, keep the $4 billion now being paid to overseas governments and put it to work right here in the United States.

Just think what could be accomplished! By my rough calculation, with the savings we could provide at least $15,000 for every textile and apparel worker displaced each year, and that's more than their current salary! Eliminate tariffs, and the transition assistance could go as high as $78,000 per worker displaced each year.

Improved Technology and Jobs

Before I leave the "jobs" question, let me make another point. You don't hear much about it, but the fact is, the vast majority of the jobs being lost in the textile and apparel industry are being lost because of improved technology, not imports.

According to the U.S. Industrial Outlook for 1985, apparel output has increased 15 percent since 1972. Productivity has increased 32 percent. Clearly, then, layoffs in that industry have not been caused just by reduced sales due to imports. The fact is, fewer employees are needed to produce more goods. No trade barrier in the world can protect workers from layoffs due to productivity improvements. Foreign competition is being blamed, but the real villains — (if you can call them "villains") — are modernization, and the strength of the dollar abroad.

As the dollar has surged to record heights in world markets, foreign goods have become an even bigger bargain. Unfortunately, the reverse is also true. American goods have been priced right out of many markets. In our opinion, the answer to the trade deficit is to tackle the root cause of the over-valued dollar, the federal deficit. The answer is *not* to substitute one bad economic policy for another, meaning, of course, more and more trade barriers.

Free Trade and a Healthy Economy

Fourth point. An open system of international trade is the very foundation for a healthy economy. Historically, this country has always been at the forefront of open trade. And it has paid off handsomely for our economy. Our economy is the envy of the world. Indeed, our European allies marvel at the amazing rate with which we create new jobs in this country.

Every time we move away from that posture, every time we indulge our protectionist whims, we pay dearly for it in terms of more job losses and a weaker overall economy. We certainly learned that lesson the hard way during the Great Depression, which was worsened by enactment of the Smoot-Hawley Tariffs back in the thirties.

The sad fact is, trade restrictions are not only an ineffective and expensive way to protect jobs, they are counter-productive. They actually cost more jobs than they "save." According to one study by the Congressional Budget Office, trade restrictions cost as many as three jobs for every one they "save," (and I use that word "save" with tongue in cheek.)

Free Trade Is Best for Consumers

Americans buy foreign-made products because they think they're a better value than any competing alternatives. They aren't in the habit of throwing money away.

Now comes a group of American manufacturers who imply that there is something wrong with buying imports. What could be wrong? . . .

The "Buy American" campaign is bad policy. It is a bid to favor workers in inefficient American industries not over foreigners, but over workers in efficient American industries, actual and potential.

So buy what you want—guilt-free. The economy works best when people are free to spend their money in their own best interest. That's what really matters.

Sheldon L. Richman, *Union Leader,* May 15, 1986.

Those jobs are lost because our overseas trading partners retaliate against our restrictions by blocking our exports with trade restrictions of their own. For example, in 1983 we restricted something like $55 million worth of cotton blouses from China. China retaliated by cancelling $500 million worth of orders for American grain.

Indeed, 40 percent of our farm products depend on overseas markets. So, the net result of trade restrictions is that we merely transfer the injury from American textile and apparel workers to American farmers or to high technology workers, aircraft workers, or workers in other industries that manufacture or produce goods for export abroad.

For a retailer, taking sides is like being forced to choose between your best customers. We don't want to make that choice. Yet the continued push for additional protection is making that choice for us every day.

Don't get me wrong. We mustn't be naive about the international trading system. We must insist on a "level playing field" for all. We must oppose unfair government subsidies, non-tariff barriers and other hidden restrictions that some countries use to protect themselves from American competition. . . .

We believe that responding in-kind to the unfair restrictions of others is like declaring economic war on our allies. For Third World countries, it's like pinning them to the ground with our foot at the same time we're extending a hand to help them up.

As someone once described the insanity of threatening trade retaliation: "It's like putting a gun to your *own* head and telling the robber: 'If you don't leave me alone, I'm going to pull the trigger.'" Believe me, if you carry out the threat and pull the trigger, it's a painful solution to the dilemma.

In our view, the President can apply many points of pressure on our overseas trading partners, without penalizing developing nations and the American consumer, and without putting our economic recovery at risk. . . .

Imports Increase Competitiveness

Point five. Imports enhance the overall competitiveness of American business! . . . American retailers, like every industry, buy some components overseas for reasons of price, quality or lack of domestic availability.

Imports help keep us competitive and the same is true for the textile and apparel industries. Indeed, many American apparel companies are now manufacturing offshore with great success. Those who continue to manufacture here at home are making tremendous gains in productivity—(faster than the national average!)—with a variety of imported machinery. In fact, to be accurate, the label ought to read "Made in America with Czechoslovakian knitting machines, Swiss looms and Japanese water-jet looms."

Dont' get me wrong. I'm not casting aspersions on anyone in the textile and apparel industry for using imports to make themselves more competitive. In my judgment, those were wise business decisions, wise competitive adjustments. In the long run, they will prove to be far more viable responses to the challenge of international competition than import restrictions, or "Crafted With Pride in America" campaigns. . . .

Our vested interest is the customer's vested interest in more jobs, lower prices, higher standards of living, more discretionary income, a stronger overall economy and greater stability in the world, because of the economic and political inter-dependence that trade fosters. . . .

If the present trend continues, whose jobs will be on the line? The answer is obvious: Not just textile and apparel workers, but farmers and high technology workers, and all of the other industries who manufacture for export. Throughout America, economic growth will be stunted.

By Bob Gorrell. Permission of News America Syndicate.

The forces which influence our businesses are becoming more international with each passing year. Try as we may to impede the progress of this trend, through protectionism and through "Buy America" campaigns, the fact remains: We live in a world economy. We operate in a worldwide marketplace. We serve an increasingly sophisticated customer, a better educated, more selective, more demanding customer.

Lee Iacocca in a London Raincoat

Take Lee Iacocca, for example. We see him on TV, urging us to be patriotic and buy his American cars and he's standing there in a Burberry raincoat, imported from England! And I'm sure each of us here today if we took inventory of our own households would find a *similar mix* of international and domestic goods. (That shows how well you've done your jobs.) The truth is, none of us can turn back the clock to a time when competition was just down the street, or just around the corner.

I am firmly convinced that our relationship with our domestic suppliers doesn't need the so-called "protection" of trade barriers to keep it intact. Our partnership has too much going for it!

American apparel manufacturers may be disadvantaged by higher labor costs, but they have many competitive advantages: Less bureaucratic red tape, reliability and proximity, shorter lead times, good old American ingenuity and creativity, advanced manufacturing technology, a skilled labor force and a natural understanding of the fashion-conscious American consumer.

Those are real competitive advantages, and their strategic challenge is to exploit them fully. My point is, if we want to be truly helpful to our domestic resources, we must support them in the most constructive way possible. Supporting their call for additional protection, in my judgment, is the least constructive way we can be of assistance.

Competition Is Best

Competition is the central force in our American economy. It always has been, and it always will be. Competition is good for our customers. Good for our businesses. Good for our society. Competition is the *essence* of the free enterprise system. It is the American way.

Indeed, the kind of "Buy America!" campaign that we should support is one that is in the best tradition of Americanism. A tradition of free and open competition where we let the customer decide.

American consumers *want* to buy American goods. They tell us so in every survey we take. But they also want American goods to be the *best*. Like us, they're disappointed when they're not. . . .

We want American merchandise to be the best quality and the best value, and we want it to be judged the best in open competition! We can't take much pride in winning a Gold Medal when the competition is limited.

Our commitment to the all-American concept of competition is one of the key reasons we strongly oppose legislation currently before Congress. It would further shelter our domestic textile and apparel industries from making the kind of tough decisions that are necessary to keep them competitive.

That legislation, ladies and gentlemen, has nothing to do with a patriotic spirit, or any "Buy America!" campaign. But it has a lot to do with the growth prospects of this country's economy, our own growth prospects and the continued prosperity of our customers. . . .

We simply must force the question: Will the American consumer be better off, or worse off, if we continue down this path? Will the economy be better off? Not just one region, or one industry, but the *entire* economy?

Our concern for the customer, and for the entire economy is what motivates us to speak out on the trade issue. . . .

Hearing the Consumers' Side

We believe competition, not protection, is in their best interests, as producers in our best interests, as retailers; and in the best interests of our mutual customers, the ones who buy *their* goods in *our* stores.

Open trade is a consumer issue. It is a jobs issue. It is a free enterprise issue. For retailers, (indeed for *all* of us!) it is a growth issue. Everyone who is concerned about those issues . . . must realize just what is at stake in the U.S. Trade Debate.

If we are to have any hope of stemming the rising tide of protectionism, we must talk about the issue to our friends, our neighbors, our employees, and even our customers—who are the constituents of our public policy-makers.

We must make sure they hear the other side of the story, the *consumer's* side, when it comes to the benefits of an open trading system, and the high cost of protectionism.

"This fixation on textbook free trade has nothing in common with the world trading system, does not reflect the trading practices of other countries, and does nothing to solve America's trade problems."

The Case Against Free Trade

Mark Anderson

Mark Anderson is an economist on the staff of the AFL-CIO Department of Economic Research. The AFL-CIO (American Federation of Labor and Congress of Industrial Organizations) is the largest labor organization in America. It lobbies for many pro-union issues, including full employment, government subsidy of industry, and trade protection. In the following viewpoint, Mr. Anderson argues that America's advocacy of free trade is unrealistic and is destroying US industry. He states that other countries heavily subsidize their industries and are able to keep prices artificially low. The United States cannot compete against them unless it, too, is offered the protections and subsidies that other countries receive.

As you read, consider the following questions:

1. What are the "devastating effects" of the trade deficit, according to the author?
2. What does the author think is wrong with David Ricardo's economic theory?

Mark Anderson, "America's Foreign Trade Crisis," *AFL-CIO American Federationist,* October 13, 1984. Reprinted with permission.

The United States is facing an unprecedented crisis in international trade. Over the last four years, U.S. exports have dropped and imports of foreign products have soared. The sharp deterioration of the international economic position of the United States has had a profound and negative impact on scores of domestic industries and millions of American workers. Left unchecked, this trade crisis poses a serious threat to the industrial base of the United States and the standard of living of all Americans.

The "hands-off" attitude of the Reagan Administration, based on a naive devotion to free markets that don't exist, has only served to accelerate America's decline. This fixation on textbook free trade has nothing in common with the world trading system, does not reflect the trading practices of other countries, and does nothing to solve America's trade problems. The U.S. trade deficit, influenced heavily by an overvalued dollar that has risen 65 percent against the currencies of our major trading partners, has increased almost fourfold since 1980 and will exceed $120 billion by the end of this year. Poor enforcement of U.S. trade law, ill-conceived monetary and fiscal policies, laws that encourage overseas production, and the absence of an effective industrial policy have all contributed to this serious problem.

The AFL-CIO believes that the goal of U.S. trade policy must be the attainment of a fair trading environment that allows this nation to remain an advanced and diversified economy. "Fair trade" means that the interests of the United States must receive greater emphasis in both the domestic and international initiatives of the nation's international trade and investment policy. To promote full employment and rising living standards, the United States must retain its manufacturing, agricultural, and service industries. Foreign trade policy and domestic economic policy must promote—not undermine—this goal.

Tragically, the policies of the last four years, rather than helping, have contributed significantly to the massive trade deficits the United States faces today. The dimensions of this problem are startling. The U.S. merchandise trade deficit for 1983 reached a record $69 billion, almost double the level experienced in 1980. This economic decline is accelerating in 1984, with the deficit expected to reach $120 billion by the end of the year. These deficits represent a significant drain on the economy and are responsible for the loss of millions of jobs. . . .

Trade and Jobs

The impact of this growing trade deficit on employment is devastating. Despite the recent expansion of the U.S. economy, there are 1.3 million fewer manufacturing jobs than in 1979. Estimates of jobs lost or not created in recent years due to the trade imbalance go as high as four million.

As dramatic as these numbers are, they may very well understate the impact of trade on U.S. employment. Many trade-related employment estimates are based on assigning a certain number of jobs for each billion dollars of net exports. For example, the U.S. Dept. of Commerce has frequently assigned 25,000 jobs for each billion dollars of exports. The use of these ratios, however, does not take into account the composition of trade and, given the labor intensity of U.S. imports and the capital intensity of U.S. exports, invariably minimizes the job losses caused by imports.

In addition, because of low labor costs in many of the countries where U.S. imports originate, a dollar of imports displaces more than one dollar of U.S. production of the same item. A factor which has made dollar-denominated measures of trade even less reliable is the sharp rise in the foreign exchange value of the dollar. The appreciation of the U.S. dollar raises the foreign price of exports, and cheapens the U.S. price of imported goods. An appreciating dollar, therefore, increases the employment loss per billion dollars of U.S. imports.

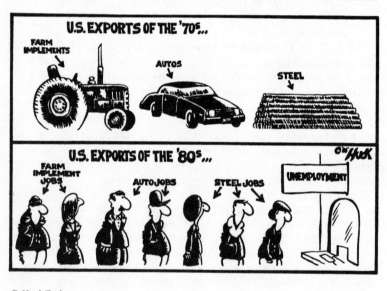

Despite this lack of accurate information, the negative impact of trade is painfully clear to millions of unemployed workers and scores of devastated communities. . . .

In 1984, the United States will record the largest trade deficit in history—more than $120 billion. Manufactured goods will account for more than two-thirds of that total. This grim economic reality, part of a longer term trend, has not occasioned any fundamental change in U.S. trade policy. As in 1960, adherence to the principles of free trade remains the government's basic policy position. The fact that as a practical matter free trade no longer exists is somehow overlooked. . . .

In 1983, when the U.S. trade deficit reached $69 billion, the *Economic Report of the President* stated:

"Trade-distorting measures, whether they take the form of protection against imports or the promotion of exports, hurt the country which adopts them as well as other countries, even when they are a response to foreign trade-distorting practices. If foreign governments limit imports from the United States and we respond in kind, the initial results will be further reductions in economic efficiency at home and higher domestic prices. If foreign governments subsidize exports, depressing world prices for U.S. products, a countersubsidy by the United States will depress prices still further. The belief that departures from free trade are automatically called for if other countries do not play by the rules is a fallacy."

National Interest Too Easily Dismissed

The tragedy of this approach is that the U.S. is frequently left defenseless in the international arena. By emphasizing, even rhetorically, the "value" of free trade, questions of national interest tend to be dismissed, or at least relegated to a lower status, and success is measured not by the health of the domestic economy, but by one's adherence to a theoretical construct.

Free-trade theory is based on principles first espoused by British economist David Ricardo in the early 1800s. Ricardo argued that a totally free exchange of goods between countries would lead to maximum utility and, therefore, universal benefit. Each nation should utilize its own comparative advantage and specialize in the production of goods in which they are relatively more efficient, and to import those goods where their production capability is relatively inefficient. His famous example involved English wool (England had a lot of sheep) and Portuguese wine (Portugal enjoyed a superior grape growing climate).

Notwithstanding the fact that international commerce in the 20th Century is somewhat more complicated than trading wool for wine, the assumptions on which free-trade theory is commonly based bear little resemblance to conditions found in today's world.

The assumptions found in the standard model include full employment, perfect competition, perfect mobility of factors of production internally but not internationally, given resources, constant technology, no transportation costs, and many others. Basically, it's a static model attempting to describe a dynamic world.

Unemployment is undeniably real. Perfect competition can't account for state trading companies, transnational enterprises, or

133

government intervention and subsidization. The static nature of the model doesn't deal with international capital flows. Ricardo did not consider swings in currency valuation. In the real world, there are unfortunately winners and losers, and the United States is increasingly going down in defeat.

These facts of life, and many others, make free trade as a foundation for public policy not just irrelevant, but harmful. The only policy truly compatible with this frame of reference is a policy of inaction so that the market can do its work. That the market really doesn't exist is somehow forgotten. Hence the charges of protectionism over any action taken by the United States, however small that action may be.

Mythical Free Market

America's trade problems have reached crisis proportions. The decline of the U.S. international economic position has caused untold hardship for millions of American workers and scores of communities, and threatens the economic health and security of our nation. Unfortunately, the Administration clings to a belief in mythical market forces and in an illusory free-trade theory at a time when positive action is desperately needed to reverse the erosion of America's industrial base.

Rudolph A. Oswald, speech given on February 19, 1985.

It should be clear by now that our trading partners have a different conception of what "free trade" is all about. Other countries see trade as a means to the larger goal of balanced economic development and full employment. While it is true that tariffs have been lowered through successive rounds of multilateral trade negotiations, a new array of non-tariff barriers has developed—quotas, stringent inspection requirements, discriminatory standards, buy-national policies, export subsidies, industrial targeting programs, and trade arrangements such as performance requirements, coproduction, offset and barter agreements.

Continued attempts by the United States to negotiate the reduction of these measures have just not been successful, and our own market remains wide open to an ever-increasing volume of imports. . . .

Foreign Trade Practices

In contrast to laissez-faire policies of the U.S., other countries manage their trade and investment flows to achieve maximum national advantage. Their focus is on domestic ramifications of trade, not adherence to a 19th-Century economic doctrine. A few examples:

- When France was recently being flooded by large quantities of Japanese video cassette recorders, customs procedures were changed to require each recorder to be individually inspected at one small customs station. A quota agreement with Japan was quickly reached.

- Italy restricts the import of Japanese autos to 2,200 cars a year.
- Japan places severe import restrictions on leather goods.
- Taiwan frequently conditions foreign investment on export requirements.
- Brazil severely limits the importation of general aviation aircraft and heavily subsidizes its own exports.
- The United Kingdom maintains strict quotas on shoe imports.
- Government-owned telephone companies in other countries refuse to buy imported products.

The list could go on and on. In general, however, the principal policies employed by other countries include high tariffs, import quotas, export incentives, discriminatory procurement, state-owned enterprises, direct government subsidies, government-supported research and development, barter trade requirements, coproduction and export requirements for foreign investment and subsidized financing.

None of these measures has anything in common with free trade or free markets. Rather they are explicit repudiations of the notion that trade and economic and industrial development exclusively reside in the private sector. . . .

No Single Answer

While there is no single answer to the trade problem, a useful beginning would be the recognition that U.S. national interest and adherence to free-trade theory is often incompatible. America must realize that it does not operate in a world of "free trade" characterized by the free market determination of trade flows according to traditional notions of comparative advantage. Other countries manage their trade and investment flows to achieve maximum national advantage. Their rejection of 19th-Century economic doctrine when it interferes with their domestic objectives is neither fair nor unfair, but sensible national policy.

With this in mind, the U.S. government must undertake a variety of specific actions to deal with the trade crisis.

First and foremost, U.S. trade law must be strengthened to reflect international trading realities. It is time to recognize that the principal approach to trade problems taken by the government—encouraging other countries to stop what are considered to be objectionable practices—has failed. While negotiations take place, injury to the American economy continues.

Secondly, the U.S. government must deal with the problems trade creates for the domestic economy.

For example, Special Trade Rep. William E. Brock, in a speech before the National Press Club, said that Japan was risking its entire trading relationship with the United States by refusing to adequately relax its quota on U.S. beef exports. He said the issue "has taken on a symbolic quality way beyond its substance." This is exactly what is wrong with the U.S. approach. In 1983, the United States had a large surplus in agricultural trade with Japan, quotas or not. The overall trade balance with Japan however was in deficit by almost $22 billion due to the tremendous imbalance in manufactured goods. That is the trade problem with Japan, not beef. Attention should be directed at substantive problems, not symbolic issues.

To help accomplish this policy reorientation, legislation is urgently needed to tighten and streamline the laws designed to relieve industries and workers injured by imports.

It is clear that the so-called "fair" and "unfair" trade remedy statutes need improvements. Both "fair" trade laws designed to alleviate trade-induced injury and "unfair" trade laws designed to counteract dumping and subsidies should have better procedures and more effective remedies.

Free Trade Is Unrealistic

It is argued that, since the end of World War II, we have had a trade policy—"free trade"—which operates in the best interests of our citizens, but "free trade" hardly describes the policies of the nations of the world. . . .

Rather than critically assess the impact of the growth of serious foreign economic competitors, our government continued to espouse and practice a policy of "free trade" while nearly all other developed nations maintained a variety of policies aimed both at limiting imports and encouraging exports.

Owen Bieber, speech before the Senate Committee on Finance, November 20, 1985.

The escape clause provisions of the Trade Act should be revised to assure quick relief from trade injury. When U.S. producers lose sales to foreign producers and reduce their production and work-forces accordingly, they know only that trade has injured their business operations. Workers feel the injury in the resulting layoffs. At this point, the injured parties don't know if the injury was caused by so-called "unfair"trade practices, by "fair" trade practices, by the rising value of the dollar, by foreign currency devaluation, or a combination of these causes. All they know is that the injury is trade-related. They should be able to receive temporary relief from the injury. And they should receive help from the government to make their case under the appropriate provisions of the Trade Act that deal with relief measures for specific "unfair" and "injurious" trade practices. Many aspects of foreign subsidy programs and dumping activities are more readily ascertainable by U.S. government agencies than by private parties injured by trade. . . .

In addition to steps that would help all industries hard hit by imports, the AFL-CIO believes that legislation should be enacted to deal with the problems of specific industries:

• Domestic content laws to help assure that the United States remains a producer of automobiles.

• Steel import quotas, provided the steel industry undertakes modernization measures.

• Action to reduce the job-destroying influx of garments, textiles and footwear now inundating U.S. industry.

• Legislation to revive the U.S. maritime industry to substantially increase the portion of cargo carried in U.S.-flag ships and to assure a strong U.S. shipbuilding base, thereby enhancing the national security.

• Policies to maintain and re-establish domestic electronic telecommunication and television industries. . . .

Industrial Policy

The government has maintained a basically "hands-off" or "laissez-faire" policy toward domestic industrial development and international trade. Other countries have implemented aggressive industrial and trade policies, with substantial success. In steel, auto, electronics, railcars, aircraft, and a host of emerging industries, Japan, the advanced industrial countries of Europe, and the new industrial countries have applied a wide spectrum of strategic government support—from low-cost credit to protection from import competition and government assistance in technology development. Manufacturing is most important for the health and balance of the U.S. economy, particularly the production of basic commodities which are essential for other production and have national defense implications. . . .

The nation must assign top priority to the channeling of resources to modernize private and public facilities and restore the national economy to a condition of balanced growth and full employment. Otherwise, the country will continue to lag in productivity growth and international trade. It will continue to leave significant portions of its human and machine resources idle for extended periods of time. It will continue to suffer a reduction in the standard of living of its people.

The AFL-CIO believes that the adoption of . . . measures—trade law reform, a restructuring of monetary and fiscal policy, active intervention in international financial markets, and the enactment of industrial policy—will help solve the trade crisis and result in achieving the basic goals of our economy: full employment and balanced economic growth.

> "We have seen that forceful, straightforward action—such as quotas on imports—work."

The US Must Restrict Foreign Imports

Joseph M. Gaydos

Joseph M. Gaydos is a Democratic member of the House of Representatives from Pennsylvania. In the following viewpoint, Mr. Gaydos argues that unfair trading practices of America's competitors are taking away American jobs and creating a monstrous and economy-damaging trade deficit. He believes the only way to bring this situation under control is to slap on import quotas for foreign goods.

As you read, consider the following questions:

1. Why does Mr. Gaydos consider the US a "debtor nation"?
2. Why does the author blame Japan for the US trade deficit?
3. Why does the author think that those people who oppose trade quotas are "traitors"?

Joseph M. Gaydos, "Congressman Says He's Proud To Be a Protectionist," *The Spotlight*, August 19, 1985.

Almost immediately after my first being elected to Congress in 1967, I began urging this body to look closely at the flow of foreign goods into this country. For nearly 18 years, I have been an outspoken proponent of limits (quotas, if you will) on goods that unfairly compete with American products in the domestic market.

Over the years that I have served in the Congress, I have been an eyewitness to the extinction and near extinction of many American industries that have been buffeted by foreign competitors—rivals that have thrived on subsidies from their home governments, rivals that have been and are wholly or substantially owned by their governments, and rivals who have shipped and sold their products here below what the cost of manufacturing was just in order to get a toehold, and then a foothold, and then the lion's share of the American marketplace.

And, because of my stand on limiting, on setting quotas on, the amount of imports to this country as a means of assisting American business, American economic growth and American workers and their jobs, I have been labeled a "protectionist."

Proud of His Label

Well, I take great pride in being tagged with that label.

In the early 1940s, when I volunteered to put on the uniform of this country's armed forces, I was sent to the South Pacific to "protect and defend" American ideals and beliefs. I believed in that cause and I was proud to be called a "protectionist."

Well, we are at war today, too. It may not be a shooting war, like that of the 1940s, but it is no less a war. And we are losing.

The US Is a Debtor Nation

Just look at what is happening. For the first time since World War I, the United States is a debtor nation. We have to depend on foreign governments and foreign investors to finance our debt—and that means our economic future is in the hand of other nations and, if we don't turn it around, we'll have to dance to someone else's tune.

We have a merchandise trade deficit that is going out of sight. [In 1984], our merchandise trade deficit hit the all-time record mark of $123.3 billion. [In 1985], the monthly deficits are even higher and the projected year-end deficit [was] between $140 and $160 billion.

What does that mean for America? It means that we are importing more goods than we are exporting. It means that these imported goods are taking a larger share of the American market—more than 25 percent of the American steel market, some 70 percent of the shoe market, more than 60 percent of the television sets and radios and nearly 30 percent of the automotive market.

But it's more pervasive than that. Those are just foreign-made goods. What about the American manufacturers who have moved manufacturing facilities offshore or who import components for products that are sold here?

Two-thirds of every IBM personal computer is made in Japan or Singapore. Half of the components of all American machine tools are manufactured overseas. The Eastman Kodak Co. sells copiers made by Japan's Canon Corp. under the Kodak name.

© Huck/Rothco

General Motors and Chrysler will be building cars jointly with Japanese and Korean manufacturers. The assembly work will be here, but the parts will be imported. The list goes on and on.

The Cost in US Jobs

And it costs us. It costs us jobs, good-paying jobs for American men and women. For every billion dollars of the trade deficit, we lose or fail to create 25,000 jobs. That means that in 1984, we lost or did not create about 3 million jobs. And, if the projections for the merchandise trade deficit for 1985 hold true, we will lose or not create between 3½ and 4 million jobs.

The components of the huge trade deficit, too, require some study. Nearly one-quarter of the 1984 trade deficit was with one country, Japan. And the picture for 1985 [wasn't] any better.

For the first three months of 1985 (January through March) our deficit with Japan worsened. Yes, it is true our exports to Japan increased overall by nearly 10 percent. But, at the same time, our imports from Japan increased by nearly 30 percent as compared to the first quarter of 1984.

What is even more disconcerting is that in April [1985], for the first time ever, Japan showed a surplus in invisibles, such items as shipping expenditures, interest and dividend payments, and licensing fees. Some are saying the $98-million surplus in the invisibles is a drop in the bucket compared to Japan's $3.3-billion merchandise trade surplus, but it's only the beginning, I fear.

The big reason for the turnaround is a surge in foreign interest income that has built up as Japanese companies send profits overseas in search of high interest rates.

And that means the United States. Japanese investors' net purchases of foreign bonds, mainly U.S. government obligations, doubled from 1982 to 1983, and doubled again last year to $26.8 billion.

Protectionist Measures in Congress

I am happy to say that more members of Congress are at long last recognizing the problem. We won three new converts to the battle. Senator Lloyd Bentsen (D-Texas) and Congressmen Dan Rostenkowski (D-Ill.) and Dick Gephard (D-Mo.) joined our ranks when they, along with a host of others, introduced legislation that would tack a 25-percent surcharge on certain goods from countries that have excessively high trade surpluses with the United States.

This legislation is intended to show the world that the Congress is seriously concerned and ready to act if the countries don't take steps to reduce those trade surpluses with us.

I want to welcome these new supporters. I am delighted that they have finally seen the light and see the danger to this country. I only wonder what took them so long to realize that our future is up to us, that we cannot wait for others to act.

The reaction to the legislation filed by these three newcomers has been predictable. The administration has labeled them "protectionist." According to newspaper quotes, this bill has been called "protectionist legislation of the rankest kind," and has been described as "patently anti-consumer, undermining the international trading system, and inviting retaliation that would cost jobs."

We have heard a lot in these past few months about Japan's efforts to open its markets to our goods. Well, anyone who has followed the trade issue knows that the Japanese government leaders have made these kinds of statements before, but that nothing has changed except in a cosmetic way.

We are still waiting for access to the Japanese market and I think

141

we'll have to wait a lot longer unless we give a couple of big sticks to our trade people. Maybe then the Japanese and other nations will take heed of our interest.

We Need Limits on Imports

There is another facet to our trade problem and it's more serious because it's coming from inside the country. We have those at home who oppose any limits on imports.

They claim to speak for the consumers and the right of consumers to choose from a variety of both domestic and foreign goods and to select on the basis of price. And they talk about retaliation by foreign governments who will impose restrictions on American goods if we set limits on their goods.

These enemies, traitors if you will, are the ones who label us as "protectionists," using the term in a negative sense as if we are the enemy of America.

They are the ones who don't see the real problem. They are the ones who fail to understand that to have consumers, you have to have people with spendable income, that you have to have people who are employed.

The enemies of protectionism say that we can retain workers who have lost their jobs. I wonder what we will train them for. The high-tech industry is beginning to feel the pinch from imports just as the steel, copper, textile, automobile, and shoe industries have, so the potential jobs in that field are going to be limited.

Restricting Imports a Vital Necessity

The consequences of the rising tide of imports and the decline in U.S. exports are being felt in all sectors of the economy through plant closings, bankruptcies, farm foreclosures, and recessionary unemployment levels. The Maine shoemaker, the Ohio machinist, the Kansas farmer, and even the so-called high tech worker in the Silicon Valley have all gained a keener appreciation of the realities of international commerce. These lessons, however, were not learned from textbooks or endless international negotiations, but from lost jobs, lost income, and lost dignity, with a massive ripple effect along every main street in America.

Lane Kirkland, before the Subcommittee on Trade, September 17, 1985.

The service industries? Sure, there will be jobs there. But service industries can't stand alone. They too, depend on manufacturing jobs as well. This country cannot survive solely on service industries.

The anti-protectionists say that the reason American goods cannot compete is because the dollar is too high as compared to the currencies of other countries and that when the dollar drops,

American goods will become more competitive abroad so our trade deficit will come down.

The value of the dollar is a factor, but even the Commerce Department says it will take a minimum of one year for the impact of a falling dollar to reflect itself in fewer imports, more exports and recovery for American industry.

Down the Drain

And what happens in the meantime? Are we to stand idly by and watch more jobs go down the drain, watch more American men and women, who want to work, unable to get work, even if they participate in the many job training programs available?

Isn't it more productive for us to keep the jobs we have than to spend billions to train men and women who have lost their jobs because of imports for new and other jobs that don't exist?

Shortly after I was first elected, and after each subsequent election, I have stood here and have sworn to "support and defend the Consitution of the United States against all enemies, foreign and domestic."

That phrase is part of the congressional oath of office.

I take my responsibility seriously. My remarks may sound jingoistic, but we are trying to be reasonable.

None of us accused of being "protectionist" has ever said that no foreign goods should be sold in this country. All we are saying is that for certain industries that we have determined to be vital to our national welfare, we want to set some reasonable limits on how much of the American market we should give away.

After all, it's not as if we are doing anything different from what the rest of the world is and has been doing for years. In fact, whether we like it or not and no matter how much we try, other nations do have barriers to American goods.

Oh, they may say that our manufacturers don't cater to their foreign audience, but that sounds like just so much verbiage to me. If they feel that's true, then just open up the market and let us compete.

Frankly, I think we get a lot of lip service from other nations when it comes to open markets or opening markets. We hear a lot of words, but there just isn't any action.

Protection and Patriotism Linked

I am a protectionist. I am proud to be one. I fully believe in what John C. Calhoun told Congress on December 12, 1811. He said that "protection and patriotism are reciprocal. This is the road that all great nations have trod."

I agree with him. I don't know why we are so afraid of it. I am especially surprised that this administration, which seems to have made a point of its patriotic flavor, has failed, like so many others, to act to protect American industry and American jobs. This administration has squandered any number of opportunities to act forcefully to "protect" this country.

We have voluntary agreements on steel that may work, only because we have the force of the administration behind them. If that fails, then the agreements will fail as well.

We have seen that forceful, straight-forward action—such as quotas on imports—work. Just a few short years ago, when the specialty steel industry was suffering, a package that included quotas and tariffs was adopted to deal with the problems.

Well, we see the results. Firms handling the specialty steel items, on which quotas were imposed, are seeing marked improvement, while those firms handling items on which tariffs were imposed and not getting any better.

We who have been elected to serve our nation have a responsibility to that nation and its people. We have taken a solemn oath to do that. And if someone wants to call me a "protectionist" because I believe I am fulfilling the duties I have sworn to do, then so be it.

I am a "protectionist" and proud of it.

"Call them tariffs, call them import quotas, call them what you will—all come down to consumers being bled via higher prices."

The US Should Not Restrict Foreign Imports

Eric Marti

Eric Marti is the managing editor of *Reason,* a monthly magazine dedicated to the concept of individual liberty in politics, economics, and the arts and sciences. In the following viewpoint, Mr. Marti argues that the two most common dangers cited by opponents of a free market—the trade deficit and the loss of jobs—are essentially imaginary concerns. The trade deficit does not really cause the US any direct harm, he counters, and, contrary to popular belief, the US has been creating far more jobs than it has lost to foreign imports.

As you read, consider the following questions:

1. Why does the author argue that the trade deficit's impact on the economy has been exaggerated?
2. What reasons does the author give to show that jobs are not being lost because of foreign imports?
3. Why is trade protection a violation of individual rights, according to the author?

Eric Marti, "Protect Us from the Protectionists." Reprinted, with permission, from the December 1985 issue of REASON magazine. Copyright © 1985 by the Reason Foundation, 2716 Ocean Park Blvd., Suite 1062, Santa Monica, CA 90405.

As all but Rip Van Winkle know, the United States is running a huge deficit in its balance-of-trade account—supposedly justifying this fall's mad rush to protectionism. But when it comes to a balance-of-blame account, we are running a huge surplus. The national mood of scapegoatism grows uglier by day, with more and more fingers pointing at foreigners, particularly the Japanese.

According to the protectionists—primarily big business, big labor, and their allies in big government—"unfair trade practices" on the part of foreign nations (such as restricting US imports and subsidizing their export industries) are harming the national interest of the United States. The ballyhooed trade deficit is Exhibit A in the case against foreign products and their makers. Exhibit B is the "loss" of American jobs.

Both pieces of evidence, however, are artifices. They suit very well the special interests mounting protectionist campaigns that are pro-worker and pro-America in rhetoric but anticonsumer in fact. But they are chock full of holes.

Exhibit A, the trade deficit, is perhaps the most misunderstood of publicly consumed statistics, though it actually tells us nothing important. The official "trade deficit" for 1984 was $123.7 billion. But what does this figure mean? In 1984, Americans spent $123.7 billion more on merchandise from foreign sellers than foreign buyers spent on American goods. But the figure includes *only* "merchandise," a statistical category that excludes "services"—things like transportation, construction, banking, and insurance, which are an increasingly important element in modern economies. In *this* category, US concerns consistently sell more abroad than are bought from abroad ($20 billion more in 1984).

Moreover, the trade deficit by itself doesn't give any clue to which specific goods Americans are buying from foreign producers. If that were shown, we'd see that oil purchases accounted for *nearly half* of the 1984 deficit. (In 1983, oil imports made up $59 billion of that year's $60-billion "trade deficit.")

Closer scrutiny of the trade deficit also reveals that it turns a blind eye to revenues that US firms earn from production and sales operations inside foreign nations. In Japan, for example, US-based firms earned $44 billion in sales [in 1984]. Though these revenues are certainly a boon to the firms' US stockholders and employees, they're not counted as export income when it comes to toting up the trade balance. Why? Simply because the data keepers don't define exports that way. When these revenues *are* counted, it turns out that Americans and Japanese, for example, bought about equal amounts of goods from each other last year ($69 billion worth).

More Accurate Statistics

Rather than getting all hot and bothered about a statistically inadequate figure like the trade deficit, the public and the politicians should be checking out other information that in fact more accurately portrays the health of the US economy in world markets. In manufactured exports, for example, the US share of the foreign market has increased from 17 to 20 percent over the last six years, surpassing West Germany for first rank on this measure. And the US share of the highly competitive Asian-Pacific market has held steady at 15 percent since 1967, while that total market has grown from $5 billion to $80 billion.

But perhaps the biggest problem with focusing on the trade deficit is that it creates a false impression about the fate of all those US dollars sent abroad for all those goodies. So what if foreigners are selling us more goods than we are selling to them? The "excess" dollars have to come back to the US economy in the end.

S. KELLEY IN SAN DIEGO UNION

Steve Kelley, *San Diego Union*, reprinted with permission.

This isn't just economic theory. The Japanese, for example, are in fact now investing enormous sums in the United States—largely profits from their US sales of VCRs, cars, stereos, etc. The whole cycle is quite understandable: as the US economy grows at its present fast clip, Americans are purchasing more and more (hence the "trade deficit"); at the same time, rapid US economic growth offers foreigners good investment opportunities and thus attracts huge amounts of foreign capital. How can we lose?

The forces of protectionism think they have the answer: Exhibit B, lost jobs. Sen. Lloyd Bentsen (D-Tex.), for example—one of the many sponsors of protectionist legislation in Congress—names "the loss of U.S. jobs" as foremost among "the trade deficit's damaging effects." And according to Democratic representative of Indiana Lee Hamilton, for his constituents the trade issue "translates into jobs." Not least because that's what the anti-free-traders keep telling all those constituents out there.

To be blunt, however, the alleged loss of US jobs is pure fiction. On the contrary, the US economy is producing new jobs at a truly phenomenal rate, 8 million since 1980, while every other major Western industrialized nation is actually losing jobs. In some US industries, it's true, jobs are diminishing—particularly factory jobs in the older, smokestack industries. But this decline is greatly offset by the explosion of jobs in newer industries. Unfortunately, the hiring of workers in thousands of personnel offices dispersed throughout the nation doesn't have the visibility—nor the six-o'clock-news appeal—of laid-off steelworkers languishing in the unemployment line.

The trade deficit and job loss, then, are useless as tools for cogent policy analysis. For purposes of making problems that are in fact entirely domestic, however, they are great.

For big-business and big-labor protectionists, equating the meaningless trade deficit with some supposed national ill enables them to divert attention from their inability or unwillingness to adapt to new economic conditions—conditions that include, for example, growing competition in basic manufacturing from newly industrialized and industrializing nations abroad and Japan's remarkable achievement in quality control.

Trade Deficit a Distraction

For protectionists in government, the trade deficit is a red herring useful in diverting attention from a host of policies that work against US exporters. In this area, public problem number one is the $200-billion-plus federal deficits: to finance its enormous overspending, the federal government borrows—and borrows—pushing up interest rates and, consequently, the foreign demand for dollars. As this rising demand pushes up the value of the dollar against other currencies, US products become more costly to foreign buyers.

And what is the government's solution to this problem? Cutting federal spending? Hah. No way. No—much more to the liking of government meddlers is international fiddling in the currency market to bring the dollar down. The Reagan administration supposedly embarked on this course in September to stave off the rising tide of protectionism in the Congress. But dollar-bashing is widely acknowledged to have no lasting effect in such matters.

Meanwhile, the forces of protectionism, which are also the sources of big political contributions, continue to have the ear of Congress. What do the protectionists want? In a word, subsidies. Call them tariffs, call them import quotas, call them what you

148

will—all come down to consumers being bled via higher prices so that some few among us won't have to lose any sleep worrying about foreign competition.

Already we're paying mightily for their untroubled dreams. Last year, American car buyers, for instance, shelled out some *$5 billion* more than they would have paid if the Japanese hadn't been pressured into "voluntarily" limiting their car exports. And that's just one for instance. Steel is used throughout the economy. Shoes. Clothing. Finished food products. The list of major and minor items now subject to unfree-trade restrictions or up for the protectionist axe is long indeed.

Raising Political and Economic Costs

There are some well meaning [Members of Congress] who have proposed bills and programs that are truly protectionist in nature. These proposals would raise the costs of the goods and services that American consumers across the land would have to pay.

They would invite retaliation by our trading partners abroad, would in turn lose jobs for those American workers in industries that would be the victims of such retaliation, would rekindle inflation, would strain international relations and would impair the stability of the international financial and trading systems.

The net result of these counterproductive proposals would not be to protect consumers or workers or farmers or businesses. In fact, just the reverse would happen. We would lose markets. We would lose jobs. And we would lose our prosperity. . . .

We do not want a trade war with other nations. We want other nations to join us in enlarging and enhancing the world trading system for the benefit of all.

President Ronald Reagan, speech, September 23, 1985.

Such intervention not only raises consumers' costs, chipping away at Americans' living standard (not to mention what it means for the foreign victims of our protectionism). It also is counterproductive: consumers who must pay more for, say, cars must now forgo buying, say, new lawnmowers—and so the US garden-equipment maker lays off workers, who can buy neither new cars nor much of anything else. Multiply these effects throughout the economy, and the true, deleterious effects of protectionism become obvious.

Protectionism Erodes Liberty

When the rhetoric and obfuscation are finally brushed away, protectionism reveals itself at bottom as a violation of individual rights. Free trade is simply part of freedom generally, the right to free association: individuals have the right to trade peacefully with whomever, and on whatever conditions, they choose. However disguised and in whatever form, trade restrictions abridge that right. Hence the price we pay for protectionism is denominated not only in dollars but in something far more dear—individual liberty.

"Japan has closed the door to free trade, and it has locked it shut."

US Trade Is Harmed by Japan's Restrictions

Pete Wilson

Pete Wilson, Republican senator from California, strongly believes that Japan's trade restrictions are harming the United States. In the following viewpoint, excerpted from a speech he made before a group of Japanese businesspeople, Senator Wilson accuses the Japanese of using unfair—and unreciprocated—trade regulations. These regulations, he states, are not only harmful to the US but to Japan as well. If Japan doesn't open its trade policies, argues Mr. Wilson, the US will be forced to retaliate with its own severe regulations and tariffs.

As you read, consider the following questions:

1. Why does Senator Wilson believe Japan's restrictions are unfair?
2. List some of the Japanese actions that Senator Wilson considers "subversive."
3. What threats does Senator Wilson make to the Japanese?
4. What does Senator Wilson urge his listeners to do?

Pete Wilson, from a speech delivered before the Japan Association of Southern California in Los Angeles, California on August 12, 1985.

Editor's note: This viewpoint is taken from a speech made before a group of Japanese businesspeople.

It is an honor to appear before this very influential group of business executives. Truly, the members of this group are influential in many ways. You offer new and exciting products to the American public—from fuel efficient cars to sophisticated consumer electronics equipment—and this influences the way that we in America live. You aggressively market your products, thereby providing increased competition that yields better products and lower prices for American consumers. And your success in our marketplace has actually enhanced the support that the principle of free trade has in the United States.

Now what I just said bears repeating, for it may run counter to what appears to be the sentiment in Washington. Americans do support free trade and, as a group, feel no ill will towards foreign supported choice. This has been true from the beginnings of our Republic, which was founded by those who were revolting from a foreign government that wanted to limit choice of all kinds—from the choice of the people we traded with to the choice of how we worshipped God.

Well, if we support free trade and take little exception to your exports to our country, why after reading press reports from our Capitol do you feel unwanted? Because, we feel that we are being denied choice by the actions of the Japanese government. We are not allowed the choice of whom we can trade with, for Japanese consumers are prevented from being our customers. And, while we do not have the power to remove those constraints on our ability to choose, we do have the power to reciprocate—we do have the power to limit your choices as your government has limited the choices of our industries.

Japan has closed the door to free trade, and it has locked it shut. And despite our efforts, and despite pronouncements to the contrary, the door remains shut.

The Key or the Fire Axe?

So, what we have come to is a question: Where do we go from here? And upon consideration, I find that the United States and Japan are presented with a choice. It is a choice between the key and the fire axe. The door to your markets will open, for it must to secure your continued access to the markets of the world.

It is simply a question of whether you will open your hands and use the key that unlocks the market barriers you have erected, or whether we must ultimately pick up the fire axe to enforce our rights to open markets with all of our trading partners. I firmly believe that the first option is preferable. However, I am just as emphatically willing to resort to the second course of action, if necessary, and so is the U.S. Congress.

By Toles for *The Buffalo News*

Some in Japan argue that your large trade surplus with the U.S. is the result of a strong dollar. Certainly, that accounts for a significant part of the problem. But a strong dollar cannot account for the trade surpluses that Japan has with the entire industrialized world. There must be more to it than the value of the dollar.

Some in Japan argue that our poor showing in your home markets is not the fault of trade restrictions. We are told that a quality product with an attractive price will sell well in Japan. I have no doubt that a well-priced, quality product would sell well in the Japanese marketplace, and actually I believe that your own government believes the same—that is why they are unwilling to give foreign companies a fair chance.

Can anyone reasonably argue that our beef and citrus products are inadequate in quality or too high in price? Cannot our air cargo carriers provide quality service when allowed to on a fair basis— that is when allowed to operate as any other carrier in the market? Do not American electronics companies offer for sale quality microprocessors, computers, and communications satellites? Are not American wines of adequate quality and low enough price that their sale must be inhibited in Japan? Are American wood products too low in quality to be permitted to be freely sold in the Japanese marketplace?

The members of this organization understand from first-hand experience the benefits of free trade. Your very presence here is a testament to them. Indeed, it is quite likely that Japan is more dependent on foreign trade for its economic health than is any other developed country. Is it so important to keep your domestic markets shut that you are willing to lose all that you have gained from free access to the markets of America and the other members of the OECD? Would it really be more painful to suffer the benefits of free trade than the certain harm of lost markets?

Impossible Barriers to Open Market

The unwillingness of your government to open markets goes beyond mere tariff and non-tariff barriers. Types of private conduct that are allowed by—and at times commanded by—the government make even a technically "open" market impossible to pierce.

The creation of Nippon Cargo Airways is a clear example of this kind of subversive governmental nurturing. It is not simply a complaint that so many competitors and customers combined to form this new entity. What is so troublesome is that an official governmental policy was responsible for the very establishment of NCA as well as the apportionment of the marketplace. If competition is truly beneficial, why should not NCA be free to compete for JAL customers as freely as it competes for the customers of Flying Tigers? I am told that NCA has cut into some JAL business, but there is in existence a governmental command that NCA concentrate on securing its business from the customer roles of non-Japanese competitors. Not only is this unfair, it is also perceived as being unfair—and it is perception that counts most in the court of world opinion.

I assume that some of you in the audience work for companies that are part owners of NCA. Indeed, it would not surprise me if everyone in this room were a part owner of this new collusive effort. But I must tell you that unless your government allows Flying Tigers the ability to operate freely in Japan, to have the same privileges afforded to Japanese cargo carriers, we must reach for the fire axe to open that closed market door—which means that we will have to restrict the business plans of both NCA and JAL within the United States.

As many of you know, there is a trade complaint pending with our Special Trade Representative over the practices of your government and your corporations in the semiconductor market. You may also know that, at my request, the Department of Justice is investigating another aspect of our trade dispute—the pricing practices of Hitachi.

What makes this trade problem so upsetting, not just to the American semiconductor industry, but to the entire U.S. government, is that while Americans have some serious doubts about the strength of some of our industries—such as steel and automobiles—we have no doubts about the competitiveness of our electronics industry when allowed to operate in a free market environment. For, while some in Japan say that our computer chips are not as reliable as those of your manufacturers, how does one explain that U.S. manufacturers command over 50 percent of the non-U.S./non-Japan market? The answer is that the world has the same high opinion of U.S. chips as do the people who make them. And, the key to avoiding a limit on the fair-priced sales of your chips in the U.S. is in your hands.

Intervening in Trade

In the world today . . . free trade is only a theory. We hear about it primarily when other nations lecture us on "the benefits of free trade." But, they don't pracice what they preach. . . .

A review of 40 recent trade studies comes up with 28 ways in which governments intervene in trade. Japan makes use of 25 of the 28 types of intervention. The U.S. uses six.

Senator Lloyd Bentsen, testimony before the House Ways and Means Committee, September 17, 1985.

Even when progress has been made in bilateral relations, we in the U.S. must be ever watchful that this which was given after long, intensive negotiations is not reclaimed by swift action of the Diet.

I have in mind the export of U.S. citrus to your markets. Real progress was made in negotiations between our two countries this past year that would raise the lid, even if slightly, on citrus imports. This was welcome news to American farmers who are proud of the food they produce not only for Japanese consumers, but for the entire world. Yet shortly after it was announced that there would be an increase in tonnage allowed in, there were attempts made to reassess the formula for allocating weight to each crate of citrus. The effect would be to take by indirect action what was negotiated directly. Such moves undercut more than just one trade agreement, they undercut the very basis of trust. Indeed, one need only reflect on this one incident—which, unfortunately, is not unique—to understand why the latest Japanese pronouncement on trade was met with such great skepticism.

It must be acknowledged that not all in the U.S. have hands untouched by protectionism. There were our restraints on Japanese cars—and I am glad that they have finally come to an end. There are now restraints on steel, which I deeply regret. But it is openly negotiated. So, while I strongly oppose these limits on imports, I find them preferable to administrative mazes such as the cer-

155

tification procedures in Japan which have stood to unfairly protect your markets.

Clearly, there is strong sentiment in the Congress to enact protectionist laws. Chief among the pending bills is one that would sharply cut imports of textiles and apparel. It has the formal support of more than one half of both Houses of Congress. So, why is it not yet law? Because, there are enough level heads in Washington—including those of the President and his cabinet—that such legislation is stalled, at least for the moment.

And there is less severe legislation pending that would, as amended, force our President to increase our access to your markets by specified amounts by using all necessary actions—including tariff increases, as well as non-tariff barriers such as difficult certification and inspection procedures. Our exports to Japan would have to increase by $4 billion the first year, $7 billion the second year, and $10 billion the third year. What is significant about this bill (Danforth—S. 1404) is that it has bipartisan support and it is directed not at the trade deficit itself, but at the level of our exports. In other words, it shows two important facets of the mood in the Senate—and I believe that this mood carries over to a majority of members in both Houses of the Congress. Specifically, it shows that we are ultimately after free access to foreign markets, not limitations on access to ours. And it shows that artificial limits on your exports to the U.S. will not answer our concerns. The real benchmark is not the deficit; the real benchmark is the level of our exports to Japan.

Deep inside, we in the Congress do not want to pass laws that restrict trade. But, the urge to enact such laws can only be stilled by the sound of the creeking hinges on the door that has for too long closed off your markets; mere silence will quiet nothing, and the sound of protectionism could not be stilled even by the most impressive efforts of the free traders in the Congress and of the President.

Free Trade in Japan's Interest, Too

I firmly believe that there are some in Japan who understand that the opening of your domestic markets serve not just the international political interests of your nation, but also the real interests of your domestic economy. I believe that Prime Minister Nakasone is the most prominent member of this enlightened group, and I commend him for his efforts to convert the nonbelievers among your citizenry. Unfortunately, his free trade views have not found their way into the bowels of the bureaucracy in the Japanese government. I do not underestimate the greatness of the challenge he has undertaken, and I do not personally condemn him for the slowness that has exemplified changes in Japanese import policy. However, changes—to the extent that there have been changes—have been too slow in coming and even

ROTHCO
LIEDERMAN.

© Liedermann/Rothco

slower in implementation.

I know that there is a feeling held by many in Japan that the U.S. has overstepped appropriate bounds when we have forcefully sought access to your markets. Some have said that we have been paternalistic in our attitudes.

In truth, we are not acting as a father would towards an errant son. Rather, we act as anyone might who feels hurt by a trusted friend. We have opened our markets as a person would open his house, and we now feel that your long stay has not been equaled by a willingness to live up to reasonably expected responsibilities.

Mutual Support Needed

In our country, a friend is a guest when received in one's home. But at some point, a friend's stay transforms the friend from a mere guest to a member of one's family. And as in any family, each member must join and make an honest effort to support the family's welfare. It is our perception of your country's lack of effort—as a member of the family of nations—that has upset not only our feelings, but the feelings of all others. It is time that Japan lives up to its global responsibilities—to both nurture those among us who are less fortunate, and to treat fairly and as equals the developed countries of the world.

When I began my speech, I told you about the great influence that you possess in our country. I just as firmly believe that you possess great influence in the country of your birth.

I cannot too strongly urge you to use your influence at home in Japan. Help your Prime Minister to lead your country to open the door to its markets, to assume its global responsibilities—and

157

help him avoid the calamity that will surely follow if we are forced to pick up the fire axe.

No Japanese citizen is better able to help than are those of you in this room, for no Japanese citizen better understands the benefits of free trade—you have seen it with your own eyes and you have reaped its rewards.

"Those people who criticize Japan's [trade practices] often lack knowledge of vital facts."

The Effects of Japan's Restrictions Are Exaggerated

Ichiro Hattori

Ichiro Hattori is president of Seiko Instruments and Electronics, one of Japan's largest electronics manufacturers and one of the largest exporter of goods to the United States. In the following viewpoint, excerpted from a speech he delivered to the Los Angeles Chamber of Commerce, he responds to the criticisms leveled at Japan's trade practices. Mr. Hattori claims that accusations of unfair trade practices are not accurate. He states that Japan is eager to cooperate with the US, that the US is as much at fault as Japan for its trade imbalance, and that both countries must work harder at mutual understanding in order to develop and maintain mutually acceptable trade practices.

As you read, consider the following questions:

1. How does Mr. Hattori refute the idea that Japanese trade practices have "stolen" American jobs?
2. What is meant by "offshore production"? Why does Mr. Hattori point to offshore production as a US-caused contributor to the trade problem?
3. What are some of the differences between the US and Japan that Mr. Hattori says contribute to the misunderstandings between the two nations?

Ichiro Hattori, from a speech delivered to the Los Angeles Area Chamber of Commerce, Business Outlook Conference, in Los Angeles, California on November 19, 1985.

Issues over trade conflicts between Japan and the United States attracted both the highest political priority and the continuous attention of the press. . . .

In response, Japan has taken several steps toward opening her market. How open is it? I cannot answer this question in quantitative terms. For the best answer, however, I would like to borrow the words of Mr. Mike Mansfield, American Ambassador to Japan and of Yoshio Okawara, former Japanese Ambassador to Washington. In an interview with *The Washington Post*, Ambassador Mansfield said the "Japanese market is not as closed as most Americans believe it is, and the American market is not as open as Americans believe." This perhaps is one-sided. You might even say that Ambassador Mansfield has become Japanese.

Commenting on the Mansfield remark, Ambassador Okawara writes that "the Japanese market, too, is not as open yet as most Japanese believe." I think the words of the two ambassadors combined offer a fair description of the present status of the Japanese market, and the perception of people thereof on both sides of the Pacific.

In the perception of most Americans, the liberalization measures, if they have been effective, must be translated into increased sales of American products in the Japanese market and into the reduction of the trade imbalance between our countries.

A huge trade imbalance still exists between us. However, we should not overlook gradual changes. The Japanese share of the U.S. external trade deficit has been declining. In 1982, one-half of the U.S. trade deficit was attributable to Japan. It was about one-third in 1983 and still less in 1984. Japan is the second largest importer of American products, next only to Canada. Contrary to popular belief, about one-half of Japanese imports from the United States comprise so-called manufactured goods; and the value of such manufactured goods increased by nearly 8 percent in 1984 from the previous year.

Need for Patience

I know Americans are getting impatient, but people do not turn around so quickly. After all, Japanese have only recently found out that their domestic products are as good as, or better than, imported products.

For a long time, Japanese used to prefer imported goods to domestically manufactured goods. It took Japanese consumers more than twenty years to rid their products of the notorious image of "cheap but inferior." This is understandable because most of the products were, indeed, not only "cheap but inferior" but at the same time often "inferior but expensive."

We have to understand that in the nature of things it takes a long time to alter consumer psychology. It does not happen overnight.

Taking that into consideration, I would like to say that the market-opening measures for manufactured products have begun to take effect.

The effectiveness of the market-opening measures, however, are obscured by the overwhelming amount of the trade imbalance. As long as the imbalance exists, the improvement scarcely reaches the eyes and ears of Americans.

Efforts to Liberalize Market

But, I would like to assure you that the efforts for opening up the market will be continuously pursued by the Japanese Government and will be supported by our business community. There are differences of opinion between the business community and government ministries regarding the extent and speed of the liberalization. It seems to me, however, that the differences more often than not promoted liberalization. Nothing new, after all, can be expected where there is just one opinion.

These efforts to liberalize the market should be further pursued, and we Japanese shall be glad to listen to recommendations or constructive criticism from foreign countries as to how it should be done.

Yet, as we all know, some of the criticism these days is hardly constructive. The notion that Japanese trade policies are unfair is alarming indeed. For example, Americans attribute the loss of jobs in the United States to Japanese trade practices and this notion has become the central tenet of the promoters of protectionism.

Reprinted by permission of Newspaper Enterprise Association.

This situation is dangerous, firstly, because it promotes protectionism which is bad for everyone and, secondly, because it jeopardizes the otherwise sound bilateral relationship between our two countries. This is a situation with which we Japanese cannot live comfortably. And I do want to make some observations now on this situation.

"Offshore Production"

In my opinion, those people who criticize Japan often lack knowledge of vital facts and make shortcuts in their thinking process. They conclude that Japan must be engaged in unfair trade practices simply because Japan has accumulated a large amount of trade surplus from the United States. But, they are overlooking many important facts about themselves.

If they would turn around from time to time and see what is happening in the United States they would see that, just as Japanese companies are beginning to come to the United States for manufacturing, American companies are increasing their offshore purchases.

It is common knowledge that Japanese color television manufacturers have set up production facilities in the United States and, recently, Korean manufacturers have started to do the same. But not much is made of the fact that American TV makers are producing almost all of their sets overseas. Calling it "offshore production," they import televisions from places like Mexico, Taiwan, and Singapore, where they are produced either through O.E.M. arrangements or in plants under their direct control.

The same phenomenon is now beginning to take place in automobile manufacturing. The newspapers report that, one after another, Japanese car makers are setting up production facilities in the United States.

Convoluted Competition

An American automobile company, meanwhile, is building a major plant in Mexico, and substantial numbers of small American-brand cars are now manufactured by Japanese and other foreign automobile manufacturers. We now are seeing American-made Japanese cars competing in the United States with foreign-made American cars.

In other words, American consumers will be asked to make a choice between a SONY TV made in the U.S. and a Zenith TV made in foreign countries, or a Honda car made in the U.S. and a Dodge car made in Japan.

Another development along the same lines is the news that American high-tech firms are moving to Mexico and other offshore sites to lower their labor costs. Mexico has severe restrictions on foreign investment, which has only been permitted with the participation of domestic capital. But, apparently, this requirement has been waived for IBM, which will own 100 percent of the plant it builds. Already the bulk of the components that go into American personal computers are imported. Just recently, *Business Week* reported that even IBM's personal computers include overseas-made parts that account for 70 percent of the manufacturing cost.

US Must Improve Own Practices

Americans increasingly single out Japan as the principal, if not the sole, villain against whom we must prevail in the world market. Japan's $37 billion trade surplus with the United States, it is said, is principally the result of countless trade distorting practices. . . .

There is no question that Japan's markets are effectively closed to many foreign enterprises. . . . Nonetheless, we should not overstate the significance of Japanese trade barriers or their relationship to the trade deficit. . . . The unpleasant truth is that, regardless of questionable Japanese trade practices, the U.S. business community needs to improve its performance in many ways. . . .

[For example], Japanese manufacturing productivity has risen almost three times faster than that of America since 1970. The Japanese savings rate is much higher than the U.S. rate . . . keeping the yen's value down [and resulting in] greater price competitiveness. . . . The large increase in the Japanese share of the world market for cars, trucks and ships reflects both cost and quality advantages. These are important differences which must be narrowed. . . . We cannot rightfully expect Japan, or any other nation, not to compete effectively in the marketplace.

US Chamber of Commerce, testimony before House Subcommittee on Economic Stabilization, June 26, 1985.

It should come as no surprise that the biggest exporter of Japanese-built computers is IBM Japan. In 1984, IBM Japan exported just under one billion dollars of products, amounting to 30 percent of its total sales. An American semiconductor manufacturer, meanwhile, has built a modern plant in Japan and is producing chips on a vast scale, both for sale in Japan and for export to the United States. These exports by American affiliates now constitute a not insignificant portion of Japan's exports. In 1984, exports to the United States by subsidiaries of American companies in Japan amounted to about two billion dollars; and exports to the United States by Japanese companies under OEM arangements amounted to five billion dollars.

Some people criticize the Japanese government for subsidizing R&D expenses of private companies. This practice, of course, is not a monopoly of the Japanese. Nearly 50 percent of all R&D expenses in the United States is paid for by public funds. The government of the United States provides a large and guaranteed market for companies in defense businesses. This is a look-alike, only on a far greater scale, of the Japanese practice of developing the telecommunication industry though the N.T.T. organization.

This may all be fine, but a sad trend in the United States is that no sooner do valuable new technologies start to create jobs within the United States than the work is snatched away and shipped abroad.

Sadder still is the fact that such freedom of shifting production abroad is mainly enjoyed by large multinational companies. Medium and small-sized companies in conventional manufacturing businesses have neither the ready access to government sponsored R&D results nor the facilities for going offshore for production. Foreign governments do not grant special concessions to small companies, while they are happy to extend them to multinational companies like IBM. In my opinion, this discrepancy, if allowed to continue, will eventually weaken the strength of the American industry as a whole.

I would like to make one more point here. *The Economist* . . . reported that, on a per capita basis, the Japanese bought $481 worth of American goods (including products made by subsidiaries of U.S. companies in Japan), while Americans spent only $287 on Japanese goods (including local production by Japanese firms in the United States).

Considering all of this, the Senate Resolution of March 28, 1985. . . criticizing Japan was, indeed, an extraordinary show. Not a single vote was cast against it. It was even more extraordinary in view of the fact that even the declaration of World War II was not carried unanimously. Free expression of minority opinion has always been the best part of a democracy. If the resolution should be interpreted to mean anything beyond a show of the Senate's muscles to the White House, then we must conclude either that the Senate completely lacked knowledge of the facts or that something, indeed, went wrong with the democratic conscience of this country.

What Is Fair?

To decide what is fair and what is unfair in international trade is no easy matter. When there is controversy between people or companies within a nation, the court of justice can decide who is unfair. But, when there is controversy between nations, they usually cannot agree on a court to judge their dispute, because a nation, especially a powerful one, cannot recede from what it believes to be its own rights.

Because America rightly believes that it is the superpower of the Western World, Americans often assume that they know the rules of the game. But, the role of America in international trade is at least a little more complicated and carries a greater responsibility than the role of the New York Yacht Club in the America's Cup Race. The rules of international trade should not be established by one nation's subjective definition of justice, but should be agreed upon by mutual consent with full knowledge of the facts that are available.

I have nothing against overseas production of American companies *per se*. I am not about to say what American companies should be doing. Japanese companies, too, shifted production to Asian nations where wages were lower. This helps expand the economy in real terms for the world. Nor do I want to make an issue out of Japan bashers who turn international economic problems into domestic political problems. But, let us be clear and agree at least on one principle; that nobody can be his own judge and, in international trade, the rules of the game by which to decide who is fair or unfair should be agreed upon by mutual consent.

Differences and Similiarities

The United States and Japan share many values. By any standard both are very democratic countries and both have a free market economy. Yet, there are also differences. The United States is a country of immigrants and Japan is a country with the most homogeneous people in the world. While the majority of the U.S. population originated from European cultures steeped in the tradition of Christianity, Japanese culture is entirely non-Christian.

There is little doubt that it will take time to create mutual consent on the concept of fairness in international trade between two different cultures. Many Americans assert that the size of the imbalance must reflect unfair practices. This assertion comes from their experience because for a long time American businessmen worked conscientiously, and there was never a country like Japan to deal with in those days.

Japanese Not Responsible

The Japanese are not responsible . . . for the revitalization of the U.S. economy. That depends on the attitudes and actions of Americans themselves.

Thomas Pepper and others, *The Competition: Dealing with Japan,* 1985.

The Japanese people strongly feel that Japan should be given more time for the change and adjustment. They, too, believe that they have been working conscientiously. While realizing the need for change, Japanese wonder if it is not unfair for other nations to force a rapid change that might cause great damage and pain to particular segments of their industry, such as, for instance, the lumber and plywood industries.

Thus, the need of deepening mutual understanding about fair practices in trade is urgently needed. But, in the meantime, we should never change our view that it is always bad to engage in protectionism. If the United States adopts protectionism against Japan, it may reduce its trade deficit with Japan temporarily at the cost of the American consumers. But, that does not mean a true expansion to either economy.

This is much like pushing one side of a balloon so that it can bulge on the other side. In Japan we call it gambling between father and son. There is nothing genuine about it. True opportunities of expansion for our manufacturing industries can only come from developing countries. These are the countries where future consumers are to be found. Some of them are just coming into the stage where protectionist economic policies may be abandoned. If we now embark on protective economic policies ourselves, how then can we ask those countries to open their doors to us when their people are ready to import our products. No nation can be so unabashed as to use such a double standard in its trade practices.

Japanese Manufacturing in the US

Coming back to our own problems, let me put forth my own outlook for our bilateral trade relations, particularly for the time after the new values for the yen and the dollar become at least stabilized, if not established.

The new rate at 200 yen plus to one dollar was welcomed by many circles in Japan. This will give at least temporary relief to the trade negotiators of both governments. The new rate, however, has made a far greater impact on Japanese industry than just buying time. This is a transformation of management thinking—a renewed conviction that Japanese industry must become more international in its manufacturing as well as in its financing facilities.

Already, Japanese companies are increasing their investment in the United States, and the circumstances for creating successful manufacturing ventures in the United States have been well documented elsewhere. In my opinion, a stronger yen and the increase of Japanese manufacturing in the United States will produce and ultimately eliminate the trade imbalance.

Positive Trends

It cannot happen next year, but I am certain that it will happen in three to four years time. The key will be increased Japanese manufacturing in the United States and this will be facilitated by other trends:

1. In Japan, employment in the manufacturing industries will be cut back. The activity level of manufacturing is related to the export activity and, hence, to the exchange rate. A strong yen combined with persistent threats of protectionism will keep Japanese

166

companies shifting their production to the United States, thereby reducing employment in Japan.

2. Short-term capital outflow from Japan will also be reduced simply because there will not be so much surplus to be invested. Instead, Japanese companies will intensify their efforts to raise capital overseas.

3. In the United States, Japanese investment will halt the offshore shift manufacturing. It is likely that more new jobs in the U.S. manufacturing industry will be created by Japanese companies than anyone else.

All of this will change the present U.S.-Japan relationship in a very favorable direction, and if we can have but 3 years to allow these factors to do their job, today's cries for protectionism will have become a bad dream hardly ever talked about any longer.

Expanding the World Economy

Finally, to conclude my talk, I would like to touch once more on a point I made earlier, which is that Americans must understand that to expand the world economy in real terms, we must have more people participate in consumption. There is a limit to the expansion of the consumer population in North America, Europe and Japan.

Increased consumption in the remainder of the world, however, cannot occur with war and violence. To expand the consumer population, a continuing peace in larger areas of the world is and will always be the vital factor. I am afraid, however, that peaceful countries and the number of their people are today less then ten years ago. Countries like Cambodia, Vietnam, Iran, Afghanistan and Lebanon have been lost as consumer markets as a result of war or other violence. The markets for consumer products in Latin America and many African countries have been diminished in size for one reason or another. We have a shrinking world in terms of the size of the consumer market. How we can turn this situation around and expand the size of the world consumer market is the crux of the problem which we all face today.

To address this problem is a mission truly worthy of the United States, the superpower of the Western World, and perhaps of Japan, also. Japan bashing and creating protective barriers may satisfy the emotion of the moment, but is neither a lasting nor a meaningful solution.

Recognizing Stereotypes

A stereotype is an oversimplified or exaggerated description of people or things. Stereotyping can be favorable. However, most stereotyping tends to be highly uncomplimentary, and, at times, degrading.

Stereotyping grows out of our prejudices. When we stereotype someone, we are prejudging him or her. Consider the following example: Lee, a labor union organizer, thinks all manufacturers are out to make a buck off America's trade situation and don't care about workers. The possibility that a manufacturer could genuinely care more about American workers than about taking advantage of open trade with Japan never occurs to her. Why not? Simply because she has prejudged all American manufacturers and will refuse to acknowledge any manufacturer who doesn't fit her stereotype.

The following statements relate to the subject matter in this chapter. Consider each statement carefully. *Mark S for any statement that is an example of stereotyping. Mark N for any statement that is not an example of stereotyping. Mark U if you are undecided about any statement.*

If you are doing this activity as a member of a class or group, compare your answers with those of other class or group members. Be able to defend your answers. You may discover that others will come to different conclusions than you. Listening to the reasons others present for their answers may give you valuable insights in recognizing stereotypes.

If you are reading this book alone, ask others if they agree with your answers. You will find this interaction very valuable.

S = *stereotype*
N = *not a stereotype*
U = *undecided*

1. Consumers are incapable of understanding trade issues.

2. Consumers are spending billions of dollars too much for imported goods and are not even aware of it.

3. American consumers are rightly concerned with stretching their family budgets. If trade protectionism makes it more difficult for them to do so, we should not adopt such a policy.

4. Foreign manufacturers are getting rich off American consumers.

5. Retailers are just as concerned about Americans keeping their jobs as workers are.

6. Consumers are never satisfied; they complain about inflation but they don't want imports jeopardizing American jobs.

7. Retailers are out to make a buck any way they can.

8. It is perfectly reasonable for consumers to complain when tariffs and taxes raise prices to exorbitant levels.

9. Those who propose trade restrictions have no idea how the world economy really operates.

10. Retailers are serving an increasingly sophisticated customer, a better educated, more selective, more demanding customer.

11. Any American worker will be better than any other worker anywhere in the world.

12. Consumers have every right to expect quality American goods.

13. Our trading partners, if they fully understand our situation, will be able to help us find solutions to trade problems.

14. Foreign exporters are interested only in the amount of money they can make, not in how their decisions affect the world economy.

15. For many reasons, the Japanese have been successful in American markets.

16. Those little Japanese are hard workers.

17. Japanese business executives are no different than American business executives; they have the same motivations, abilities, and handicaps.

Periodical Bibliography

The following list of periodical articles deals with the subject matter of this chapter.

Richard Alm — "Free-Trade Flight," *U.S. News & World Report*, September 23, 1985.

George J. Church — "The Battle over Barriers," *Time*, October 7, 1985.

Dollars & Sense — "Trading Woes, Trading Blows," January/February 1986.

I.M. Dressler — "Protesting Congress or Protecting Trade?" *Foreign Policy*, Spring 1986.

Pete duPont — "Kamikaze Economics," *Policy Review*, Fall 1985.

Stuart F. Feldman — "Out of Balance and Out of Hand," *American Legion Magazine*, April 1986.

Yoichiro Ichioka — "U.S.-Japan Frictions," *World Press Review*, June 1986.

The New Republic — "Free to Shoes," September 30, 1985.

The New Republic — "Protectionism by Any Other Name," June 16, 1986.

Jane Bryant Quinn — "What Does It Cost to 'Buy American'?" *Women's Day*, October 15, 1985.

Ronald Reagan — "U.S. Trade Policy," *Vital Speeches of the Day*, October 15, 1985.

William Schneider — "Free Trade: Fury Grows in Congress," *Los Angeles Times*, September 22, 1985.

U.S. News & World Report — "Is Free Trade Good or Bad for U.S.?" September 23, 1985.

Ezra F. Vogel — "Pax Nipponica," *Foreign Affairs*, Spring 1986.

Murray L. Weidenbaum — "The High Cost of Protectionism," *Vital Speeches of the Day*, October 1, 1983.

George F. Will — "Hands Off My Life-Style Concept!" *Newsweek*, May 13, 1985.

World Policy Journal — "Beyond Protectionism," Winter 1985-86.

5 CHAPTER

Will Farms Survive the Economic Crisis?

"Suicide, alcoholism, drug use, broken families, child abuse and child neglect show unprecedented increases—all caused by the strain of farm foreclosures."

The Farm Crisis Is Real

Edward M. Kennedy

Edward M. Kennedy, Democratic senator from Massachusetts and brother of the late President John F. Kennedy, is a member of a wealthy and highly active political family and has been considered a presidential candidate. Senator Kennedy, a staunch liberal, has supported many measures intended to improve the lives of poor Americans. In the following viewpoint, he describes the desperate economic plight of many American farmers and argues for governmental support to keep this segment of the American population from starvation and bankruptcy.

As you read, consider the following questions:

1. What irony does Senator Kennedy see in the use of food stamps by many of the farmers he visited?
2. Does Senator Kennedy see any causes for the crisis faced by these farmers?
3. What remedies does Senator Kennedy believe are essential?

Edward M. Kennedy, "The Farm: One Time A National Treasure," *Los Angeles Times*, February 23, 1986. Reprinted with the author's permission.

"Senator," said 16-year-old Renee Fenski, "it's as if we don't exist. We're suffering so much . . . and no one hears our cries for help." An elderly woman in large rubber boots, munching a sandwich in the high school cafeteria, told me, "It's no longer a crisis. It's a way of life."

Signs of crisis were everywhere. Hunger is at a 15-year-high in parts of the nation's breadbasket. Soup kitchens and emergency food pantries in Missouri reported a 24% increase in requests for emergency food assistance in 1985 compared with 1984—and a 45% rise in rural parts of the state.

This was the Christmas season; my sons Teddy and Patrick, my nephew Mark Shriver and I were in Memphis, a small farm community in Scotland County in northern Missouri. We had been invited to visit a farm and learn about what many there simply call "The Depression."

Suicide, alcoholism, drug use, broken families, child abuse and child neglect show unprecedented increases—all caused by the strain of farm foreclosures. Health care is neglected; insurance policies expire; treatments and checkups are postponed. The shortage of rural doctors is rising as more and more communities are unable to support a practitioner.

The student body at Scotland County High School has declined 27% in four years, as families abandon blighted towns and farms. Principal Leroy Huff told us, "Not since the 1930s has a cloud of such proportions hung over rural America."

Collapse of Farm Economy

The source of the cloud is the collapse of the farm economy, brought on by rising farm costs, falling farm prices and plunging farm exports—the result of massive federal budget deficits, high interest rates and a still-high dollar. Yet this is one of America's richest agriculture areas. Bill Heffernan, a farm expert and a University of Missouri rural sociologist, told me, "If you can't make a living farming here, you can't make it anywhere."

Not a single farm foreclosure was recorded in Scotland County between 1973 and 1980. In the next five years, 45 farms in the county went on the auction block; in other nearby counties, the figures reported are worse. Overall, one out of every five farms in Missouri has been lost since 1980.

Much of the food saving lives in Ethiopia and other parts of Africa is grown by American farmers. Yet, many of these farmers and their families bought holiday dinners with food stamps; many others have become refugees from their own farms and homes, forced out by declining markets and mounting debt.

The families we met resent the suggestion that their own inefficiency has caused the crisis. As one farmer told us, "You don't work a farm for 50 years and then all of a sudden become inefficient."

We spent a night in the farmhouse of Bill and Donna Shoop. Bill had been named the county's best farm manager in 1975 and won two statewide awards in the '80s. Now, his farm and home are in bankruptcy. Bill explained why he invited us: "We hope we can convey that we are honest, hard-working people out here under severe pressure."

The fundamental decency, strength and character of American farmers were obvious in this community; the courage of these families and hundreds of thousands like them is challenging Congress to develop a sensible food and farm policy that respects their dignity, hard work and commitment to their country.

Several farmers I met had worked through the night before we arrived, fighting cold and snow to salvage crops. "Every minute counts now," explained Donna Shoop. "If we get another three inches of snow on top of what we already have, we'll probably lose everything that's left in the fields, and that's a lot."

Yet they may soon lose everything. At a small meeting with nine families in the Shoop's living room, senior citizens Herbert and Mary Jones of Hamilton, Mo., spoke last. They have already lost their farm and may lose their house this spring. They worry about themselves, about Jones' 84-year-old mother, who has had a stroke, and about their two sons. The younger son had been farming rented land, but had to stop when his equipment was repossessed. The older son is retarded. When the bank foreclosed, it ripped out fences and demolished useful buildings. Holding back tears, Herbert Jones gave us snapshots of the damage.

One of the most frequent complaints concerned the credit practices of lenders, including the Farmers Home Administration (FMHA) and banks. In recent years, many farmers have had to accept variable-rate loans that allow a rise in interest on short notice. Sudden higher costs are often the final straw. In a market already swamped with distress sales, more foreclosures and bankruptcies produce a domino effect; land values go down and the worth of the collateral put up by those still in farming also declines, impairing their future ability to borrow. Shoop's 1983 bankruptcy followed a variable-rate loan. He had borrowed $200,000 at 10% in 1979, then saw the rate rise to 18% in 1980, 21% in 1981.

In January the FMHA threatened to call in any loan more than $100 behind in payments; 90,000 farmers, a third of all those who have FMHA loans, fall into this category. As many as 45,000 farms could be lost if the FMHA proceeds.

We ended the two-day visit with a trip to the food caves in Kansas City, Kan., the enormous man-made caverns carved from a limestone cliff and converted into the world's largest refrigerator and underground food storage complex.

The U.S. Department of Agriculture uses the caves, operated by private industry, to store 300 million to 400 million pounds of surplus butter, cheese and other foods, including milk, juices and cereals.

Surplus and Desperation

The contrast between the vast caves of surplus and the desperate plight of farmers was a symbol of the contradiction in America's agriculture policy. The new farm bill, by reducing price supports, will be a death knell for many more farms.

There are no simple cures for the farm depression, in a country that spends $20 billion a year to subsidize farming while thousands of farmers are broke.

But something has to be changed when American farmers produce food in extraordinary abundance—enough to feed starving millions around the world—but face hunger in their own homes. There is a flaw in a policy that obliges government to purchase and store millions of pounds of dairy products and billions of bushels of grain, but cannot get food to the needy in cities across the country. There is a fallacy in farm lending programs that force farmers out of business and depress land values for those who remain.

There is much we can do now, and all of it is familiar to those who deal with the farm crisis. Priorities should include: halting harsh interest-rate escalations and premature foreclosures; adjusting Medicaid and food-stamp requirements so that farmers do not have to sell their land in order to qualify for help, and emphasizing bankruptcy work-outs rather than liquidiations, so that farmers will have a fighting chance to keep farming. Unless we do at least this much, the crisis will become a catastrophe.

But even if we take these immediate steps, much will remain undone. Most of all, we must see to it that farmers receive a fair price in the market. During the debate on the 1985 farm bill, I supported measures which would allow wheat, corn and soybean growers to agree on acreage set-asides and production controls, in return for a reduction in farm subsidies. That would have saved money—and farmers, too. Unfortunately the Administration's plan prevailed: it cut prices further and raised taxpayers' costs higher.

Needed: Far-Reaching Reforms

We need far-reaching reforms in the farm credit system to permit renegotiation of current debts. We should deal with the absurd irony of the food caves by enlarging the food-stamp program, not curtailing it as we are doing now.

American farmers are still the best in the world; the bounty they produce is a national treasure. We will move from irony to tragedy if we don't ensure our capacity to produce and enable the fruits of our harvest to continue feeding the world's hungry. As Bill Shoop's neighbor, Gary Anson, told me on his farm, "I'm raising hogs out here, doing it the way our government wants us to. I'd like you to do something about it."

I intend to.

"How many times can the American taxpayers be asked to bail out those who refuse to learn the most basic economic facts?"

The Farm Crisis
Is Exaggerated

T. F. Leonard

Freelance writer T. F. Leonard, a farm wife in northern Michigan, believes that most of the farmers who are in desperate plights are there because of their own lack of common sense. She writes in the following viewpoint that these people foolishly feel that they have to have every new piece of equipment that is developed even when the size of their land or the condition of their present equipment doesn't warrant it. She also argues that government programs, supposedly designed to aid farmers, have only aggravated the situation by allowing farmers to believe that no matter what happens, money will be available. Those farmers who are prudent and self-reliant, she writes, may not live in luxury, but they do survive.

As you read, consider the following questions:

1. What does the author mean when she writes that many farmers suffer from "new-paint disease"?
2. What does she mean when she writes that each new generation must "earn the farm in its turn"?
3. Why does Ms. Leonard believe that government intervention is more damaging than helpful to farmers?

T.F. Leonard, "Down on the Farm—I, Bravo, David Stockman," *National Review,* June 28, 1985. Reprinted with permission from National Review, Inc., 150 East 35th Street, New York, NY 10016.

A neighbor, call him Steady Eddie, slowed up in his brand-new, two-tone, four-wheel-drive pickup. Steady Eddie just wanted to laugh a little longer as he approached my husband, Bob, who was walking the ground to pick rock before coming onto our field with the planter. Steady Eddie never bothers to pick rock. He clangs and bangs full-tilt over stones and small trees with his brand-new $6,500 planter. This is rough on machinery, but Steady Eddie doesn't really own his planter, anyway. He had signed for it the previous fall with a deal that put off the payments for six months, no interest, until his next loan came through, courtesy of the American taxpayers. Without these loans, Steady Eddie couldn't keep farming because he is handicapped. He has what is known around here as "new-paint disease." New-paint disease is what keeps a farmer buying great big, brand-new, fancy farm machinery that he doesn't need, and can't pay for, because it makes him feel like a hero, high-rolling past the neighbors on the long haul to a 37-acre plot of poor, sandy ground that he can't afford to farm.

"New-Paint Disease"

Steady Eddie is not the only farmer in our county who suffers from new-paint disease. Quite a few of them know about all the new government programs before the bureaucrats do, and they line up in front of the farm-loan office the very morning the funds become available. The money, of course, already has been spent. The tax dollars only need be *expected* to be allocated in order for some debt to crop up to justify the taxpayers' generosity. A farmer always has some piece of machinery he's itching to replace or buy outright. New-paint disease is the moral hazard of government loans to farmers. Easy money encourages the over-indebtedness it is meant to relieve.

Farmers must walk the fine line between conservative and progressive outlay of capital. Agriculture has changed from a labor-intensive to a capital-intensive industry. In order to compete, modern farmers have to carry more debt than their grandfathers did. The successful ones temper their willingness to invest with a little of Old Grandpaw's prudence. Farmers who can't are in trouble. In 1980, Steady Eddie was still buying up land and four-wheel-drive air-conditioned tractors with stereos because, he said, land here was going to $1,000 an acre, and corn and wheat would soon break the $5- to $6-a-bushel mark. Another farmer said, "Well, I've been farming 35 years and that hasn't happened yet."

It won't happen, because the laws of economics defy anyone to make a good living and an excellent return on a big investment by working six months of the year to grow and harvest a crop of corn. Nor can a farmer keep afloat by using technology just to shorten a workday. Fancy machinery makes it tempting to farm on weekends, but a part-time farmer cannot expect to make the machinery pay for itself. Anybody who wants to stick with farming only forty acres had better keep the mule, too. The same crops on the same acres cannot support Old Grandpaw in his retirement and his progeny. Each generation must earn the farm in its turn. A continuous process that favors the most cost-efficient farms (these are not always the largest) sorts out the farms to fallow from the farms to follow.

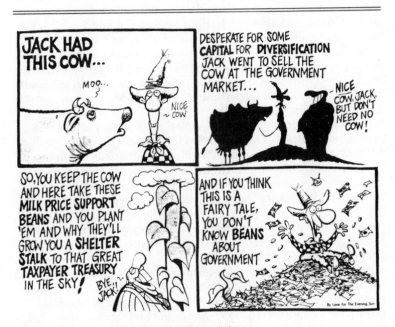

Mike Lane, *The Evening Sun*, reprinted with permission.

Farming is a risky business. There are good years and bad years. Farmers must endure the uncertainties of weather, new technology, disease, pests, and politicians. Not all farmers can be winners all the time. When government intervenes to protect farmers from loss, it prevents the market from rewarding farmers for success. Change is rapid; too much shielding is a bad thing. A farmer can't farm wearing blinders, but during the Seventies, many tried. Then high inflation and low real interest rates kept farmers' net worths bullish on paper. It seemed investments didn't have to provide cash-flow; prospects gleamed rosily even if a farmer produced nothing. Many farmers who are in trouble today didn't lose their shirts farming. They lost their shirts speculating on land. It looked like everything was going to hell in a handcart, but a guy could make a buck getting there. Steady Eddie and his lender bet the farm that President Reagan couldn't stay the course. Steady Eddie lacked faith. And if there's one thing a farmer has to have, it's faith.

Bailing Out Those Without Common Sense

Faith can't be legislated. Neither can wisdom. But how many times can the American taxpayers be asked to bail out those who refuse to learn the most basic economic facts? What goes up must come down, etc. The unpalatable truth is that many farmers every bit as earnest and attached to their land as Gil and Jewell Ivy in the movie *Country* are being foreclosed upon for loans they never should have taken out in the first place. Billions and billions of dollars' worth of emergency loans already have been made, to no avail. A good housecleaning is long overdue out here in the heartland, and the Federal Government cannot afford to postpone the day of reckoning any longer.

I speak for the two-thirds of American farmers who think to themselves, "Bravo, David Stockman," and then quietly go back to their work. I speak for the two-thirds of American farmers who get on nicely without government handouts, who are busy with spring planting, who therefore will not be circling the White House on tractors. I speak for the vast majority of American farmers who herald a return to market-oriented agriculture, which allows private action based upon the laws of supply and demand, rather than government direction, to determine production, price, and promotion of our commodities.

If farmers voted their short-term interests, they all would pull the big lever next to the little donkey. When Uncle Sam is greasing the wheels, the economy can show some hellish spurts. Like during the Seventies: Farmers went nuts buying land and equipment; dealers couldn't keep pace and sold by quota; some manufacturers overexpanded. But wise farmers, and their wise suppliers, knew that business at a landoffice pace wouldn't last. It couldn't last. Those were not normal times.

These are normal times. Uncle Sam is no longer luring back to the land those who seek lifestyle, romance, and tax advantages. Lenders no longer encourage would-be farmers who are already floundering to try to fix things by going deeper in debt. The sorting process, continuous in any healthy, progressive economic sector, now is discouraging those who for many years were willing to operate at a loss.

What is important to remember is that ag lags. The agricultural sector is slower to go into a recession (that's why Steady Eddie still was piling up debt in 1980), and it is slower to come out. Farmers can lead the way to make the Reagan Revolution com-

FARM BELT ECONOMIC GROWTH
Trends 1982-85

	Personal Income Total	Per-capita Income Current $	Constant $	Constant $ 1977-80 Growth
U.S	24.5%	21.0%	8.4%	4.3%
9 Grain-Belt States*	23.4	22.1	9.4	3.7
20 Top Farm (Non-Oil) States	25.6	21.5	8.9	4.1
*9 Grain-Belt States				
Nebraska	28.6	27.2	14.0	4.7
Minnesota	26.9	25.1	12.1	4.7
Iowa	20.2	20.9	8.4	4.5
Missouri	24.8	22.5	9.8	0.9
South Dakota	22.6	20.1	7.6	3.8
North Dakota	20.9	18.6	6.3	9.9
Kansas	21.7	19.7	7.3	7.4
Arkansas	24.1	21.2	8.6	-0.3
Illinois	20.8	20.2	7.7	3.8

Source: Department of Commerce Bureau of Economic Analysis Survey.

Reprinted with permission of *The Washington Times*.

plete, or they can try to turn back the clock to what only seemed like better times.

Remember the uproars over pesticides, fertilizers, antibiotics, technology? Remember consumer rights, labor rights, animal rights, and water rights? Remember well-fed suburbanites carrying signs that read, "Food Is for People Not for Profit"? Those people and their agendas haven't gone away: They are in Washington right now, with Jessica Lange and Jane Fonda, lobbying for bailouts for farmers. Later on, when farm income rallies again, as it did in the mid-Seventies, they will lobby for intervention that favors consumers instead of producers. Their allegiance is not to farmers but to big government. Study the history of U.S. farm policy and note this: The more government becomes involved with agriculture, the more and greater powers it soon usurps in all phases of our lives.

Farm-reform movements always have been vulnerable to championing and betrayal by lovers of big government. This is because farmers work eight-day weeks, bouncing over rough ground on hard seats, and sometimes, with the stress and fatigue and loneliness, their self-esteem falters. Then farmers wonder whether they're valiant, rugged, entrepreneurial stewards of the land, or mere boorish, overworked victims in need of a union. But unions aren't the answer, because farmers are employers, not employees. Opportunity is abundant in the heartland, but farmers see too many who want positions and too few who want to work. Rural America cannot afford to cultivate among its young the attitude, "Well, if they're giving handouts, I may as well put my hand out like everyone else." Work enables all Americans to create and contribute, not just farmers. America's traditional values are rooted in churches, not barns. Farmers must turn a profit farming, or we'll all be as bankrupt as the notion that farmers are society's benefactors and deserve to be rewarded by government largesse.

Government Must Not Subsidize More Foolishness

Controversy could rage for months over how much the government should help farmers already in trouble. Places like Iowa have been buffeted by drought, and land values there skyrocketed higher and fell harder. This much, however, is clear: Government must not help any more farmers get into trouble than it already has.

This spring Bob hauled out of the tool shed his 26-year-old tractor and 47-year-old grain drill. The old drill planted another 250 acres of barley without breaking down. When the inevitable, final breakdown comes, the machine will be replaced with money that's been budgeted for decades. But the old drill and tractor will be there with the rest of the machinery, the newest ten years old, bought used, and brought up to dependable, top condition with a lot of hard work, as long as they do the job.

Bob put in another fine stand of barley in long, gently rolling fields. I looked up and saw, soaring over Bob and his antiques, a flight of T-37 jet trainers, quick, white flashes from the Strategic Air Command base near our farm. On my knees in the garden, I was thankful that all the aircraft flying overhead were friendly—and Steady Eddie slowed up as he drove past.

> "In order for the family farmer to survive, the administration and the Congress must realize that the family farmer has to be supported through tax incentives and other measures."

Government Must Support Farmers

Charles M. Fischbein

Charles M. Fischbein is a correspondent for *The Spotlight,* a weekly newspaper which calls itself "populist and nationalist." It speaks out on a variety of issues, claiming to stand for the point of view of the majority of Middle Americans—"the hardworking, misled, exploited and brainwashed American producer . . . who pays the bills for the super-rich and the very poor." In the following viewpoint, Mr. Fischbein describes the American farmer as being the victim of conflicting government and banking policies. He argues that to save the family farmer, the government must intervene with tax incentives and other economic measures.

As you read, consider the following questions:

1. What are some of the policies Mr. Fischbein cites as being causes of the farmers' problems?
2. What must be done, according to Mr. Fischbein, to enable the family farm to survive?
3. Why does Mr. Fischbein think that the family farmer is so important?

Charles M. Fischbein, "U.S. Policy Anti-Family Farm," *The Spotlight,* February 3, 1986.

Gramm-Rudman, the new budget balancing law, is placing further strain on the family farmer at a time when massive farm foreclosures are being readied by the Farmers Home Administration.

The law, which calls for a 4.3-percent reduction in domestic spending for fiscal 1986, will cause a $1.26-billion cut in aid to already beleaguered farmers.

At the same time, the government is cutting price supports to farmers, it is pushing for programs that will drastically reduce the demand for U.S.-grown crops in Third World countries. In the past, farmers could always count on the Third World to absorb part of our surplus grain production.

The drop in Third World demand is the result of sales of new technology by agribusiness corporations and chemical companies. Credit is being extended to Third World countries by internationalists at the World Bank that allow these high-risk countries, already defaulting on their loans, to get additional credit to purchase high-tech agricultural know-how and products from the major chemical and agribusiness firms.

High-Tech Sales

Instead of developing programs that would make it easier for foreign countries to purchase American farm products, the government gives massive incentives to the multinational chemical companies to go into Third World countries and sell high-tech programs to starving people.

While it is true that these countries are in desperate need of help to feed their people, the technology sold with the backing of the U.S. government is usually designed for massive farm enterprises with sophisticated personnel, rather than for the small family or tribal farm unit.

Instead of supporting a program that allows developing countries to purchase farm produce while at the same time learning basic farming techniques, which would help both the American farmer and Third World people, the government follows the dictates of the executives and stock holders of the major agribusiness and chemical companies.

These policies are designed to cause further hardship to the family farmer and come at a time when basic price supports for wheat are being cut from $2.40 a bushel down to $2.30, and the corn loan program is reducing supports from $1.92 a bushel to $1.84.

Government's Choice

While it is true that the farmer must realize that problems of reduced demand, increasing costs and falling subsidies will force many farmers off the land, the government must decide whether to save the family farm or to continue a policy that will assure that only large corporate farms will survive.

With the philosophy in Congress that bigger is better and big business should be supported at any cost, the price will be the loss of the family farm.

While the government has been looking toward big business interests, the small farmer has been looking toward the government for help. Farmers are now starting to fight back.

© Kirk/Rothco

Farmers are beginning to say "no" to the chemical company representatives that are peddling toxic fixes for their production problems and are looking toward natural solutions. The concepts of healing the land, of producing less but higher quality crops, of marketing to local suppliers instead of the mass markets are all being looked into by farmers who for decades refused to consider these alternatives.

In order for the family farmer to survive, the administration and the Congress must realize that the family farmer has to be supported through tax incentives and other measures. Members of state legislatures and governors of farm states must develop populist alternatives to the bottom line orientation of the present administration. The government's bottom line orientation, started by former Budget Director David Stockman, looks only at the balance sheet.

What this type of policy ignores is the value of the individual family farm in terms of community spirit and support of local business. The bottom line policy also disregards the value of the practical knowledge of the family farmer, who in most instances can solve production problems in innovative and cost effective ways.

If we can support endangered animals at the cost of millions of dollars a year, we owe at least as much to our farmers. The government must realize that the family farmer is of unique value to the country, not only in a historical way but in a very current way. Today the family farm represents a socio-economic unit that should be preserved, a unit that supports many small town businesses, and a unit that underscores the American values of hard work and moral worth.

"It is time to get the government out of farming."

Government Must Leave Farmers Alone

Don Doig

Don Doig based the following viewpoint on a study he did for the Cato Institute, a Washington, DC-based public policy research foundation which is concerned about the intervention of government in what they believe should be private economic situations. Mr. Doig argues here that government subsidies for farmers should be stopped. They are more harmful than helpful, he says. He believes that if farmers return to competitive freemarket principles, both the economy and farmers will benefit.

As you read, consider the following questions:

1. In what ways does Mr. Doig say that government farm-support programs have harmed both farmers and society?
2. Why, according to Mr. Doig, will farmers be better off if the government stops intervening?

Don Doig, "Washington Should Get Out of Farming," *Human Events*, December 31, 1983. Reprinted with permission.

The U.S. government's farm-support programs have not contributed any clear-cut, lasting benefits to American agriculture. Evidence is accumulating that these programs may have created more problems than they've solved, by damaging the economic well-being of family farms, indirectly subsidizing environmental ruin, and soaking taxpayers for yet another subsidy of special business interests.

Programs to support farm prices have been in place since the New Deal. But recently the costs of those programs have soared, from some $4 billion in 1981 to an estimated $21.8 billion in 1983.

Cattle ranchers Wayne and Jim Jenkins, interviewed about problems down on the farm, spoke candidly of hypocritical attitudes. Regarding some farmers, the Jenkinses voice the sentiment that, instead of farming their farms, these people are farming Washington.

Wayne said: "I've got a friend down here who paid for his farm four times over with government checks." He said his neighbors "complain about other people living on welfare" and "call for an end to government 'overregulation' and in the same breath demand the government provide better price supports, storage loans, and disaster payments."

Are the subsidies really too low? Or is their very existence at the heart of the problems?

It is true that producers of long-subsidized commodities, such as cotton, wheat, rice and corn, often do tend to be facing economic hardship. Interestingly enough, though, many other producers—generally those who produce nonsubisdized commodities such as hogs, fruits, vegetables, eggs and turkeys—are all doing well. There is a connection to be made here.

Over-Production and Prices

Whenever a commodity is overproduced in relation to demand, its price naturally tends to drop. Lower prices then decrease the incentive to produce that commodity.

If, however, the government undertakes to artificially raise the price paid to producers for a commodity, the effect will be to encourage overproduction. Surpluses will acccumulate, which will tend to depress the market price still further.

The effect is the same when the government subsidizes the economic survival of marginal producers. Their additional production damages the economic viability of all producers, including the more efficient ones.

Ultimately, the U.S. farm policy supports large corporate farms at the expense of family farms. Tax benefits, heavily regulated marketing mechanisms, and subsidies all favor big agribusiness concerns. In 1978, just 3 per cent of the producers soaked up 46 per cent of all subsidies handed out by the federal govenment.

Other federal farm programs have also been dismal failures. The payment-in-kind program, or PIK, was created to alleviate the problem of huge government-owned commodity stockpiles. Farmers rushed to cash in on the largess, and the program depleted the stockpiles. Now, ironically, the government will be forced to buy more commodities on the open market to transfer to participating farmers—at a cost to taxpayers of $9 to $12 billion.

Destructive Policies

The USDA also encourages the introduction of new land into the cropland base. Commodity price supports and other subsidies increase the attractiveness of growing wheat or other grains compared to grazing livestock, and so such subsidies promote "plowdown" of Western rangeland. This practice destroys the prairie grasses whose tightly packed roots provide resistance to wind erosion. Subsidy-induced plowdown of rangeland threatens to recreate the dust-bowl conditions of the 1930s.

By Bob Gorrell. Permission of News America Syndicate.

Free or low-cost insurance and disaster loans offered by the government have encouraged risky management decisions. The availability of these loans has artificially encouraged utilization of marginal croplands, including many western rangelands—again, to the detriment of the environment.

Government-subsidized irrigation projects also enable a few privileged agribusiness concerns to expand their production; such

189

expansion aggravates an already serious excess of farm commodity production.

Farmers are businessmen. Like other businessmen, they compete to offer a product or service to consumers. If the market is allowed to operate freely, the price mechanism transmits relevant information concerning supply and demand. Information flows quickly and furnishes clear incentives for business people to act on that information and move resources to their highest valued uses.

In a free market, resources—capital, land, manufactured equipment—tend not to be sequestered by inefficient producers but rather to move, as marginal producers go out of business, to where they can best be used.

Benefits of Free Market

Free, unregulated, unsubsidized markets offer no guarantees of profits or success. In this way consumers are best served; and in the long run, the economy benefits. Price controls, subsidies and regulation subvert this natural process.

The distortions and dislocations of current agricultural policy arise directly from ill-advised attempts to manipulate markets and to subsidize a small group of businessmen. Many farmers, adapting to political pastures where they graze on taxpayer greens, have learned the subsidy game well. But most farmers and ranchers have been harmed, not helped, by these policies.

It is time to get the government out of farming. The long-term economic health of farmers and ranchers, as well as the quality of the environment, hangs in the balance.

"In the long run, the less government does to protect farmers, the better off farmers will be—the better off all Americans will be."

Farm Set-Aside Programs Harm Farmers and Taxpayers

James Bovard

James Bovard wrote the following viewpoint for *Reader's Digest*, a monthly magazine which publishes original and condensed articles from a variety of sources. In this viewpoint, Mr. Bovard argues that farm subsidy programs such as PIK (payment-in-kind) have only succeeded in bilking taxpayers out of billions of dollars. Far from aiding farmers, such programs encourage overprotection and higher prices thereby leading to unsaleable surpluses and to economic crisis for farmers.

As you read, consider the following questions:

1. According to Mr. Bovard, what was PIK designed to do? How successful does he believe the program has been?
2. How does Mr. Bovard say PIK has harmed exports?
3. What long-term harm does Mr. Bovard say PIK is causing farmers?

James Bovard, "Fiasco on the Farm," *Reader's Digest*, April 1984. Reprinted with the author's permission.

- South Lake Farms, in Kings County, California, is a subsidiary of the Bangor Punta Corp., a Connecticut-based conglomerate that turns out planes, boats and firearms. Last year the U.S. Department of Agriculture (USDA) gave South Lake $2.4-million worth of government-owned cotton.
- National Farms is a huge agri-business operating in Nebraska, Texas and Arkansas. In 1983 Uncle Sam gave it $3.5 million in federal corn and wheat.
- Belridge Farms in Kern County, California, is a subsidiary of the Shell Oil Co. Last year it received more than $2 million in free USDA wheat and cotton.

These corporate giants and hundreds of thousands of other farmers are beneficiaries of a strange new federal program called Payment in Kind (PIK) that gives farmers government-owned surplus crops—which they can then sell—in return for leaving their own crop lands idle. U.S. farmers were given nearly $10-billion worth of PIK commodities in 1983. As their part of the deal, they kept some 48 million acres—roughly the size of Nebraska—out of production. Declares Sen. Larry Pressler (R., S.D.), "Never in the history of mankind has there been such a massive effort not to grow food."

Giving farmers free harvests left much of the world's best farm land unplanted last year. Hundreds of fertilizer, farm-equipment and seed dealers had to close shop because PIK resulted in sales losses of up to 50 percent. An estimated quarter-million jobs were lost among suppliers, farm laborers, and in farm-related industries such as canning, milling and transportation. PIK, plus last summer's drought, drove feed prices up, devastating poultry, pork and cattle growers. PIK will cost American business billions in lost farm-export sales and could add another $20 billion to $30 billion to consumer food bills in 1984.

Subsidy Fiasco

PIK is only the latest fiasco in a 50-year effort to increase farm income and stabilize commodity markets by paying price supports to farmers. Government subsidies had dipped low by the mid-70s because, with inflation, price supports were at or below rising market prices. Then the Carter Administration hiked support levels, and payments escalated to $3 billion a year. Now, during the Reagan Administration, subsidies have gone through the roof, increasing sixfold to *$19 billion*—with PIK adding another $10 billion on top of that! "We are spending more for farm subsidies," complains Budget Director David Stockman, "than we are for welfare for the entire poverty population of the country."

The PIK story begins with farm legislation enacted in 1981. Under that bill, farmers were promised a set price for their major crops—corn, wheat, cotton, rice and grain sorghum—regardless of what the market price was. Because the USDA assumed that inflation would continue, these supports were scheduled to increase automatically each year for four years.

But the USDA was wrong. Inflation abated, and soon government prices were far above market levels. With the government obligated to buy the high-priced crops that farmers couldn't sell on the market, government-owned surpluses began piling up to record levels. How did Congress react to the crisis? With elections coming, they *raised* price supports for corn and wheat still higher, encouraging farmers to grow even more.

By Borgman for The Cincinnati Enquirer

Reprinted with special permission of King Features Syndicate, Inc.

It was to deal with the massive resulting surpluses that President Reagan unveiled PIK in early January 1983. The program was designed to reduce surpluses by giving farmers government-owned crops in return for not growing their own. By limiting production this new way, the Administration sought as well to reduce outlays under the price-supports program by driving up market prices.

Profits From Idle Land

But the USDA was operating in the dark. Without a single survey to see how farmers would react, the department estimated that PIK would idle 23 million acres. When the returns from PIK and other USDA programs were tallied in January 1984, farmers had left a total of 77 million acres—*one-third of all the eligible crop land in the country*—unplanted.

193

PIK promised to give wheat farmers 95 percent of what they would normally grow, and corn, cotton, rice and grain-sorghum farmers 80 percent. Since farmers were saved normal outlays for labor, seeds, fertilizer and fuel, they often netted far more than they would have from planting. Ultimately, 60 percent of wheat farmers, 90 percent of rice producers, 85 percent of cotton and 56 percent of corn producers went on the government dole.

PIK benefits were supposed to be in proportion to acres planted and crops harvested in previous years, but some farmers exaggerated their figures, claiming land that didn't meet PIK qualifications or even more land than they actually had available. In California, the USDA allowed cotton planters to claim the unplanted strips between rows of cotton as "idle" land eligible for PIK payments!

PIK is already haunting consumers at supermarket checkouts. Chemical Bank analysts say food prices will rise by as much as eight percent by late 1984, largely because of PIK. Agricultural economist Clifton B. Luttrell estimates that PIK will add $300 to the annual food bill of a middle-income family. Moreover, because PIK has depleted food reserves, the program greatly increases the risks of a 1985 food-price explosion if there is poor weather again this year.

Reducing Prosperity

The prosperity of American agriculture is heavily dependent on exports. In 1980 more than 40 percent of all the cash earned by U.S. crops came from abroad. Since then, however, USDA subsidy programs have driven up the prices of U.S. commodities. The volume of agricultural exports is down nearly 20 percent since 1980, and it's expected to drop another 3 percent this year. America's share of the world grain trade has fallen from 55 percent to 49 percent.

PIK will make the export situation worse. When American producers cut their planting last year, farmers in every other major exporting nation increased their output. Said Sen. Max Baucus (D., Mont.), "Argentina is jumping for joy over PIK."

And the story goes on. Last year the USDA spent $10 billion on PIK to help drive prices up. It also committed $4.8 billion to export subsidies, thus allowing U.S. farmers to sell crops to foreign countries at *below-market* prices. Pure insanity: one program to drive prices up for U.S. consumers; another program to drive prices down for foreign consumers!

Agriculture Secretary John Block defends PIK. It has "improved the quality of the environment," he claims, because so many millions of acres have been set aside for "conservation use." But most farmers have done little or nothing to conserve idled lands, and the USDA has not complained. A survey by 12 Midwestern-state agencies found 20 percent of PIK acreage unprotected from erosion, and another 37 percent protected only by last year's crop residue or weeds. To Rep. Ed Jones (D., Tenn.), chairman of the House soil-conservation subcommittee, Block's claim that PIK has helped the environment "is a joke."

Poor Justification

Attempts to justify PIK as income assistance for the struggling family farmer are no more successful. Since payments are based on number of acres idled, our many small farmers get little, while our few large and successful farmers reap a bonanza. (Federal law prohibits the USDA from giving more than $50,000 a year to any single farm. The USDA evaded this statute by claiming that since it was distributing commodities instead of cash, no limit applied. The General Accounting Office said this violated the law, but it possesses no judicial power to restrain the USDA.)

Even so, PIK marches on. This year the wheat program will pay farmers 75 percent of the average yield for set-aside acres. Programs for cotton, corn, grain sorghum and rice will also be driving down production and inflating prices.

Farm Aid Helps Wealthy

Subsidies seldom help ordinary farmers, benefiting instead wealthy "agribusinessmen" with Washington connections. Such political fixes shift tax money to a relatively few big farms, thus undercutting small farms at the market.

Columnist Warren Brookes notes, for example, that taxpayers this year will shell out $1.8 billion to have 850,000 dairy cows slaughtered. This will drive up dairy prices, penalizing consumers and enriching large dairy conglomerates. (One "dairyman" got $9.9 million to slaughter his entire herd.) These 850,000 cows also will glut the beef market, with evil consequences for livestock ranchers. As always, the federal subsidy helps the politically advantaged at the expense of the politically powerless. No wonder we have a farm crisis.

Editorial, *The Washington Times,* June 19, 1986.

And for what? Soybeans, our largest export crop, prove that extensive government protection is not necessary. In 1930 U.S. farmers planted 1.1 million acres each of peanuts and soybeans. Then government decided to protect peanuts and leave soybeans to the ravages of the marketplace. Today, American farmers grow 1.4 million acres of peanuts—and over 65 million acres of soybeans. In recent years corn and wheat exports have been decreasing, while exports of soybeans have soared. Yet the only difference between the corn and wheat industries and the soybean industry is that the former two get massive government aid.

Next year all the nation's agriculture laws expire, and Congress must draft comprehensive new legislation governing commodities. On the one hand, we must stop encouraging farmers by paying them more than their crops are worth; on the other, we must stop discouraging them by paying them for not working. In the long run, the less government does to protect farmers, the better off farmers will be—the better off *all* Americans will be.

"This is an appropriate time to create a new, modern farm program," says former Agriculture Secretary Clifford M. Hardin, "one that eliminates counterproductive price supports and production controls, one that utilizes to the fullest the efficiency and high productivity of the American farmer."

"Farm set-aside programs [such as PIK] make as much sense as paying unemployment compensation to workers."

Farmers Need Set-Aside Programs

Eleanor Zimmerlein

Eleanor Zimmerlein from LaMoille, Illinois, wrote the following viewpoint as a letter to the editors of *Human Events*, a conservative weekly newspaper. She wrote in response to an article by James Bovard (author of the previous viewpoint) which attacked the PIK program. Ms. Zimmerlein argues that it is not PIK that has harmed farmers; it is government policies which discourage practical export of farm products. She believes that the desperate farmer needs programs such as PIK in order to keep going.

As you read, consider the following questions:

1. For what reason does Ms. Zimmerlein believe farm exports have dropped?
2. List some of the reasons Ms. Zimmerlein uses to justify such programs as PIK.

Eleanor Zimmerlein, "Further on PIK: Illinois Farmer Takes Exception," *Human Events*, July 14, 1984. Reprinted with permission.

Regarding James Bovard's article, "PIK—The Agricultural Subsidy Disaster," *Human Events, May 26:*

Farm exports have tumbled, but mainly because embargoes have ruined our markets. We had four embargoes in a 10-year span, and the U.S. is no longer regarded as a reliable supplier.

When President Nixon imposed the first embargo, it cut off a major portion of Japan's food supply. That nation immediately invested billions of dollars in Brazil to increase their production of soybeans, vowing they would never again depend on the U.S. for its food supply. Brazil has increased its production tenfold, and is now second only to the U.S.

The straw that finally broke the farmer's back was the Carter embargo of 1980. Prices plunged—again; the surplus mounted—again; and farmers were left holding the bag, again.

The strength of the American dollar is a very big factor in pricing grain to our overseas customers. If the price of a bushel of corn today were exactly the same as it was four years ago, it would cost the foreign customer 50 per cent more because his currency is worth that much less in relation to the U.S. dollar.

U.S. laws to protect our domestic textile industry caused the Chinese to cancel huge orders of wheat. Domestic content legislation now in Congress will, if passed, prompt other countries to retaliate in like fashion against our grain.

U.S. laws require a certain percentage of the grain produced in the U.S. to be transported in U.S. flagships. Shipping costs are triple those of foreign flag ships.

PIK Not Out of Control

The PIK program did *not* give farmers 80 per cent of their usual production for idling their land. Only 50 per cent of the corn acreage in a county could be idled. A farmer could bid as much as 80 per cent of his base acreage, but in most counties that bid would not be accepted because of the 50 per cent total acreage limitation.

My county, Lee, in north central Illinois had bids ranging from 49 per cent to 79 per cent, with only the lower bids being accepted.

Furthermore, there is no way the base acreage could be inflated, as every year farmers are required to report acreage to the county ASCS office. This is a part of the permanent record there.

Aerial photos and on-farm visits are taken to verify farmers' reports. Our farm participated 100 per cent in the PIK program. In 1982 we raised 25,000 bushels of corn. Under the PIK program, we received 15,000 bushels of corn.

Even if acres are idled, there are still many, many expenses to be covered and hours of labor involved. Seed, tillage and mowing costs for idled acres, land payments or cash rent, taxes, interest, insurance, machinery payments, and fuel are a part of the expenses.

If the surplus of grain was to be reduced, large farmers had to be included in the program. They received more money because they had more acres and consequently more expenses. The payout per acre would be the same as the small-size farm.

Farm machinery sales have fallen since 1981. Poor farm prices forced most farmers to eliminate or postpone in the one area where they could. A great share of the PIK money went to pay overdue notes because of the losses prior to PIK.

Can't Eat Net Worth

A farmer can't eat his net worth. That is all tied up in land and equipment. Very few farmers can take a loss for a few years and still remain in business.

In 1973, net farm income was $33 billion. The individual farmer received about the same as the non-farmer at that time. Since then, farm income has dropped by at least a third, while non-farm income has more than doubled.

Dana Summers, *The Orlando Sentinel*, reprinted with permission.

The farmer has a huge amount of capital invested in his business, 10 times as much as the capital investment required for an auto worker. He needs some return on his investment and to replace worn-out machinery. It takes five people to supply the needs of one average farmer. A prosperous farm economy benefits the whole nation.

Grain prices too high? In the past 10 years, machinery costs have tripled; most other costs have at least doubled. Yet prices for corn and beans today are lower than in 1973.

The farmer's share of the consumer dollar has dropped from 37 cents in 1973 to 27 cents in 1983. In the meantime, labor's share has risen to 33 cents.

Why do you predict higher food prices when all signs point to a surplus of grain again this year?

Food Prices Less Than Other Inflation

Food prices over the past several years have gone up less than the rate of inflation. You maintain the PIK program will drive up food prices. How much do you attribute to last year's drought? How much have food prices been held down because of embargoes?

Farmers have *not* significantly increased their plantings in recent years. Approximately 350 million acres were under cultivation a generation ago, compared to 300 million today. Also, according to Orion Samuelson, WGN farm director, the farmer debt-to-asset ratio is the worst it has been since the '30s. Even *U.S. News & World Report* says the farmer is still in trouble.

Your figure for agricultural programs for last year must surely include the cost of food stamps, as the cost of the PIK program itself was much, much less. Does it also include lending programs, but not the amount that farmers pay back? Payments scheduled for farmers for this year have been cut in half.

Should Congress abolish all subsidized loan programs to farmers? Loans to the small businessman can go for as low as 3 per cent. I don't know of any farm loan interest rate that comes anywhere near that figure. How about grants for public transportation, urban renewal, city water and sewage systems, enterprise zones, etc.? If all subsidies should be taken away from the farmer, then let's play fair and take them away from everyone else.

Farm set-aside programs make as much sense as paying unemployment compensation to workers, while at the same time driving up wages by raising the minimum wage and other legislation that encourages union monopolies. The federal Davis-Bacon Act and the Illinois prevailing wage act fall in the same category.

"Free Market" Doesn't Exist

We do not have a free market system. When our government can turn our exports off and on at will, force agricultural products to subsidize our merchant marine, then we should expect our government to pay for the damage it has caused.

The Ability To Empathize

The ability to empathize, to see a situation from another person's vantage point, is an important skill. When we empathize, we put ourselves in someone else's position. This helps us look at a problem in a new way, one that we perhaps have not considered before. It also aids us in understanding an opponent's viewpoint and in deciding how to effectively respond to him or her.

Imagine the following situation: A new bill to aid farmers is presently being discussed in Congress. The bill would give farmers the option of putting off payments on all loans taken out for farm land and equipment. If the bill passes, farmers would have up to five years before they resume payments on such loans. As they usually do when considering legislation, the legislators will be listening to testimony from all kinds of people regarding the pros and cons of the bill. Among the testifiers on this particular bill are the following people:

Senator Edward Kennedy — author of Viewpoint 1 in this chapter

T.F. Leonard — author of Viewpoint 2 in this chapter

John Peterson — a Kansas farmer recently foreclosed on because he defaulted on loan payments

Helen Koosman — a Detroit auto worker who has been laid off for the last five years and who also has lost her home because she couldn't make all of her payments

Deborah Adams — one of the President's economic advisors who is seriously concerned with the national budget deficit

Nathanial Edelman — a member of Americans Concerned for Freedom, a strongly conservative organization which promotes free enterprise and which believes there is too much government involvement in matters that should be taken care of by individuals

Andy McMahon — president of Jersey Farms, Inc., a 60,000 acre farm conglomerate in California; although the corporation is making profits of several hundred thousand dollars a year (much of which is reinvested in the farm system), it also owes nearly a million dollars in loans.

Try to put yourself in the place of each person listed above. List the advantages and disadvantages each would see in the proposed bill. Which way would each urge the legislators to vote? How would *you* vote?

Periodical Bibliography

The following list of periodical articles deals with the subject matter of this chapter.

Heather Ball and Leland Beatty	"Blowing Away the Family Farmer," *The Nation,* November 3, 1986.
Doug Bandow	"Free-Market Farming?" *The New American,* January 20, 1986.
Dennis Bechara	"The Continuing Plight of Agriculture," *The Freeman,* May 1986.
Business Week	"How PIK Is Poisoning Farm Policy," August 8, 1983.
Susan Dentzer et al.	"Bitter Harvest," *Newsweek,* February 18, 1985.
Aloysius Ehrbar	"Facts vs. the Furor Over Farm Policy," *Fortune,* November 11, 1986.
Laurence Grafstein	"Farms Control," *The New Republic,* 1983.
Devorah Lanner	"A Farm Bill by and for Farmers," *The Nation,* July 6/13, 1985.
John J. McManus	"Roots of the 'Farm Problem,'" *The New American,* May 5, 1985.
The New Republic	"Breaking Eggs," November 11, 1985.
Robert J. Samuelson	"The Farm Mess Forever," *Newsweek,* November 18, 1985.
Dero A. Saunders	"The Yields Were Spectacular," *Forbes,* January 27, 1986.
Jim Schwab	"Saving the System, Not the Farmers," *The Nation,* January 18, 1986.
Kenneth R. Sheets, John Collins, et al.	"Ailing Farm Economy—Damage Spreads Wide," July 29, 1985.
U.S. News & World Report	"As U.S. Farmers Struggle for Foreign Markets," March 14, 1983.
U.S. News & World Report	"It Looks Pretty Bleak For a Lot of Farmers," interview with John Block, the Secretary of Agriculture, February 18, 1985.

How Can the US Ease the World Debt Crisis?

> *"Cancellation of these debts is fully justified and would permit the developing countries to make a fresh start."*

The US Should Cancel Foreign Debts

Gus Hall

Gus Hall, general secretary of the Communist Party USA, believes that lending countries, primarily the United States, have imposed crippling and unfair terms on the debtor nations. Their motives, he states, are not generosity but greed and political domination. He argues that it is impossible to expect the less developed nations to repay such extravagant amounts of money and that the only realistic, fair solution is to cancel the debts.

As you read, consider the following questions:

1. What does Mr. Hall mean by "financial imperialism"?
2. Mr. Hall states that the US has become the world's debt enforcer. What means does he say the US uses?
3. How would Mr. Hall rationalize cancelling the debt even though that would mean that the lending institutions would never get repaid?

Gus Hall, "New Tentacles of Financial Imperialism," *Political Affairs,* January 1986. Reprinted with permission.

Financial imperialism has become the largest source of plunder of the developing countries, which are treated as neocolonies by the United States, Japan and Western Europe.

Yearly, $100 billion is drained from the developing countries to pay the interest alone on $750 billion of debts—half paid by Latin American countries, the remainder by Asian and African nations. During the past ten years the debts have multiplied five times and the interest burden nearly ten times. This has a paralyzing impact on the economies of the developing countries.

The ruling circles in the debtor countries have used part of the borrowed sums to pay for imports of armaments and luxury products and to finance investments that lead to further exploitation of their own very low-paid workers. Other loans went to the transnational mining, manufacturing and trade companies to expand their investments and increase the booty extracted from these countries and the exploitation of their workers. The tax-free status of the transnationals adds to corporate profits and the debt crisis.

U.S. multinational corporations reap $2.50 in profits for every dollar they have invested in Latin America. Every year the Latin American affiliates of multinationals transfer nearly $40 billion in profits out of these countries.

Sacrifices from the People

On the other hand, very few dollars are invested for the needs of the people in the debtor countries. In fact, the more loans are made to these countries, the more sacrifices are squeezed from the people through extreme austerity programs imposed on the debtor countries by the imperialist corporations and banks, and by the International Monetary Fund.

With the world capitalist economic crisis of the '80s, the price scissors operating against the developing countries widened. Prices of the products they imported rose rapidly while their receipts from sales to the industrialized countries decreased.

Overvaluation of the dollar increased the dollar-dominated debt and interest charges and the cost of imports. By 1982, the payments required of Brazil, Mexico, Argentina, the Philippines, Ivory Coast and other countries reached impossible levels. The costs of servicing their foreign debt reached a level that made it impossible to import materials needed to run their industries. The resulting crisis caused the workers of the debtor countries extreme suffering.

The share of developing-country borrowing which is from private foreign banks has gone up dramatically, from 16 per cent in the early 1970s to 80 per cent at the beginning of the 1980s. Per capita external debt jumped from 85.5 dollars in 1971 to 1,000 dollars in 1984.

The large financial institutions are the main profiteers from this

Reprinted from *USA Today*, January 1986. Copyright 1986 by The Society for the Advancement of Education.

enormous interest windfall. Over the years they have reaped more in interest alone than the amount of the original loans. Cancellation of these debts is fully justified and would permit the developing countries to make a fresh start.

However, the imperialist banks, their affiliated International Monetary Fund (IMF), and their governments are doing everything they can to ensure continued collection of all interest, regardless of the drain on the debtor countries. While U.S. banks are owed 30 per cent of the total, the U.S. acts as enforcer for the world's gang of creditors.

Through its domination of the IMF, U.S. finance capital has imposed crippling terms on the debtors. Through intervention in Nicaragua, Angola and Afghanistan, massive military bases and political dominance of the Philippines, as well as the invasion of Grenada, the U.S. delivers warnings and threats that non-payment may be met by invasion or by imposition of puppet military dictatorships.

Through generous support of the murderous regimes in Central America and through big loans to dictators like Pinochet in Chile, the U.S. reinforces the most reactionary, militarist and fascist groups in the debtor countries. In many ways, U.S. finance capital tells the governments and ruling classes of the debtor nations they will be richly rewarded if they impose terrorist regimes that collaborate with the transnational banks and corporations.

For example, through the IMF, Washington and Wall Street have forced on Mexico, Brazil and Argentina—the largest Latin American debtors—"austerity" programs in order to guarantee interest and repayment on debts to the banks.

Oppressive Effects of the Austerity Programs

The common feature of all these "austerity" programs is the forced cut in real wages of workers, in some cases a 30 per cent cut in the wages of workers who are already paid as little as one-tenth of U.S. wages. This dooms tens of millions more to hunger and extreme poverty, joblessness, homelessness, lack of medical care, education and housing.

The ruling capitalists and military of these countries tend to accept these orders because they, too, make profits from the low wages of their workers.

They also betray their own national interests by pouring billions into the U.S. and other "safe" countries, thereby canceling much of the "savings" in foreign exchange they get as a result of the "austerity" programs. The ruling circles of the debtor nations fear that any defiance of the bankers will lead to confiscation of their ill-gotten profits.

The deepening crisis of capitalism, the gross imbalances in international trade, the destablilization of currencies, all are factors that have contributed to the failure to achieve any easing of the international debt crisis, even in this period of partial economic recovery. It is bound to become more acute with the next cyclical crisis, which looms on the horizon. . . .

The plunder of developing countries by financial imperialism also costs U.S. workers. It forces reduction in sales of U.S. goods to debtor countries, throwing thousands of U.S. workers out of jobs. By further forcing down wages in developing countries, it encourages transnationals to close more U.S. plants, to move more production to where wages are super-low.

But there is a fightback against the bankers, the IMF, the transnationals and U.S. imperialism. Demonstrations and strikes are being carried out by workers in Brazil, Argentina, the Philippines and many other debtor countries. Protest actions in Peru and Bolivia have caused those governments to cut payments to the bankers. U.S. workers are beginning to see the connections between big corporations that exploit them and their transnational offspring that exploit workers in other countries.

The plunder can not be collected indefinitely. Sooner or later the crisis will be basically resolved when anti-imperialist forces, headed by the working class, come to power in the debtor countries and take radical corrective measures in defiance of the financial leeches.

The Wall Street banks raise the false alarm of bankruptcy if they don't get their interest payments, while their profits rise to new highs each year. What they want is government guarantees of bailouts for defaults. . . .

It is in the interests of U.S. workers to support the people's struggles and their demands to cancel the debts. The enemies of the people of the debtor nations are also our class enemies—the exploiters, the banks and racists.

Remove Debt Cancer

"Unless the cancer [i.e., the debt] is removed it will kill all democratic processes. . . . The breakdown comes quickly, very quickly. . . . I believe that we'll have many allies among the industrialized countries if we can convince them that this [cancellation of the debt] is in their interest because it will mean more employment, greater use of industrial facilities, more world trade, and capitalism can emerge from this crisis."

Fidel Castro, press conference, July 7, 1985.

It is also the internationalist duty of U.S. workers to support their fellow workers in developing countries, to follow the historic example of human rights advocates, of peace advocates who have opposed U.S. colonialism for over a century. Today the political heirs of those who opposed U.S. aggression against countries like Cuba and the Philippines are demonstrating in the same spirit.

Easing the Economic Situation

The Communist Party, USA calls for:
• Nationalization of the major banks and central banking system of the U.S., under the democratic control of workers'

209

representatives.

The trillions of dollars of their resources must be used to finance essential improvements in the infrastructure—public housing, education, health, transportation, recreation, etc., for no-strings-attached aid to developing countries to enable them to recover from the poverty and unbalanced development imposed by centuries of colonial and neocolonial control.

• Support of all measures taken by the workers and progressive forces of developing countries to reduce or eliminate the debts and interest burden that is oppressing masses and crippling national economies. This calls for the unconditional cancellation of the debts of Latin American, Asian and African countries, debts that have in reality been repaid many times over as a result of the looting by financial and industrial transnationals.

• An end to all intervention in the internal affairs of these countries. An end to all direct and indirect invasions, to all support for or imposition of military dictatorships. Remove all U.S. troops from all foreign bases.

• Implementation of the United Nations New International Economic Order, which provides for closing the price scissors and paying equitable prices for the commodities supplied by developing countries.

• Provision of long-term interest-free capital for use by debtor countries in developing their own industries in their own interests. Recognition of their right to expel transnational exploiters and to take back national ownership of appropriated properties.

• Immediate cancellation of all "austerity" programs imposed to pay the massive interest and debts.

Finance capital works to have it both ways—to keep squeezing the developing countries financially and economically, and to get the government to guarantee their profits and protect their investments.

Finance capital is ready to do anything as long as it can continue its loan sharking. Any concept that lets finance capital, the most ferocious sector of monopoly capital, off the hook, is of necessity at the expense of the working class.

The Communist Party urges and supports the establishment of direct cooperation between the U.S. working class and the workers of the developing, debtor nations, through trade union support of their struggles. It calls for an end to the intervention and provocative schemes of the CIA and its agents in the trade union affairs of the U.S. and the developing countries.

"It is clear that the LDCs [less developed countries] must reform their domestic economies and curb corruption and bribery."

Debtor Countries Must Reform Themselves

George B. N. Ayittey

George B. N. Ayittey, a native of Ghana, is assistant professor of economics at Bloomsburg University in Pennsylvania. In the following viewpoint, he points out that lending nations have put billions of dollars into the less developed countries' economies but to little avail. He argues that the world debt crisis is not the responsibility of the US or other lending countries. The debtor nations must reform their own economic systems before more help is given them.

As you read, consider the following questions:

1. What is "capital flight"? How does Mr. Ayittey believe this has contributed to the debt crisis?
2. What are some of the reforms Mr. Ayittey states the LDCs must make?
3. What evidence does the author use to show that it is not greedy lending nations that have caused the debt crisis?

George B.N. Ayittey, "The Real Foreign Debt Problem," *The Wall Street Journal*, April 8, 1986. Reprinted with the author's permission.

Many leaders of nations saddled with a burdensome foreign debt find it convenient and popular to blame their plight on Western banks and governments while they allow rampant corruption and counterproductive economic policies to continue.

Peruvian President Alan Garcia—who has limited debt repayments to 10% of his country's export earnings—said recently: "Economic subjugation and foreign debt are the modern forms of what occupation and military blockade were in the past. The debt . . . has become a modern expression of imperialism." He described interest on foreign debt as a "brazen attempt to collect foreign currency and cover the deficit of the wealthy countries, expecially the most powerful country."

Even those leaders of less-developed countries (LDCs) not given to overheated rhetoric propose solutions that address only the international aspects of the debt crisis. For example, the key proposals of the Cartagena Group of 11 Latin American debtor nations include lowering real international interest rates, securing concessionary terms on existing debt, and increasing annual International Monetary Fund lending to keep pace with international inflation. Debtor representatives are also using the IMF and World Bank meetings . . . to ask for more lending on easier terms. Nowhere is there a concrete set of proposals by the debtor nations to tackle some of the worst domestic causes of the debt crisis: economic mismanagement, inflation, corruption, excessive government control of economy and capital flight.

Capital Flight

Capital flight—the legal or illegal export of foreign exchange—is perhaps the largest single obstacle to a resolution of the Third World debt crisis. Journalist Lenny Glynn writes that "there is growing evidence that capital flight from LDCs was a major factor behind the cash shortages that drove several of them to the brink of bankruptcy." James S. Henry, an economist writing in the New Republic, reports that "More than half of the money borrowed by Mexico, Venezuela, and Argentina during the last decade has effectively flowed right back out the door, often the same year or even month it flowed in."

What is the source of this capital? A great deal of it represents money invested abroad by those who have little or no faith in the management of their countries' economies. But much of it consists of tens of billions of dollars spirited out of the LDCs by corrupt officials since the 1970s. Owing to its clandestine nature, precise figures on much of the capital exodus are hard to come by. But in *Canadian Report on Business* magazine, Mr. Glynn cites a revealing confidential study carried out by a New York bank. After examining the balance-of-payment accounts of 23 debtor nations from 1978 to 1983, it was discovered that while those nations added $381.5 billion to their foreign debts, $103.1 billion flowed back out as capital flight. Some examples from that five-year period:

- Argentina incurred $35.7 billion in new loans while $21 billion left the country.
- The Philippines added on $19.1 billion in new debt as $8.9 billion left.
- Venezuelans spirited $27 billion out of their country while that nation's debt load rose by $23 billion.

These findings are corroborated by another study by the Bank for International Settlements. It found that, excluding Venezuela, some $55 billion left Latin America between 1978 and 1982.

Reprinted with permission from *The Washington Inquirer.*

If anything, capital flows are even greater today. At a recent Manhattan Institute luncheon, Walter Wriston, the former chairman of Citicorp, reported that in February alone, $3 billion in capital was sent out of Mexico. According to Mr. Wriston: "Most people believe that the flight of capital from Latin America on deposit in New York and Miami exceeds the total capital remaining in those countries." This hemorrhaging of financial assets means that further solutions to the debt crisis must come from the debtors themselves. As Mr. Wriston says: "There is no point in lending money to Mexico if they don't let their currency float, bring their inflation down, and reduce their deficit. There is nothing that a lender can do to help."

Capital flight is, of course, not unique to Latin America. Billions of dollars were whisked out of Africa by corrupt government officials in the late 1970s and early 1980s. A recent Nigerian

213

government investigation estimated that at the height of the oil boom in 1978, corrupt politicians were transferring $25 million a day abroad. President Mobutu Sese Seko of Zaire is reported to have amassed some $5 billion in Swiss bank accounts—a fortune large enough to pay off his nation's entire foreign debt of $4.4 billion.

Besides naked looting by corrupt officials, there are other ways to strip a country of its capital. One is to persuade a foreign contractor to inflate a project's cost and deposit the surcharge in the foreign bank account of an official. In 1974, Argentina's then minister of economics, Jose Galbard, had two foreign companies deposit $4 million in a Swiss bank account after he agreed to purchase a nuclear reactor they had built. In the Philippines, Imelda Marcos was nicknamed "Mrs. Ten Percent" for the cuts she allegedly took off big government contracts.

Another way of transferring capital abroad is to over-invoice imports. Here a foreign supplier is persuaded to inflate the cost of an import item and place the difference in a minister's foreign bank account. An investigation by the government of Ghana in the early 1980s revealed that the country was losing at least $60 million a year through over-invoicing of imports.

Under-invoicing of exports and smuggling also rob an LDC of much-needed capital. Diamond smuggling—75% of which is done through the VIP lounge at the Luanda airport—costs the Marxist government of Angola some $70 million a year in lost foreign exchange.

The foreign loan or aid money that is not shipped out of the recipient country is often used to build expensive show projects and to pay bloated government bureaucracies. Nigeria has spent four years and billions of dollars on its proposed new capital of Abuja. Its cost will equal the $24 billion total sovereign debt of Nigeria. Foreign loans are also often channeled into inefficient and corrupt state-owned enterprises. In Ghana, for example, the state-owned sector received more than 90% of the foreign loans while much of Argentina's $50 billion in loans went to the military and a collection of 353 state enterprises.

LDCs Must Reform

While the international aspects of the debt crisis are important, it is clear that the LDCs must reform their domestic economies and curb corruption and bribery. If wealthy Argentines would repatriate the estimated $30 billion they have hoarded abroad, their country's $50 billion debt crisis would be dramatically eased. If rich Mexicans returned the $45 billion they hold in property and bank accounts abroad, according to Mexican government statistics, Mexico's debt would be halved.

It is within this context that the plan proposed by Treasury Secretary James Baker in October [1985] to grapple with the debt crisis should be assessed. The Baker Plan envisages a pledge of $29 billion in new loans from Western commercial and development banks to the debtor nations. In return, the debtor nations would be required to pursue sound anti-inflationary policies and institute major structural reforms to reduce the role of the state in their economies, liberalize trade and arrest capital flight. . . . The World Bank and IMF will begin implementing this plan by setting up an initial $3.1 billion lending program largely for nations in sub-Saharan Africa.

In essence, the provisions of the Baker Plan do not differ radically from the austerity measures the IMF often already prescribes as conditions for its aid. Those conditions have been assailed in the past by LDC leaders as "offensive" and "politically suicidal." It is no surprise then that the reaction of the debtor nations to the Baker Plan was cool and disheartening. Only Argentina, Ecuador and Mexico expressed guarded willingness to endorse some of its aspects.

Reforms Must Be Made

[Recent political events have] focused attention on the wealth that Third World oligarchs have plundered and stashed abroad. . . . In some cases, the wealthiest classes of poor countries have actually sent more money out of their countries than foreign borrowing has brought in—and often it's the same money. . . . As Third World leaders and international bankers warm up for another chorus of moaning about the debt crisis, they need a forcible reminder that the solution may lie in their own hands. Countries like Mexico should get no more money until they have enacted reforms to ensure that the dollars we lend them don't come right back again in the bank accounts of rich private citizens.

James S. Henry, *The New Republic,* April 14, 1986.

While leaders of the debtor nations overwhelmingly reject Mr. Baker's initiative, they don't propose a substitute that deals with the domestic side of the debt crisis. It is tragic that so many countries that struggled so long for their independence from colonial powers are now led by people who must wait for outsiders to come up with realistic solutions to their domestic economic problems.

That progress is possible is shown by the experience of Brazil. Even the modest reforms initiated by that country's new democratic government have paid large dividends. In 1985, Brazil had a balance-of-trade surplus of $11 billion and a real growth rate of 8%—double that of the U.S. As Mr. Wriston says: "Two years ago, they were saying the beads over Brazil. . . . If you handle your affairs correctly, the capital of your own people will come back.

If your own people don't trust you, why should anybody else?"

The notion that debtor nations are the innocent victims of greedy international bankers is patently false. Three of the richest people in the world are current or former leaders of LDCs: President Mobutu of Zaire (estimated wealth of $5 billion), the Marcoses of the Philippines (estimated wealth of up to $10 billion), and President Suharto of Indonesia (estimated wealth of $3 billion). Many of these leaders wouldn't dream of sharing their wealth with their own people. Yet, they want the rich nations to share theirs with the Third World. And they are often all too willing to make paper promises of reform in exchange for another foreign-loan fix.

It takes very little common sense to realize that pouring water into a bucket full of holes is pointless. Similarly, without genuine efforts by the LDCs to address the domestic side of the debt crisis, an international rescue package of loans will flow right back out of the debtor nations in the form of capital flight and booty.

"Added together, American foreign aid and the West's lost loans have cost more than a trillion dollars. . . . It is time to stop."

The US Must Stop Bad Lending

Patrick J. Buchanan

Patrick J. Buchanan, Chief of Communications for President Ronald Reagan, argues that the world debt crisis was caused by a combination of faulty foreign policy decisions and unwise lending by banks. He writes that this kind of error-based decision-making cannot continue. The only solution is to stop throwing good money after bad. Even in the unlikely case that all the debtor nations default, he believes that the economies of the lending nations will comfortably survive.

As you read, consider the following questions:

1. According to Mr. Buchanan, what caused the world debt crisis?
2. What seems to be Mr. Buchanan's attitude toward making loans to communist countries?
3. How does Mr. Buchanan answer those who say that refusing to loan more money would be disastrous?

Patrick J. Buchanan, "Let's Freeze the Debt Bomb," originally published in *Future 21: Directions for America in the 21st Century*, edited by Paul Weyrich and Connaught Marshner. Greenwich, CT: Devin-Adair, 1984. Reprinted with permission.

In 1973 the Warsaw Pact nations, harnessed together in the Kremlin counterfeit of the Common Market called Comecon, had $9.3 billion in debts outstanding to Western Europe and the United States. By 1983, Pact debt had risen ninefold to $80 billion. With Yugoslavia added, Communist Europe owed $100 billion to the governments and financial institutions of the West. The equal of half a dozen Marshall Plans had been consumed; and at the decade's end half the Communist regimes were illiquid, insolvent or bankrupt. Poland, Rumania and Yugoslavia were rudely demanding a rescheduling of old loans and new infusions of Western capital, while threatening a general default that would send the great banks of West Europe toppling like a line of dominoes.

In Latin America, three nations—Argentina, Brazil and Mexico—had accumulated $210 billion in debt. Interest alone on the Mexican debt was running at $250 million a week.

"The figures are beyond comprehension," wrote scholar William Quirk in the *New Republic.* "In June of 1982, according to Treasury Secretary Donald Regan, the poor countries owed $265 billion to Western private banks. Latin America alone owed $168 billion to the banks. Including loans from Western governments and international agencies, the poor countries owed $500 billion. Counting in loans to companies in poor countries, the total was $626 billion of which $400 billion was owed to the banks. . . . Half of that poor country debt is due. . . . "

This, then, is the essence of the debt crisis:

After a decade of improvident or, more precisely, lunatic lending, Western governments, financial institutions, and banks held $700 billion worth of paper representing loans to the Soviet Bloc and the Third World. Three dozen countries on four continents were in "technical" default; *i.e.,* they had failed repeatedly to meet the original terms of their loans. If these "non-performing loans" had to be written down or written off, as normal banking and accounting procedures require, there would ensue a worldwide banking collapse.

How did we arrive at a juncture where the United States is presented this apparent Hobson's choice: Either accept the indefinite siphoning of your wealth into the looted vaults of the communist and socialist world to enable them to "service" their debts, or call a halt to the income transfers and risk collapse of the international financial system, the crash of the Big Banks, and a repeat of 1933? . . .

Roots of the Debt Crisis

The Bank crisis is rooted in two events: the "detente" summit at Moscow in May of 1972 and the Yom Kippur War in October of 1973.

"A generation of peace" is what President Nixon hoped would

follow from detente; "restraint" on Soviet behavior was the more modest return anticipated by Henry Kissinger. Nonetheless, the deal was struck. In exchange for an end to Soviet adventurism, Russia and her vassal states were accorded unrestricted access to the warehouses of the West.

As the Bloc was without hard currency, and could earn only limited foreign exchange selling furs and vodka, oil and gas and coal, there was a need for credit. Western bankers like David Rockefeller moved with alacrity to provide it.

"Just because a country is technically called Communist," said Mr. Rockefeller, "doesn't mean that capitalist institutions such as the Chase bank can't deal with them on a mutually beneficial basis, and, indeed, we do deal with most of the so-called Communist countries of the world on a basis that has worked out well, I think, for both of us." . . .

By the end of 1982, with new credit drying up, the Russians were said to be considering a general default. Eighty billion dollars—gone!

The Great Re-Cycling Scam

Third World Debt, which eclipses Bloc Debt by a factor of six, is traceable to the run-up in oil prices in the aftermath of the October War.

Bear Losses if Necessary

Banks made loans to the debtor countries at terms they considered profitable, taking full account of the risks involved. Had all gone well, they would have reaped the profits. If any loans go sour, the banks (i.e., their stockholders) should bear the loss, not the taxpayers. If government socializes the losses, it will inevitably end up socializing the profits. Neither the banks nor the rest of us can have our cake and eat it.

Milton Friedman, *Newsweek*, November 14, 1983.

Even in retrospect, the numbers astonish. From $2.50 a barrel in 1973, the price of light Arabian crude, benchmark for the OPEC cartel, rose to $34 by 1982—prodded along by Western panic and hoarding after the collapse of the Shah.

The magnitude of the wealth transfer is detailed by Professor William Quirk: "In 1972, the Arabs received $24 billion from the rest of the world. In 1982, they received $230 billion. Since all oil prices followed OPEC's lead, in the U.S. the cost of oil went from $20.3 to $225 billion in 1982. . . . The Arabs with the banks brokering the deal had made a major withdrawal from the West."

But these legendary windfall profits presented the OPEC Arabs with a problem: where to park the billions so that they would remain secure and grow.

The answer presented itself. Where better than those most solid of institutions, the European and American banks?

The immense and mounting deposits from the Persian Gulf presented the Big Banks in turn with their own problem: where to lend the money so it would earn a higher rate of interest than the bankers were paying OPEC for the privilege of holding it.

This answer, too, presented itself: Why not turn around and lend the money to the Third World which could then use the funds to pay their escalating oil bill and expand their import purchases from the West?

Thus began the great re-cycling scam of the Seventies. The cartel would collect and package petrodollars pouring in from Europe, Japan, and the United States. The packaged monies would be placed on deposit in the great banks of Tokyo, London, and New York. The Big Banks—with the Americans in the van—would turn around and lend the funds at a bit above the LIBOR rate (London inter-bank offer rate) to the Third World which would use the money to buy more oil from the cartel and more imports from the West.

Hemorrhage of Western Capital

With this steady hemorrhaging of its investment capital—life blood of a free economy—Western economies faltered while the cartel flourished and the Third World boomed. Bankers bored with nursing along loans to the dying industries of Smokestack America reveled in night flights to exotic sites like Buenos Aires and Brasilia to be feted by the finance ministers of the countries of the future.

The money was lent without regard to ideology. "Who knows which political system works?" is how Thomas Theobold, heir presumptive at Citibank, casually dismissed a reporter's question from the *Wall Street Journal*. "The only thing we care about is how they pay their bills." . . .

But, surely, there was a huge economic risk in lending hard currency, without collateral, to socialists and communists: Not to worry, said Leland Prussia, Chairman of the Bank of America. "Countries are different from individuals. We can go bankrupt and disappear. Countries can't do that."

So, in the Seventies and early Eighties, the seed corn of the U.S. economy was scooped up and carried off to be poured onto the sandy soil of the socialist South and the rocky ground of the Soviet Bloc. Back home, interest rates soared, economic growth was stunted, per capita income, for the first time since the Great Depression, began to fall. . . .

There is a rule taught young journalists: Never overestimate the knowledge of your reader; nor underestimate his intelligence. The American people may not be schooled in matters of international finance, but they are not fools.

When American businesses starved for capital were failing at the Depression rate of 500 a week, when a cab driver in San Francisco was being required by the Bank of America to pay 19 percent for an "unsecured personal loan," Americans began to inquire what their Congress was doing shoveling our investment capital out to maintain the credit rating of Mr. Ceaucescu of Rumania and Mr. Kadar of Hungry.

What happens to cooperating Congressmen when Americans awaken to the knowledge that the "non-aligned" dreck that treats their country like kitty litter at the U.N. is not only subsidized with our foreign aid, but is being carried on the books of our biggest banks? When the American people discover that the Soviet nuclear arsenal targeted on Europe and North America was underwritten with Western credit? "How will it be with kingdoms and kings?" asked Edwin Markham.

Gamble in *Florida Times Union*.

To those of us making this case, the pragmatists have what appears to be an irrefutable retort. It runs as follows:

"Agreed, the banks made stupid loans in the decade past. But consider the consequences of blocking future bailouts, of forcing countries like Mexico and Argentina into default.

"If they walk away from their debts, the Big Banks will have to write off billions in bad loans. Bank profits will disappear;

dividends will be eliminated; bank stock will plummet. Huge slices, perhaps the whole, of bankers' equity will be eliminated. As equity vanishes, and loan loss reserves mount, new lending in the United States as well as overseas will come to a halt; savings will be threatened; a run on the banks by depositors will follow. We are looking at 1933, when 10,000 American banks went under."

"The National Interest"

John Chamberlain, the bard of capitalism, argued the case from the national interest as follows: " . . . despite the outraged feelings of the Populist New Right, Ronald Reagan is not in a position to let Mexico go down the drain. It is not Reagan's fault that the bankers, big and little, mined the whole territory at our southern border before he took office. He must be cursing the day that the Chase bank ever let Mexico have a nickel, but he can't say anything out loud. He can only tell his State Department to tip the world bankers off to their 'duty' which is to bail and bail and bail. . . . It's going to be a long and painful business . . . [but] we are stuck with the bail-out business."

Are we indeed between Scylla and Charybdis? Must we acquiesce in construction of a giant pipeline from Middle America through the I.M.F. into the Third World and back to the Big Banks to maintain the fiction that the loans are good—or risk implosion of the banking system and our own financial ruin?

So the bankers and global bureaucrats would have us believe. Voltaire's description of history comes to mind: " . . . a pack of lies agreed upon." But we are *not* bereft of choice. We are *not* condemned to perpetual pillage of the savings of the American people with the connivance of their own Congress. "There *are* simple answers," Ronald Reagan used to say in the campaigns of 1976 and 1980. "It is just that there are no easy ones." That native wisdom is needed.

The right answer is, indeed, a simple one. It consists, first and foremost, of facing up to, and acting upon, the truth.

Facing Facts: The Money Is Gone

The money is gone; it is never coming back. We will no more see again the $80 billion in outstanding credit given the Warsaw Pact than we will see again the World War I billions lent the Triple Entente or the World War II billions sent to J.V. Stalin in Lend-Lease.

You could send a naval expedition up the Congo River and you would find Kurtz before you find a trace of the billions sent to Joe Mobutu.

Americans were had once again. For ten years we poured the seed corn of the American economy into the drainage ditches and slit trenches of the Third World and reaped for our inebriate's generosity a harvest of insolence and ingratitude. That is the truth. And it is necessary to recognize and act upon the truth if we are not to re-enact the folly.

Prepare to Write Off Bad Debts

The first piece of business is to notify the Soviet Bloc and the Non-aligned that the game is over, that no more good dollars will come chasing their bad debts, that we are prepared, if necessary, to write off the whole investment, that the United States is not so terrified of default as some would have led them to believe. True, the evening the U.S. Congress rejects the next bailout, the lights will be burning late at the Bank of America and Chase Manhattan, Citibank and Manny Hanny. But it will not be the end of the world. The lights will go on again, soon. The paneled offices will be reoccupied—only by different men heading up less ambitious institutions than the Gonzo Bankers who preceded them.

Despite the atmosphere of crisis that has been created, the principal losses threatened by a general writing down, or writing off, of bad loans to the Soviet Bloc and the Third World are to bankers' profits, their shareholders' dividends and their own jobs, salaries, bonuses and perks.

End Counterproductive Aid

As long as counterproductive bank lending and multilateral "assistance" continue, the "lesser developed countries" are going to stay that way. In fact their condition will deteriorate, as it has done in the two years since the last debt scare.

By contrast a Third World default now would be salutary. The welfare states would be forced to make it on their own, which is the only way that prosperity can be attained. At the same time our own economists and development experts might learn a useful lesson about the fundamentals of economic life.

Tom Bethell, *The Washington Times*, August 14, 1985.

As Paul Craig Roberts, formerly of Treasury, has testified, the entire exposure of the nine largest U.S. banks in the Third World is 222 percent of total capital; their exposure to the three largest debtors, Argentina, Brazil and Mexico, is 112 percent of their capital. While writing down the banks' bad debts might wipe out bank equity, the bad loans are only a fraction of the hundreds of billions in solid performing loans in the bank portfolios.

As former Chase Chairman George Champion has recommended, the American banks should be permitted—if not required—to raise their tax-deductible loan loss reserve from the 1982 level of 1 percent of loans outstanding to 5 percent. While the Treasury would sustain a loss in revenue, the reserve would cushion the banks to take the blows that are coming. Second, rather than increasing their exposure, the banks should cease all lending to the Soviet Bloc and to any Third World nation deep in arrears on its debt. Third, bank dividends should be pared back or eliminated to leave the banks more capital to deal with the default loans. Fourth, the enormous and no longer necessary overhead of the Big Banks—the salaries, bonuses, country-club memberships, travel expenses, foreign loan departments, excess officers and employees—should be eliminated, as in other enterprises going through the winnowing process that lies ahead.

In the last analysis, if there is need for a bailout of any U.S. bank, or any particular Third World country like Mexico, it should be done directly by the government of the United States, not through an institution like the I.M.F. for which we receive nothing of value in return. If certain countries allied to or supportive of the United States are *in extremis,* send the money directly, and receive in return tangible assets like naval bases, C.I.A. stations, assistance in U.S. diplomatic initiatives, ouster of Russian or Cuban diplomats or "technicians," or support at the United Nations.

US Can Handle Debtors' Defaults

The men who tell us "you have no choice," who view any default anywhere with fear and trembling, are most assuredly men with a stake in the game.

True, a debtors' cartel might default collectively and shake America to its foundations, but with a three-trillion-dollar economy, the United States of America could accept the shock and remain erect.

But, consider the predicament of our enemies if they walked away from their loans.

The Soviet Empire would be reduced to autarky, total self-reliance. No longer would the West's machinery and technology be coming East on the easiest of credit terms. Any new loans the Bloc received would reflect in the exorbitant interest rate the real risk the bank was taking in lending to an unreliable Communist regime. Should the West Europeans continue sending capital East, in the knowledge it would never return—*i.e.,* that it was disguised foreign aid, capitalist tribute to purchase "peaceful co-existence'—then it is time we recognized the symptoms of Finlandization and reset our course accordingly.

The Marxist-Leninist states and the London School of Economics models would at least be confronted with the consequences of their inherently unworkable economic and political systems. If disorder in the East Bloc followed, and upheaval in the Third World, if half the membership of that tyrants' club known as the Organization of African Unity ended up decorating lampposts from Accra to Dar es Salaam, it would not be more than many deserved.

There is a rising tide of nationalism in the United States, the visible return of a healthy spirit of patriotism, a belief again in America First, if not forsaking all others, at least *before* all others. The time is ripe not only to reject the I.M.F. as over-banker to all mankind, but to discard the husks of institutions that no longer correspond to the needs of our time or conform to the spirit of the age.

Since 1945, the United States has poured out a quarter of a trillion dollars in foreign aid. Most of it went directly, but more and more goes indirectly through the United Nations and the World Bank and such progeny as the Inter-American Development Bank and the Asian Development Bank. For what purpose? These international institutions are museum pieces, absurd antiquities like coal scuttles and chamber pots.

In ten years, for instance, the World Bank has quintupled its annual lending to more than $13 billion with India the great beneficiary. What do we have to show for it?

The myth that serves the vast foreign aid constituency is "another Marshall Plan"—the recurring hope that somewhere in the subcontinent of Asia or tropical Africa we shall one day replicate the miracle of Europe. But the preconditions for a successful Marshall Plan were peace, a democratic political system, a market economy and people who share the work ethic of the West. Free Asia alone excepted, in what region of the Third World can these be found?

Added together, American foreign aid and the West's lost loans have cost more than a trillion dollars, more than a thousand billion dollars wasted, the wealth of an empire sunk, a sum vast enough to wipe out the national debt of the United States. Gone.

It is time to stop.

"The [US] should . . . establish standards to encourage debtor countries to move toward market-oriented policies."

The US Must Encourage Freemarket Systems Abroad

Esther Wilson Hannon & Edward L. Hudgins

Esther Wilson Hannon is a policy analyst and Edward L. Hudgins is Walker Fellow in Economics, both at the conservative Heritage Foundation in Washington, DC. They believe that the only way to end the world debt crisis is to get the debtor nations into the freemarket system and away from dependence on outside capital. In the following viewpoint, excerpted from a report they wrote for the Heritage Foundation, they make several recommendations for US economic policy to encourage movement toward growth-oriented market policies.

As you read, consider the following questions:

1. Why do the authors believe the debt crisis is threatening the trend toward democracy that has been prominent in recent Latin American politics?
2. The authors list several policies they believe the US should follow in order to lead the debtor nations toward a freemarket system. What are they?

Esther Wilson Hannon and Edward L. Hudgins, "A US Strategy for Latin America's Debts," The Heritage Foundation *Backgrounder*, April 7, 1986. Reprinted with permission.

The international debt crisis began in August 1982 when Mexico failed to make interest payments on its borrowed funds. Shortly thereafter, most other Latin American countries joined Mexico teetering on the brink of default. The International Monetary Fund's (IMF) attempts to deal with the crisis have failed to get to the roots of the problem. U.S. observers periodically have heralded the end of the crisis, only to see it rear its head anew. Latin American countries owe nearly $400 billion, with Brazil's debt at $104 billion, Mexico's at $98 billion, and Argentina's at $50 billion.

The debt crisis has economic and political aspects that affect vital U.S. interests. Continuing economic stagnation in Latin America, for example, has reduced the region's purchase of U.S. goods. U.S. exports to Latin America dropped from $41.9 billion in 1981 to just $25.2 billion in 1983. The Latin American debt, moreover, poses serious problems for U.S. banks, which fear huge defaults. More generally, an economically depressed Latin America is a heavy drag on the world economy.

Threat to Democracy

The past five years have seen a dramatic spread of democracy in Latin America. After years of dictatorship, for example, Argentina, Brazil, Uruguay, and Guatemala, among others, have held free elections. Yet the economic hardships resulting from the debt crisis threaten this democratic trend. Leftists and communists, including Cuban dictator Fidel Castro, are using the debt crisis and U.S. support for IMF austerity policies to drive a wedge between Third World debtors and "imperialist" America.

The U.S., however, deserves very little direct blame for the debt problem. To be sure, many U.S. banks behaved irresponsibly in the 1970s by making vast sums of credit available to Latin American countries which were becoming ever less credit worthy. More at fault were attempts by the IMF to encourage private lending to less developed country (LDC) governments. The major blame lay with the socialist and statist economic policies of the recipient governments. These policies, as those elsewhere in the Third World, inhibit economic growth, investment, and entrepreneurism and almost ensure that loans from the West will not be used productively. . . .

The Reagan Administration should . . . establish standards to encourage debtor countries to move toward market-oriented policies. Specifically, a U.S. strategy for dealing with the Latin American debt should:

1) provide technical information, preferably through the World Bank, on how to privatize state enterprises;

2) explore the possibility of converting parts of the Latin American debt into equity shares in enterprises in debtor countries;

3) encourage more trade between the U.S. and debtor countries,

and among the debtor countries themselves, by reducing trade barriers;

4) spotlight and reward those countries that move toward market policies;

5) refuse to grant additional funds to multilateral lending agencies unless these funds are used to promote effectively market-oriented policies. . . .

Recommendations

Latin American debtor countries can help themselves economically by restructuring their economies along market principles, with sharp reductions in the size and scope of government. The U.S. can help them in a number of ways. Among them:

1) *The Administration should develop standards to determine the degree to which debtor countries are adopting market-oriented policies. . . .*

Detailed guidelines need to be developed. Such guidelines should focus on debtor countries' policies toward taxes, foreign investment, trade, state-owned enterprises, and business regulations. The advantages of the market approach, along with the disadvantages of statism, should be highlighted. Since change will be slow, special attention should be given to what constitutes acceptable progress. Initially these principles should be based on the strictest market philosophy. Application to the circumstances of each country would be made later. The more the international debate focuses on the principles of economic growth, the better for the forces of free enterprise.

Key to Prosperity

Among Third World states there are a few who've found the secret of rapid growth and high living standards. The key is capitalism.

Although it gets little play in the major press, there are free market countries in the Third World. A few adopted pro-market strategies at independence. Others turned to free enterprise when their Socialist economies collapsed. Together, these nations have posted astonishing economic gains; gains that prove that the market can produce prosperity as surely for Asians, Latins and Africans as it does for Americans.

Dan Dickinson, *Human Events,* January 21, 1984.

---

2) *The World Bank should make information on how to privatize state enterprises available to debtor countries.*

Debtor countries wishing to privatize costly state-owned enterprises face technical and political difficulties. For example, there must be guarantees that the transition not unduly disrupt essential services. Resistance from employees and customers of state enterprises, politicians, and state bureaucrats must be overcome. For example, attempts by Argentina's President Raul Alfonsin to privatize such state enterprises as the telephone company and several oil and steel companies met with resistance within his own cabinet and political party.

Techniques and strategies for privatization have been developed in the U.S. and Britain. Successful privatization efforts have yielded valuable lessons. Yet much of this information is unavailable and unknown in debtor countries. The World Bank itself has experts knowledgeable in these matters. Until now, however, their services have been underutilized. The Bank should devote substantial resources and efforts to the collection and distribution of information on privatization.

Capitalize the Debt

3) *Banks should explore the possibility of capitalizing the Latin American debt.*

A partial solution to the debt problem would involve banks forgiving loans owed by debtor countries in exchange for equity shares in state-owned, Latin American enterprises. Along these lines in Chile recently, Bankers Trust was able to convert Chilean foreign debt notes into local currency, which was then applied to the purchase of a private pension fund. Although in this case the debt was converted into private equity, it set the stage for conversions of debt into public equity. Such a solution would not only ease the debt crisis but would jibe with efforts to privatize state enterprises: portions of such companies could be set aside for debt liquidation efforts. Certain U.S. regulations would have to be changed to permit U.S. bank participation. Three-party deals also might be worked out where the banks sell portions of their Latin American loans (no doubt at less than face value, as a means of writing down these bad loans) to other private companies. Such companies would in turn forgive these debt portions in exchange for shares in the LDC state companies. Newly privatized companies with shares held by private foreign companies also would have better access to much needed capital for expansion and modernization.

Such a plan would meet with much initial resistance from all sides. Banks would be reluctant to sell loans at less than face value. Debtor countries dislike foreign ownership of equity in their domestic enterprises. But given the fact that both the debtor governments and the imprudent banks are in part responsible for the current crisis, this solution would be equitable and would not require the U.S. taxpayer to foot the bill.

4) *There should be a new emphasis on freer trade between the U.S. and the debtor countries.*

Free trade, essential for economic growth, is crucial for debtor countries. To gain the hard currency needed to pay debts as well as to invest in future growth, these countries must export. If the U.S., the major market for many debtor countries, erected protectionist barriers, these countries simply could not earn the needed funds and would default. Free trade must be a two-way street. Latin American countries must open their markets more to U.S. goods. The U.S. should offer to negotiate Free Trade Areas with any Latin American country that desires completely open markets.

A Market Solution

A solution to the debt problem requires a market system based on the idea of private property rights. . . .

If there is a return to a free economy, individuals, by pursuing their own self-interest, will direct resources to the production of those goods and services demanded by consumers. As consumer demands are satisfied, the returns to investment (profits) insure an ever expanding economy. Through this process, savings can be set aside which will service and eventually repay the debt. As government, reduced to its function of protecting life and property, is removed from the economic scene, its need and ability to borrow will be eliminated. The individuals, whom the government is required to protect, will pay for this service with some form of taxation. . . . There are only two alternatives: a free economy based on private property rights or a command economy in which the state exists at the expense of the individual. The latter leads to economic chaos and social instability. Only the former results in peace and prosperity.

Michael Adamson, *The Freeman*, December 1985.

5) *Debtor countries should attempt to promote freer trade.*
Latin American countries have harmed themselves not only by restricting the import of U.S. goods but by keeping their markets closed to one another. After World War II, Western European countries formed a common market to promote their own economic growth and freer trade with one another. The Latin countries, in contrast, have made only half-hearted efforts to liberalize trade. The U.S. should promote freer trade between the debtor countries as a major part of its debt strategy and a condition for U.S. assistance. President Febres Cordero of Ecuador is currently seeking freer trade with his fellow Andean Group countries of Bolivia, Chile, Colombia, and Peru. The U.S. should aid this effort. The U.S. should also focus attention on the Latin American Free Trade Association, which includes Argentina, Brazil, Chile, Mexico, Paraguay, Peru, Uruguay, Colombia, and Ecuador, and encourage this group to move ahead with their stated aim of trade liberalization.

6) *The good debtor nations should be pointed to as good examples.*

When debtor countries follow growth-oriented policies, the Administration should praise them publicly, noting their achievements, encouraging imitation by others, and increasing state visits and other forms of prestige boosting. If necessary, economic changes beyond the Baker Plan, such as special trade arrangements, should be made.

Currently Ecuador stands out as most deserving of such treatment. Ecuador's President Leon Febres Cordero is committed to free market principles and has sought not more handouts from banks or multinational lending agencies, but rather, direct foreign investments.

Limit Lending

7) *The Administration should not grant additional funds to the World Bank or to other multilateral development banks.*

The current debt crisis is not caused by a past lack of international lending. To the contrary, the staggering size of the debt indicates that too much was lent irresponsibly. The World Bank actually has a surplus of funds. Additional funds or loan commitments to multilateral development banks will contribute little to the resolution of the crisis and might well be counterproductive, perpetuating irresponsible lending.

The Administration should support replenishment only if the World Bank, under its new President, can carry out . . . growth-oriented policies. In the long run, if debtor countries adopt such policies and invite direct foreign investments, the World Bank itself could be privatized. Since most of the Bank funds are currently borrowed on the market, the Bank would simply take the next logical step and become a private concern.

Conclusion

Imprudent lending practices of the U.S. banks and U.S. banking laws that drove capital overseas themselves were in part responsible for the Latin American debt crisis. Yet the growing magnitude of the debt, which has reached around $400 billion, stems primarily from the statist economic policies of the debtor countries themselves. Restrictions on direct foreign investments, costly import substitution schemes, inefficient state-owned industries, high taxes, and counterproductive state regulation of the market have led to the need for massive government borrowing as well as to the waste and squandering of such borrowed funds. The only long-term solution to the debt crisis is to move the Latin American debtors away from socialist policies and toward market-oriented growth policies.

A shift away from destructive IMF-imposed austerity measures and toward the growth-oriented market policies envisioned by the Baker Plan offers some possibility for meaningful economic change. The IMF should work with the World Bank to promote such market policies. And the new World Bank President, Barber Conable, should make implementation of the Baker Plan philosophy his top priority.

The Latin American debt crisis poses a serious threat to the U.S. and the world economy. Dealing with this crisis is a formidable task. Yet the causes of the crisis are known and the market policies necessary to solve the problem are clear. The debtor countries themselves now recognize the folly of many of their socialist policies. If the Reagan Administration, the World Bank, and the IMF work with Latin American leaders to promote and implement market policies, the debt problem could be solved once and for all.

"We propose freezing the debt for ten years, that is, refusing during this period to pay either principal or interest."

The Debtor Nations Should Put a Moratorium on Repayment

Athos Fava

Athos Fava is general secretary of the Communist Party of Argentina, one of the countries most deeply in debt. In the following viewpoint, Mr. Fava writes specifically about Argentina but the views he expresses are similar to those of many people in the other debtor nations as well. Mr. Fava writes that Argentina is the victim of the greed of the United States, acted out through its control of both private and public lending institutions such as the International Monetary Fund (IMF). He believes that the only way to end the hopeless debt is to put a moratorium on repayment and to use the resulting money to advance the individual nations' economies.

As you read, consider the following questions:

1. Why does the author view the foreign debt problem as central to his country's future?
2. According to the author, how does the U.S. use much of the money the debtor nations repay?

Athos Fava, "'No!' to Imperialism's Debt Bondage," *Political Affairs*, November 1985. Reprinted with permission.

The U.S. imperialist policy of plunder directed against developing countries, Latin American ones included, is a widely known fact condemned by the overwhelming majority of the world community. The "great northern neighbor" has long treated Latin American republics as a habitual sphere of plunder and economic subversion. Their peoples, like other peoples of the Third World, not only overpay for finished products and raw materials purchased from monopolies but virtually bear the brunt of the economic crises of capitalist powers as a consequence of unequal financial relations, primarily fettering debts. Latin America's foreign debt, which is mounting at a dizzy rate, exceeds 360 billion dollars now. One of the main victims of this bondage is my country [Argentina], whose development recently entered a new stage, with the class struggle going on against the background of a revival of civilian institutions. . . .

Legalized Plunder

The dilemma confronting Argentina—freedom or dependence—can not be resolved without settling the problem of foreign debt. This problem is nothing new to us Communists. . . . It fully reveals the contradiction between the interests of U.S. imperialism and the Argentine nation, which will not ease off in spite of likely changes in both the Argentine and U.S. governments.

The foreign debt, a new way of modernizing and increasing dependence, is the chief topic of an intense political and social controversy on the continent, whose outcome is bound to have a notable impact on constitutional stability and the future of democracy.

The debt is one of the forms of neocolonial dependence aggravating all our problems. There are two prospects now: one, staying dependent and obeying the dictates of the IMF, and two, resisting userers and rescheduling payments on both principal and interest for ten years. The latter solution is the only one acceptable to the people, since it would pave the way for liberation. . . .

We need not cite many figures to show the plight of the Argentine people. Wages are not enough to meet even elementary human needs (they only cover 30 per cent of family expenditures, according to the National Institute of Statistics and Censuses). Inflation exceeds 1000 per cent annually and literally swallows the people's incomes. The demand for labor has fallen off by nearly 40 per cent. The number of industrial workers had diminished by 500,000 and over one million are unemployed or hold part time jobs.

Eight million Argentines live in poverty. In Buenos Aires alone (the richest city), 1.8 million children are underfed. Official data indicate that in 1970 poverty affected about 10 per cent of our compatriots; today their proportion is set at 30 per cent. It is certainly due to dependence that in terms of per capita income

Argentina has slipped from tenth place in the world in 1928 to fiftieth today. Technologically, we are lagging farther and farther behind developed countries; this is also true of agriculture, into which some innovations have been introduced.

Instrument of Imperialism

The external debt is an instrument used by imperialism in alliance with the old and new domestic oligarchy in an effort to increase and perpetuate dependence by shifting the burden of its current crisis and the insane arms race onto somebody else's shoulders. The foreign debt of Argentina, a country of 30 million people, averages 1600 dollars per inhabitant.

Over the past five years the republic has spent about 22 billion dollars on interest payments, or three times more than it owed in 1976. . . .

However, economic plunder by imperialism and its Argentine partners goes further than that. In addition to the 5.5 billion dollars exacted from us every year in interest payments, we make other payments under fraudulent deals designed to pump out money, with the result that we annually lose another 14.7 billion dollars. Plunder has made Argentina, a creditor country before 1947, one of the world's biggest debtors.

THIRD WORLD DEBT: SIZE ISN'T THE ONLY PROBLEM

A sampling of debtor nations and their ability to pay through exports

Country	Total external debt (1984)*	Annual debt payments as a percent of yearly export earnings
Brazil	$104.4	46.5%
Mexico	96.3	51.6
Argentina	47.8	95.6
Korea	43.1	20.9
Venezuela	34.9	27.7
Indonesia	32.5	18.6
India	31.8	14.3
Egypt	27.3	46.7
Philippines	25.9	48.3
Peru	13.4	51.7
Kenya	3.0	30.6

Source: Institute of International Finance   *in billions

Reprinted with permission of *The Washington Times.*

The long term plunder of national resources is made worse by high interest rates, an excessive exchange rate of the dollar and a great discrepancy between the low prices for raw materials exported by developing countries (including Argentina) and the high prices for the finished products imported by them. Here is how prices for our exports have been going down: Whereas in the 1976-1977 agricultural year we needed 156 tons of wheat to purchase one tractor in the world market, in 1984-1985 we need as much as 270 tons. As regards plant, spare parts and other imports, the terms of trade turnover have deteriorated even more strikingly.

Developing countries consider that the fundamental requisite for their progress is to establish a new international economic order (NIEO), making it possible to end an unjust state of affairs and opening a new chapter in world economic relations.

The struggle against debt bondage is inseparable from the battle for a NIEO, which the UN decided on in 1974. The main purpose of a NIEO is to safeguard national sovereignty over national resources and the economic inequality of nations and establish a system of trade favorable to developing countries in order to improve their financial position.

Paying for the Arms Race

The imperialists want to make us pay for the arms race. Their policy tells on us directly in the form of an increasing external debt. The U.S. government raises interest rates and the dollar exchange rate to obtain from other countries money needed to meet its deficit, caused by enormous military expenditures. These expenditures rose to 391 billion dollars in 1984 and are expected to stand at 597 billion dollars by late 1989. To support Washington's war preparations, the peoples of the nonsocialist world, including the working class of the United States itself, must pay as much as 1.5 billion dollars a day from their pockets.

The foreign debt of our republic offers U.S. finance capital powerful levers for influencing either directly or through the IMF, the long-term orientation of the economic policy of our state, primarily in respect of industries from which the USA can derive huge profits, as it now does from the oil industry, the service sector and finance. The fact that most credits are short term (half of them fell or will fall due between 1984 and 1986) and that they can not be repaid compels Argentina to renegotiate its debt time and again and makes the country still more dependent.

No country tied to the IMF by treaties may alter parity of its currency without the consent of the IMF (or, in other words, without U.S. approval). Argentina, which joined the IMF after the 1955 coup, is likewise denied the right to make sovereign decisions on its currency. It follows that ever since it came into existence, the IMF has been an instrument of capitalist, primarily U.S., expansion (this is particularly true today).

236

The IMF makes the signing of a treaty with any country conditional on lowering wages, increasing unemployment, expanding exports to the detriment of domestic consumption, devaluing the national currency, abolishing protectionist measures, restricting the public sector, reprivatizing industries and cutting expenditures for social needs, that is, investing less in public works, education, health services, and so on.

System of Traps

The technique of granting loans is a refined system of consecutive traps. First a country finds itself unable to pay its debt and so is granted an "interim credit," which adds to the debt; thereupon the debtor is offered new and increasingly harsh terms of granting loans needed to pay interest. The result is an endless period of debt bondage, inflation and mounting privations for the people. An important spring of this mechanism is the policy of inadequate adjustment of wages, intended to prevent them from keeping pace with inflation.

Exploitation Calls for Moratorium

In the long run, Latin America virtually finances the U.S. federal deficit, because about half of the sums paid in interest goes to the U.S. Treasury, the president of Brazil's National Association of Investment Banks said recently. "We are willy-nilly taxpayers of the Reagan Administration," he added.

The debt bondage of the Latin American countries is a result of their inequitable economic and commercial ties with the United States that have developed over the decades, and of Washington's predatory imperialist policy in the region. . . .

The extremely high interest rates have led to the enormous growth of Latin America's foreign debt, with about 85 per cent of it created by short-term private bank credits which have, in recent years, been granted mainly for the repayment of foreign debts.

Pyotr Nikolayev, *New Times*, June 1984.

It is typical of the current stage in the development of imperialism that capital is exported mainly by the private and not the public sector, investments going above all into finance and not the production sphere. This also applies to Argentina, which borrows chiefly from private banks generally engaged in speculation. In the 1977-1982 period, the debt grew more than 90 per cent, mainly as a consequence of purely financial transactions involving no purchases of machinery or other products.

About 70 per cent of the debt is owed by the public sector; moreover, the money has been lent on the security of state enterprises. The rest, or 30 per cent, is owed by the private sector and the state is going to pay it, using the device of underwriting exchange rate losses. This mechanism of plunder and this method of granting credits may be described as the principal factor for debt growth. Today mortgages shackling our country add up to 48.42 billion dollars. This debt is close to 70 per cent of the value of the gross national product and is all the more dramatic because in 1975 it equalled only 10 per cent of the GNP.

A considerable part of the debt owed by the private sector is a result of fictitious loans taken by enterprises and individuals; they remit their funds abroad (mainly to the USA and Western Europe), only to bring them back in the form of loans allegedly granted by foreign banks. After doing shady business on the home market, speculators export the same funds without declaring this to be in payment of the debt. In this way 9.524 billion dollars was exported before 1982; the Central Bank of the Argentine Republic recorded them as "flight of unaccounted capital."

Furthermore, in the 1967-1983 period, our economy lost about 30 billion dollars, which was spent on purchasing property in Canada, Spain, the USA, Brazil, Uruguay and Paraguay or was deposited in U.S. and European banks. The Argentine economy virtually found itself bled white.

Debtors as Creditors

The reason why domestic supporters of the IMF insist so strongly on repaying the debt is they are also creditors, for they export capital and then lend it to our country on guarantee. In other words, they grant "themselves" loans which become part of the foreign debt.

As a means of paying the debt, they propose selling public enterprises and ceding control of oil (whose reserves are nonrenewable), and ultimately declare for a complete sellout of the country to ensure that the upper section of Argentine society is paid interest abroad, along with imperialist monopolies and big banks.

The main lines of economic development for the 1985-1989 period, worked out by the present Minister of the Economy, provide for payments on the debt as a purely technical matter. This approach may have fatal consequences, since five years from now interest payments on loans will amount to 23.5 billion dollars, plus another 6 billion dollars in the form of dividends and license payments. In other words, the nation will lose 29.5 billion dollars. Yet part of this amount, or 25 billion dollars, would be enough to pay wages in both the public and private sectors for over a year. It would be enough to raise real wages by 20 per cent in the next five years. As for the rest, or 4.5 billion dollars, it could solve the housing problem of 750,000 poor families. Should the official plan materialize, this would compel the country to solicit in five years' time a further loan amounting to 5.6 billion dollars. As a result, Argentina's debt would exceed 50 billion dollars.

Noted economists and officials of Argentina have submitted proposals for ways of effectively opposing IMF claims. The demand for a moratorium is gaining ground among the progressive forces of the country, which must either go on taking its cue from the IMF and so increase dependence, or desist from the current practice.

© Kemchs/Rothco

The point at issue is whether our people are to work for themselves or for the U.S. monopolies and the domestic oligarchy. A struggle is under way over who is to foot the bill of the crisis, whether we, as has been the case so far, or they. This is why we Communists say that the implementation of unfair agreements with the IMF must be blocked and that all debtors must come out jointly against paying the shackling debt and, first of all, demand an *immediate moratorium*. We proceed from the fact that all the terms of refinancing through a standby or "interim credit" now under a discussion are mere varieties of the IMF dictate. We therefore propose *freezing the debt for ten years, that is, refusing during this period to pay either principal or interest, and spending the funds released on advancing the national economy, raising wages, creating jobs and meeting social needs.*

The "recommendations" of the IMF are certain to disrupt the nation's economic life. To follow them is tantamount to unconditionally accepting the dire legacy of the dictatorship and clearing the decks for another "strong government," another coup aimed at "restoring order" after deliberately creating a state of chaos.

The fact is that Argentina's technological lag, which would increase as a result of applying IMF recipes, would aggravate the socioeconomic situation to the utmost.

Should our country continue paying interest, it would be left with less money for internal investment, real incomes would decline, the exchange rate of the dollar and interest rates would go on climbing, with inflation as a consequence, the tax burden put on the people would become heavier and unemployment would grow. The home market would shrink still more and this, in turn, would hamper production while monopoly concentration would assume greater proportions due to the failure and closure of numerous small and medium enterprises.

The pursuit of an IMF-imposed "policy of adjustment" would lead to the sale of all or some of the paying public enterprises, the steady growth of tariffs and public service charges, a reduction of internal credits and the abolition of state regulation and controls vis-a-vis the subsidiaries of transnationals and powerful domestic groups in the interest of "free enterprise and a free market."

Realistic Solution

Prompted by the widespread opinion that Argentina can not repay its foreign debt, we propose a realistic solution. An unrealistic thing to do would be to stay tied to the ominous system under which we must pay interest on interest, draining the country of its lifeblood and incurring an ever steeper growth of the debt.

Contrary to our adversaries' most pessimistic forecasts, a moratorium on the debt of the Third World would not cause a worldwide financial and economic collapse. While the debt is staggering, it falls short of even ten per cent of the value of the annual GNP of industrial capitalist countries. The loss of this sum would not be irreparable for them while for us it is tantamount to ruin. The moratorium would, in particular, put world economic activity and trade on a sounder basis and help remove the effects of debt accumulation, which generally express themselves in decreasing consumption, growing inflation and unemployment and a reduction of investment. . . .

The debt is a problem that does not concern Argentina alone, but the whole continent. It is an economic and political issue and is becoming a revolutionary issue in step with developments, as Fidel Castro has said. The struggle to settle it is one of the major tasks facing the peoples of Latin America today. It will undoubtedly be backed by the broadest sections of society; it will contribute to continental unity, which José de San Martin and Simon Bolivar dreamed of, and will be part of the common battle of developing countries for their definitive independence, for the establishment of more equitable economic relations in the world.

"It's time for some initiative on the debt question."

The US Should Encourage Innovative Methods of Repayment

Robert Wesson and Jon Basil Utley

Robert Wesson, author of Part I of the following viewpoint, is a senior research fellow at the Hoover Institution at Stanford University and the author of *Politics, Policies, and Economic Development in Latin America.* Jon Basil Utley, author of Part II, is associate editor of *The Times of the Americas* and a former correspondent in South America for *The Journal of Commerce.* In the following viewpoint, the authors state that there are a large number of possible and partial solutions to the world debt crisis that, with a little imagination, could prove successful.

As you read, consider the following questions:

1. List several of the debt solutions suggested by each author. Which ones seem like they would have a real impact on the debt crisis?
2. Review the more drastic solutions suggested by the other authors in this chapter. If you had to make a recommendation about American policy to the US President, what kind of program would you suggest to alleviate the world debt crisis?

Robert Wesson, "Imagination Can Ease World Debt Crisis," *Los Angeles Times,* August 8, 1985. Reprinted with the author's permission.

Jon Basil Utley, "How to Ease International Banking Crisis," *Human Events,* August 18, 1984. Reprinted with permission.

Seldom, if ever, has economic catastrophe been so starkly visible on the horizon as the problem of the Latin American and African debt, which is obviously far beyond the capacities of the debtor countries. The international financial community stubbornly resists recognizing this fact, taking any patch of clear sky as reason to hope that the storm is receding, because acknowledging reality—classifying non-performing loans as non-performing, and writing off loans to major borrowers—would be disastrous.

It is not necessary, however, to choose between pretense and fatalism. Imagination may suggest many alternatives. One put forward has been a reduction of interest rates, amounting in effect to a partial write-off. Another has been applied by the Soviets, who take Peruvian manufactures in lieu of cash, with the result that Peru is paying something on its debt to the Soviet Union and nothing on its debt to Western creditors. It is, of course, much easier for the Soviets to do this, because they have ample demand at home and have no need to worry about disruptions of markets. However, with some ingenuity, banks should be able to devise means of getting something out of a quantity of Peruvian textiles, perhaps by exchange deals or sales non-competitive with U.S. producers. At the same time, the Peruvian economy would be stimulated rather than deprived. Generally speaking debtor countries would be far more prepared to furnish goods than money.

Debt Payments to Investment Funds

It has been suggested that part of the debt obligations be taken in shares of state enterprises of debtor nations. This is hardly practical, because politicians cannot propose turning over major parts of the economy to foreign capitalists (anyway, most state enterprises produce losses). It would be acceptable to most nationalists, however, for debt payments to be made into a fund managed by a consortium of banks or an international agency to make new investments in the debtor country. This would give the banks equity, and conceivably could be profitable in the long term. It would have the enormous advantage of activating instead of depressing debtor economies—the usual effect of the conditions that the International Monetary Fund tries to impose.

Another approach stimulatory to debtor economies would be to give some credit against debt charges for imports of goods from other debtor countries. One of the ill effects of the debt burden is that debtors are pressed to reduce imports; Brazil thus cuts down purchases from Argentina, and vice versa, with bad effects for both. To the contrary, Brazil should be encouraged to buy from Argentina, and so forth, thus helping both economies and making funds available for Argentina to apply to debt service. Or perhaps Argentina could use the sum to make purchases in Peru.

Each exchange would help the economies of countries on both sides.

A further possibility would be to permit the debtor countries to redirect portions of their payments to internal economic improvements, such as covering costs of privatization of inefficient state enterprises, or reducing taxes on exports. It is much preferable to facilitate or reward actions that will ultimately strengthen production and increase the capacity to pay, rather than trying to prescribe policies that are inevitably unpopular.

If they undertake to do so, intelligent professionals of creditor institutions could doubtless devise other schemes for getting something from the debtor countries in ways that do not compress but,

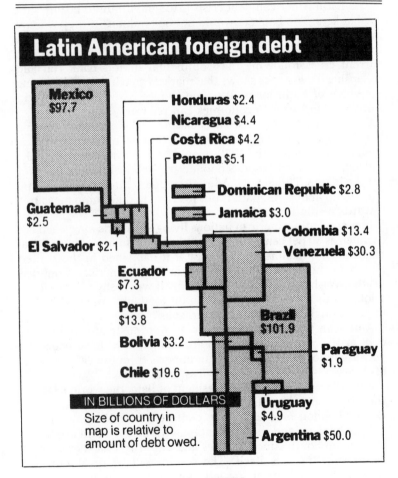

Horn in The Christian Science Monitor © 1986 TCSPS.

preferably, expand their productive capacities.

When investors go into communist countries lacking foreign exchange (or unwilling to expend it unless absolutely necessary), they apply much ingenuity to finding ways to compensate themselves, such as sharing in the output of the enterprise that they finance, taking local currency to procure goods for export, or making triangular swaps. The case of creditors wanting a return on their loans to overburdened Third World countries is really not very different, and it should be approached in the same spirit—not of insisting on the impossible but making the best of a very difficult situation.

II

The Latin American debt crisis is too important to be left with the bankers. The bankers would not be "human" if they weren't more concerned about their pensions and not being blamed for the current mess than they are with the nation's interests. The current crisis following the Continental Illinois bank run and collapsing bank stocks shows that markets are already discounting the value of Latin loans. It's time to face realities so the Latin American and world economies can recover.

Conservatives can't just sit back and complain about the big banks and even wish them ill. An international monetary collapse such as happened in the 1930s would be a disaster for everybody. Indeed, "capitalism" (and economic and political freedom) would get the blame. The Reagan Administration so far has shown little leadership about the matter, but it's time to take some measures towards a solution.

In many Latin American nations living standards have been cut as much as 50 per cent. They are on the brink. Imagine the political chaos such a decline would cause if it happened in the United States. As the Brazilian delegate of the Latin American Congress visiting Washington last May warned, "It will cost you Americans a lot less to lower interest rates a bit for Latin Americans than to pay to fight against new Nicaraguas."

American jobs and industry are also seriously affected by the debt crisis. Some 700,000 jobs are estimated to have been lost because of lower Latin American imports from the U.S. and tens of thousands more because of less Latin tourism.

John Wleugel, senior vice president of Bata, the world's largest shoe company, described the situation at a recent *International Reports*/London *Financial Times* conference in Washington:

"U.S. bankers and the International Monetary Fund are trying to force on South America taxes and austerity that they'd never dare try in the U.S. itself. The results will be revolution and extreme nationalism of the left or right, and the overthrow of democratic governments. Worse things can happen than debt default, and then the debts would be repudiated anyway, especially if there is a totalitarian takeover." (Cuba repudiated all its debts to U.S. banks *and* seized all Americans' properties when the Communists took over.)

Fortune magazine last November criticized the IMF for pushing upon debtors policies of "slashing imports and boosting exports similar to the prescription of beggar-thy-neighbor policies that destroyed world trade in the 1930s." It is time for supply-siders to propose possible solutions to the Latin debt crisis, not just to complain about the IMF and more of the same old tired statist solutions.

Many Possible Solutions

There are many possible solutions which can be taken up without waiting for default or a world economic crisis. All cost something, but they are manageable.

First, Washington (the banking authorities) needs to change banking regulations to allow banks to write off over a period of years any concessions made to Latin American borrowers. The big fear for the banks is having to write off billions in just one year, an action which would wipe out most of their equity capital. Such a write-off would be disastrous for Americans, too, because it would severely restrict the banks' ability to fund new loans to anybody.

Creative Solution Needed

Third world debt is simply unpayable as structured. We cannot continue to ask debtor countries to ruin their economies by putting all their dollars into debt repayment. But we also cannot pass the full burden back to the banks, thereby risking widespread financial instability. Nor, in this era of $200 billion budget deficits, can we expect the United States Government to foot the bill.

What is needed is a creative solution under which the burden is shared among debtors, banks and governments.

Charles E. Schumer, *The New York Times*, March 10, 1986.

Various proposals have been put forth. Most would involve a U.S. government role. One currently being seriously considered in Washington would have the U.S. government take over the debts from the U.S. banks, paying 70 cents on the dollar for the face value of the loans. In return, the U.S. banks would receive 8 per cent non-negotiable Treasury bonds. Then the Latin nations would be able to pay off their debts over 30 years at a fixed 8 per cent rate.

The U.S. banks would be allowed to write off their 30 per cent loss over a period of years for tax and reserve purposes, thereby not infringing upon their liquidity. The plan originates from the procedures used in the 1920s to write down European post-World War I debts owed to the U.S.

Other proposals suggested by Latin Americans, international traders and bankers follow:

• Restructuring all debt service payments to limit them to not more than 20 or 25 per cent of a nation's export earnings, a number equal to the region's average debt service costs during the last decades. Such a solution, it is argued, would give both debtors and creditors a mutual interest in the debtors' economic growth. Bankers might even start recommending "supply-side" reforms and stop financing state socialism in the Third World.

• A two-year moratorium on all debts and interest payments, and then some form of restructuring. Such a program would involve some sort of forced allocation to share losses.

• Converting all debts to a 15-year term with a few years' grace period initially, and lower "capped" interest rates, adding any excess to the principal amounts of debts.

• Increasing the resources of the International Monetary Fund and the World Bank to provide new funding to help bail out the banks. This, however, would not provide more than a temporary and costly (for taxpayers) solution if past evidence is any guide.

• Simply cutting the face value of all loans by, say, 30 per cent.

More original solutions include the following:

• Trading parts of bank debt for equity in Latin America's giant state-run industries such as steel, cement, airlines, electricity, oil, etc. Most of them are money-losing monstrosities sucking the life-blood of their respective nations. Several governments might be happy to give up an equity interest to foreign banks which might then be used as an excuse to control corruption, gain efficiency, and cut their subsidies.

• Payment to the banks in part with local currency into blocked accounts. The banks could then sell money from the accounts at some discount, perhaps 20 or 30 per cent, to importers of a host nation's non-traditional exports or to investors who might then invest in new industries in the host nations.

• Simple default of outstanding loans, followed by the debtor governments using current export earnings for repayment of new trade credits and new (post-default) loans. The Federal Reserve or Federal Deposit Insurance Corp. might then accept the Latin paper from banks in trouble, at some discounted value. This would, however, be the costliest solution for everyone, involving tremendous losses for U.S. banks and massive lawsuits and trade disruption with Latin America.

Costs of Solutions

All the solutions cost something, but the banks too bear plenty of responsibility for their poor management and for what they helped inflict upon their debtors. All are better than the alternative of default and reprisals, spreading trade warfare, new Communist revolutions and possible world depression.

It's time for some initiative on the debt question for both the short and long run. "Otherwise," in the words of Manuel Ulloa, Peru's former finance minister, "there may not be a long run," even until November.

There are solutions around, but they better start being looked at or the problem will solve itself with far more misery for all Americans in both hemispheres.

On the positive side, an orderly restructuring of the Latin American debt crisis would also remove a major uncertainty from the stock and bond markets. They could respond in an explosive way to any reasonable debt solution which allowed the Latin economies to recover.

Evaluating Sources of Information

A critical thinker must always question sources of information. Historians, for example, usually distinguish between *primary sources (eyewitness accounts)* and *secondary sources (writings or statements based on primary or eyewitness accounts or on other secondary sources)*. A diary kept by a spy is an example of a primary account. An article by a journalist based on that diary is a secondary source.

In order to read and think critically, one must be able to recognize primary sources. However, this is not enough. Eyewitness accounts do not always provide accurate descriptions. Historians may find ten different eyewitness accounts of an event and all the accounts might interpret the event differently. The historians must then decide which of these accounts provide the most objective and accurate interpretations.

Test your skill in evaluating sources of information by completing the following exercise. Pretend that your teacher tells you to write a research report about foreign debts. You decide to include an equal number of primary and secondary sources. Listed below are a number of sources which may be useful in your research. Carefully evaluate each of them. Then, *place a P next to those descriptions you believe are primary sources.* Second, *rank the primary sources* assigning the number (1) to what appears to be the most objective and accurate primary source, the number (2) to the next most objective, and so on until the ranking is finished. *Repeat the entire procedure, this time placing an S next to those descriptions you feel would serve as secondary sources and then ranking them.*

If you are doing this activity as a member of a class or group, discuss and compare your evaluation with other members of the group. If you are reading this book alone, you may want to ask others if they agree with your evaluation. You will probably discover that others will come to different conclusions than you. Listening to their reasons may give you valuable insights in evaluating sources of information.

P = primary
S = secondary

1. an editorial by the president of a US lending bank encouraging other US banks to stop lending to Third World governments

2. a letter requesting postponement of loan payments, from the president of Argentina to a lending bank in the US

3. a *New York Times* article reporting on the terms of a new US loan to Zaire

4. a novel about a poverty-stricken family in Guatemala that struggles to survive in an economy racked by foreign creditors and war

5. film footage of a demonstration and strike by Brazilian workers that resulted in the Brazilian government cutting its interest payments to US banks

6. transcript of a speech by the president of Peru explaining why he limited debt repayments to 10 percent of his country's export earnings

7. an article by the general secretary of the Communist Party USA titled "New Tentacles of Financial Imperialism"

8. an editorial in a Philippine newspaper complaining about the impossible payments required by European and US banks

9. an article in *The Wall Street Journal* about the International Monetary Fund's warnings to Third World debtor nations to pay back their loans

10. statistics showing the balance-of-payment accounts of 23 debtor nations from 1980 to 1985

11. a report issued by the Nigerian government detailing the results of its investigation into how much money corrupt politicians were transferring abroad at the height of the 1978 oil boom

12. an editorial in an Argentine newspaper titled "A Gang of Bullies: the US as Enforcer for the World's Creditors"

13. an article in *Time* magazine explaining which nations of the world owe the US, how much interest each one has paid, and how much of its loan each nation has outstanding

Periodical Bibliography

The following list of periodical articles deals with the subject matter of this chapter.

The American Legion	"Should the U.S. Increase Its Contribution to the International Monetary Fund?" January 1984.
Tom Bethell	"The Return of the Debt Crisis," *National Review,* August 23, 1985.
Commonweal	"Third-World Debtors' Prison," July 13, 1984.
Andy Feeney	"Sacrificing the Earth," *Environmental Action,* November/December 1985.
S.C. Gwynn	"Adventures in the Loan Trade," *Harper's,* September 1983.
James S. Henry	"Where the Money Went," *The New Republic,* April 14, 1986.
Mark Hulbert	"Will the U.S. Bail Out the Bankers?" *The Nation,* October 16, 1982.
Stephen Koepp	"Baker Steers a New Course," *Time,* October 21, 1985.
Stephen Koepp	"The Gathering Storm," *Time,* July 2, 1984.
Penny Lernoux	"Tio Sam's Big Financial Stick," *The Nation,* March 22, 1986.
Stephen Schwartzman	"Banking on Disaster," *Multinational Monitor,* June 15, 1985.
Sara Sleight	"Latin America's Debt," *Report on the Americas,* July/August 1984.
Kenneth S. Smith	"World Bank, IMF—Do They Help or Hurt Third World?" *U.S. News & World Report,* April 29, 1985.
J. Antonio Villamil	"Is Latin America Headed for Another Debt Crisis?" *USA Today,* January 1986.

Glossary of Terms

balance of payments the ratio between a country's income (from exports, loans, etc.) and its outflow of payments (imports, debt repayment, etc.)

base currency the currency (money) on which a country's money standard is based; e.g., in the United States, the present base currency is the dollar

central bank the bank—sometimes part of the government, sometimes a private bank—used by the government to issue money, determine the value of the country's money, and regulate the amount of money in circulation

COLA cost of living allowance; used for **social security** and other social programs as a way to determine how much money recipients need to live

Cost-of-Living Index the Consumer Price Index prepared by the US Bureau of Labor Statistics; the Index measures changes in the cost of living month by month, year by year

currency used by consumers (e.g., paper money) to buy and sell goods and services, reflecting the value of those products

deficit the amount by which the money spent by a company or country exceeds its income

demand-side economics economic theory stressing the demand side of the **supply-and-demand** equation based on the idea that an increased demand for goods creates markets and the need to supply those markets; according to demand-side theorists, taxing and redistributing big corporate profits and maintaining wage protections enables a much larger segment of the population to buy goods, thereby stimulating growth on both sides of the equation

"the Fed" Federal Reserve Banking system; the central bank of the United States; the Fed sets interest rates and regulates the money supply

fiscal policy actions taken by the Federal government to stabilize the economy by increasing or decreasing Federal spending, increasing or decreasing taxes, and increasing or decreasing the deficit or surplus in the Federal budget

flat rate tax a tax system in which all persons are taxed the same percentage regardless of earnings

GATT General Agreement on Tariffs and Trade; established as an agency of the UN in 1948, its members are pledged to work together to reduce tariffs and other barriers to international trade and to eliminate discriminatory treatment in international commerce

GDP Gross Domestic Product; the value of all goods and services produced within a country over a given period regardless of who owns the production facilities

GNP Gross National Product; the value of all goods and services produced by an economy over a given period (usually a year); the production facilities must be owned by residents of the nation

gold standard basing a country's money system on the value of gold; i.e., using gold itself as money or using paper money or some other substitute that would be based on the value and amount of gold that is held in reserve by the country; the paper money could be exchanged for gold

inflated dollar when the dollar is overvalued in the world market US investors can buy more foreign goods with the dollar than they can US goods; this means an influx of more dollars abroad, and more goods in the domestic economy; related to the *strong dollar*, which again means the dollar's purchasing power is valued too highly; too many dollars abroad could bring about a *devaluation* of the dollar, producing **inflation** at home and a **trade deficit** in the world economy

inflation a relatively large increase in the price level of goods and services, usually caused by a shrinking supply of goods or an increase in the amount of currency beyond the needs of trade; usually steep inflation like that of pre-WWII Germany (2500% in one month) leaves money virtually worthless and can lead to economic collapse

IMF International Monetary Fund; a specialized consulting agency of the United Nations which encourages international monetary cooperation, facilitates balanced growth of international trade, assists member countries in correcting **balance of payment** deficits, and promotes foreign exchange stability

Keynesian economics named after its major proponent, John Maynerd Keynes, this approach called for limited government interference in an essentially capitalist system to insure a healthy economy (high employment, low **inflation**)

LDC less developed country; has relatively poor transportation and communication systems and relies on other countries for refined goods (i.e., technology)

macroeconomics the part of economics concerned with the operation of a nation's economy as a whole

markets particular goods and services are exchanged at a price, with the traders free to swap or not swap what they have for what they want

MDB Multilateral Development Bank; a bank contributed to by a number of different countries which loans and grants money to member countries to aid in their development; the **World Bank** is one example

microeconomics the part of economics concerned with specific sectors of the economy

monopoly complete control of a product by one seller or producer

national debt the total amount of money a country owes other countries and private investors

OECD Organization for Economic Cooperation and Development; a primarily European organization whose goals are to promote the economic and social welfare of its members and to coordinate and stimulate member assistance to developing countries

PIK payment-in-kind; a federal program designed to pay farmers for not producing as much as they normally do but still allow them the same profit; designed to reduce surplus and keep prices at reasonable levels; for example, grain farmers are given government stocks of grain (which they may then sell) in exchange for leaving part of their land fallow

political action the expenditure of substantial amounts of effort and money by unions, businesses, and organizations to promote their political causes; their rationale is that what is gained at the bargaining table can be taken away through legislation

private goods and public goods private goods (food, autos, cigarettes) are paid for directly by the buyer and are sold for profits; the cost of public goods (highways, public beaches) is shared by the taxpayers and the "profits" (good roads, access to the ocean) are more intangible

private sector that part of the economy made up of privately-owned businesses

privatization having the private sector do things currently done by government; e.g., some cities have eliminated city garbage pickup, turning over that service to private companies

progressive tax a tax system in which those who make more money pay a higher percentage of their earnings than those who make less

protectionism policies designed to protect a country's industries from foreign competition; might include import tariffs or quotas, **subsidies** for domestic products, and other kinds of support for domestic industries

public sector the government; that part of the economy made up of federal and other organizations which are the shared responsibility of the public

real wages wages expressed in terms of what today's dollar will buy; a common way of determining buying power is through the Consumer Price Index

refinancing debts new loans granted to help pay off current debts

rescheduling debts changing or postponing the dates on which debt payments are due in order to create additional time to repay a debt

Smoot-Hawley Tariff Act passed by Congress in 1930, this brought tariff levels to their highest point in US history; other countries retaliated by raising their tariffs and US foreign trade declined sharply

subsidy a grant by the government to a person or company to support an enterprise deemed advantageous to the public; e.g., farm subsidies are given to farmers to enable them not to plant all their land and still make profits; this is designed to stabilize farm prices by steadying the supply of farm goods and preserve the land by resting it

supply and demand the core concepts of old-style (market) economics; supply is the quantity of a good that would be *offered* at different prices; demand is the quantity of a particular good that would be *purchased* at different prices; the law of **supply and demand** holds that the cost of goods is determined by the ratio of supply to demand

supply-side economics an economic theory claiming that a supply of goods creates demand for them and that the proper role for government is to stimulate production, or the supply side of the **supply and demand** equation; reducing tax rates and proving incentives for corporate development are two things most supply-siders suggest to achieve this

trade credits short-term loans granted to finance the purchase of specific goods

trade deficit when a country imports more goods than it exports

trickle-down an economic theory which postulates that if the wealthy are unimpeded by harsh taxes and other limiting laws, their wealth will "trickle down" to the poor through increased investment, more jobs, and a healthier economy

World Bank a worldwide banking organization that provides funds for the economic development of member nations

Organizations to Contact

The editors have compiled the following list of organizations which are concerned with the issues debated in this book. All of them have publications or information available for interested readers. The descriptions are derived from materials provided by the organizations themselves.

American Federation of Labor/Congress of Industrial Organizations (AFL/CIO)
815 16th St., NW
Washington, DC 20006
(202) 637-5000

The AFL/CIO, made up of 95 labor unions, 51 state federations, and 742 city bodies, is the largest federation of its kind. Its publications include the weekly *AFL/CIO News*.

American Federation of State, County and Municipal Employees (AFSCME)
1625 L St., NW
Washington, DC 20036
(202) 452-4800

The AFSCME is a union with more than a million members which publishes the *Leadership Newsletter* and the *Public Employee Newspaper* monthly.

Cato Institute
224 Second St., SE
Washington, DC 20003
(202) 546-0200

The Institute sponsors programs designed to assist scholars and laymen in analyzing public policy questions. It is dedicated to extending social and economic freedoms. The Institute publishes a variety of publications, including the monthly *Policy Report* and the *Cato Journal*.

Center for Corporate Public Involvement
1850 K St., NW
Washington, DC 20006
(202) 862-4047

The Center for Corporate Public Involvement encourages social responsibility in life and health insurance companies. It does this by providing assistance, providing a public accounting of insurance companies, and sponsoring health education and promotion programs. Its publications include the bimonthly *Response* and the annual *Social Report*.

Citizens for a Debt Free America
2550 S. Sunny Slope Rd.
New Berlin, WI 53151
(414) 782-1305

The Citizens for a Debt Free America, founded in 1983, are intent on eliminating the national debt through massive private contributions to the US Department of the Treasury. By doing this, it hopes to ensure hope and opportunity in the US. Its newsletter, *Silver Linings*, is published four times per year.

Citizens for a Sound Economy
122 C St., NW, Suite 700
Washington, DC 20001
(202) 638-1401

Citizens for a Sound Economy is an advocacy group dedicated to returning economic decision making to citizens. It publishes a large number of issue analyses, issue alerts, capitol comments, and news releases on many economic issues.

Committee for Economic Development
477 Madison Ave.
New York, NY 10022
(212) 688-2063

The Committee for Economic Development is a research organization made up of economic experts. Through its studies and reports, it seeks to increase employment, improve living standards, and increase opportunities for all. It provides statements on national policy, digests, discussion guides, reports, films, and filmstrips to interested parties.

Committee for a Responsible Federal Budget
220 1/2 E St., NE
Washington, DC 20002
(202) 547-4484

The Committee for a Responsible Federal Budget is a nonprofit, educational association whose membership is committed to educating the public regarding the budget process, the deficit, and other issues that have significant fiscal policy impact. Among its publications are two booklets on the deficit.

Council on Economic Priorities
84 Fifth Ave.
New York, NY 10011
(212) 420-1133

The Council on Economic Priorities gathers information on the social responsibility of corporations and disseminates it through its monthly newsletter, reports, and studies. The Council also compares different corporations' levels of responsibility. Its recent publications include a book on Hazardous Waste Management, and one called *Good Business* which carefully compares the performance of American corporations in the area of social responsibility.

Eagle Forum
Box 618
Alton, IL 62002
(618) 462-5415

Eagle Forum is a conservative organization headed by anti-feminist Phyllis Schlafly. The organization publishes a monthly newsletter.

Foundation for Economic Education (FEE)
30 S. Broadway
Irvington, NY 10533
(914) 591-7230

This organization focuses its research efforts on freemarket theory and society without government interference. FEE also maintains a speakers bureau, a library with related materials, and publishes *The Freeman* monthly.

Foundation for Rational Economics and Education (FREE)
P.O. Box 1776
Lake Jackson, TX 77566
(409) 265-3034

Made up of individuals who wish to study the Constitution, economic freedom, and personal liberty, the Foundation for Rational Economics and Education conducts seminars for high school and college students and produces a number of publications including the monthly *Freedom Report*.

The Heritage Foundation
214 Massachusetts Ave., NE
Washington, DC 20002
(202) 546-4400

The Heritage Foundation is a conservative public policy research institute. It produces a tremendous number of research and position papers on current policy issues along with publications like the *Backgrounder.*

International Institute for Economic Research
1100 Glendon Ave., Suite 844
Los Angeles, CA 90024
(203) 208-7735

The International Institute for Economic Research educates students and the general public in the area of economics. It sponsors reports on economic problems, radio and television series on issues, and the monthly publication, *Broadcast.*

Invest-in-America National Council
Architects Bldg.
117 S. 17th St., Suite 906-907
Philadelphia, PA 19103
(215) 568-7311

The Invest-in-America National Council works with teachers, students, and education-oriented organizations to increase understanding and appreciation of the American free-market system. It presents American capitalism as a very positive system and stresses people's personal opportunities in it. It sponsors institutes at universities and circulates films throughout schools.

Public Service Research Foundation
8330 Old Courthouse Rd., Suite 600
Vienna, VA 22180
(703) 790-0700

The Public Service Research Foundation is dedicated to the ongoing support of research projects and studies on the issues of public sector labor relations and unionism. The Foundation's program disseminates the results of these studies to the media, public officials, educational organizations and the general public. Its purpose is to enhance understanding and stimulate discussion on controversial events and topics in governmental labor relations. It issues a fortnightly newsletter, the *Government Union Critique,* and the academic quarterly, *Government Union Review.*

Reason Foundation
P.O. Box 40105
Santa Barbara, CA 93103
(805) 963-5993

The Reason Foundation's purpose is to provide a better understanding of the intellectual basis of a free society. It promotes individualist philosophy and freemarket principles through all its outlets. These include the publications, *Fiscal Watchdog* and *Reason Magazine.*

Rockford Institute
934 N. Main St.
Rockford, IL 61103
(815) 964-5053

The Rockford Institute is a conservative research center which studies capitalism and liberty. It publishes three periodicals, *Chronicles of Culture, The Rockford Papers,* and *Persuasion at Work.* The Institute has also published occasional papers on nuclear freeze and antinuclear activism in the United States.

Union for Radical Political Economics (URPE)
155 W. 23rd St., 12th Fl.
New York, NY 10011
(212) 691-5722

The Union for Radical Political Economics (URPE) seeks, through political economic analysis, to present a continuing critique of the capitalist system and of all forms of exploitation and oppression while helping to construct a progressive social policy and create socialist alternatives. URPE publishes a quarterly journal, *Review of Radical Political Economics,* and has published a variety of pamphlets for use in teaching and research.

United Farm Workers of America (UFW)
LaPaz
Keene, CA 93570
(805) 822-5571

The United Farm Workers is a labor organization which advocates for the rights of farmworkers and consumers. It seeks to give farm laborers pride in their work by improving working and safety conditions and wages. The UFW's monthly publication is entitled *Food and Justice.*

Bibliography of Books

American Federation of State, County, & Municipal Employees — *Passing the Bucks: The Contracting Out of Public Services.* Washington, DC: AFSCME, 1984.

Robert L. Ayres — *Banking on the Poor: The World Bank and World Poverty.* Cambridge, MA: The MIT Press, 1983.

Joseph N. Beldon et al. — *Dirt Rich, Dirt Poor.* London: Routledge and Kegan Paul, 1986.

Wendell Berry — *The Unsettling of America: Culture and Agriculture.* Washington, DC: Sierra Club Books, 1977.

Center for Popular Economics — *Economic Report of the ~~President~~ People.* Boston: South End Press, 1986.

Robert W. Crandall et al. — *Regulating the Automobile.* Washington, DC: Brookings Institution, 1986.

The Debt Crisis Network — *From Debt to Development.* Washington, DC: Institute for Policy Studies, 1986.

Martha Derthick and Paul Quirk — *The Politics of Deregulation.* Washington, DC: Brookings Institution, 1985.

Edwin Diamond et al. — *Telecommunications in Crisis: The First Amendment, Technology, and Deregulation.* Washington, DC: Cato Institute, 1983.

George W. Downs and Patrick Larkey — *The Search for Government Efficiency.* Philadelphia, PA: Temple University Press, 1986.

Robert Eisner — *How Real Is the Federal Deficit?* New York: Free Press, 1986.

Robert E. Hall and Alvin Robushka — *The Flat Tax.* Stanford, CA: Hoover Institution Press, 1985.

John D. Hanrahan — *Government by Contract.* NY: W.W. Norton & Co., 1983.

Gary Clyde Hofbauer et al. — *Trade Protection in the United States: 31 Case Studies.* Washington, DC: Institute for International Economics, 1985.

Dwight R. Lee ed. — *Taxation and the Deficit Economy.* San Francisco: Pacific Institute for Public Policy Research, 1986.

Thomas K. McCraw — *Prophets of Regulation.* Cambridge, MA: Harvard University Press, 1984.

J. Tevere MacFadyn — *Gaining Ground: The Renewal of America's Small Farms.* NY: Holt, Rinehart, Winston, 1984.

John H. Makin	*The Global Debt Crisis: America's Growing Involvement.* New York: Basic Books, 1984.
John C. Moorhouse	*Electric Power.* San Francisco: Pacific Research Institute for Public Policy, 1986.
Michael Moffitt	*The World's Money: International Banking from Bretton Woods to the Brink of Insolvency.* New York: Simon and Schuster, 1983.
Steven Morrison and Clifford Winston	*The Economic Effects of Airline Deregulation.* Washington, DC: Brookings Institution, 1986.
John J. Nance	*Blind Trust: How Deregulation Has Jeopardized Airline Safety and What You Can Do About It.* NY: William Morrow, 1986.
Maxwell Newton	*The Fed: Inside the Federal Reserve, the Secret Power Center That Controls the American Economy.* New York: Times Books, 1983.
Jay Olnek	*The Invisible Hand.* Washington, DC: Liberty Library, 1985.
Joseph Pechman	*Who Paid the Taxes, 1966-1985?* Washington, DC: Brookings Institution, 1985.
Public Agenda Foundation	*Taxes: Who Should Pay and Why?* Dayton, OH: Domestic Policy Foundation, 1985.
Paul Craig Roberts	*The Supply-Side Revolution.* Cambridge, MA: Harvard University Press, 1984.
E.S. Savas	*How to Shrink Government: Privatizing the Public Sector.* Chatham, NJ: Chatham House Publishers, Inc., 1982.
Irwin Schiff	*The Great Income Tax Hoax.* Hamden, CT: Freedom Books, 1985.
Herbert Stein	*Presidential Economics: The Making of Economic Policy from Roosevelt to Reagan and Beyond.* New York: Simon and Schuster, 1984.
Joan Kennedy Taylor	*Free Trade: The Necessary Foundation for World Peace.* Irvington-on-Hudson, NY: The Foundation for Economic Education, Inc., 1986.
Lester C. Thurow	*The Zero-Sum Society.* New York: Basic Books, Inc., 1980.
Ingolf Vogeler	*The Myth of the Family Farm: Agribusiness Dominance of U.S. Agriculture.* Boulder, CO: Westview Press, 1981.

Index

Adamson, Michael, 230
Alperovitz, Gar, 16-22
American Federation of State,
    County, and Municipal Em-
    ployees (AFSCME), 42, 45
Anderson, Mark, 130-137
Anderson, Robert G., 98
Andres, William A., 121-129
AT&T, 33, 37
Ayittey, George B.N., 211-216

Baetjer, Howard Jr., 94-99
Bartlett, Bruce, 75-79, 112-117
Bentsen, Lloyd, 155
Bergland, David, 96
Bethell, Tom, 223
Bieber, Owen, 136
Bovard, James, 191-196, 198
Browning, Edgar K., 86
Browning, Jacquelene M., 86
Buchanan, Patrick J., 217-225
budget deficit
    see deficit, federal
bureaucracy, federal
    and corruption, 27
    and privatization, 41
    and private enterprise, 18, 26,
        29
    costs of, 28
    defined, 27
    evils of, 23-29

Carter, Jimmy, 17, 63
Castro, Fidel, 209
charitable deductions, 88
    need for, 91
Conable, Barber B., 89-93
Congressional Budget Office
    (CBO)
    and privatization, 42
    on research and development
        tax credit, 114
    on trade restrictions, 125
    predictions of, 63, 68-69, 77
    study of air fares, 38
corporations
    investments of, 108-111,
        112-116
    research and development

spending of, 113-116
taxation of
    as bad, 112-116
    as good, 108-111
Crane, Philip M., 84-88

Davis, Bill, 46
debt crisis, world
    and debtor countries
        economies of, 206
        privatization in, 228-229
        reforms needed in, 211-216
    beginnings of, 227
    causes of, 218-219
    solutions to, 242
        cancel debts, 205-210
        creative payment plans,
            241-247
        encourage internal reform,
            211-216
        free-market system,
            226-232
        postpone payments,
            233-240
        stop lending, 217-225
defense spending
    as good, 63
    cuts in, 57
    need for more, 78
deficit, federal
    and farming, 173
    and Japanese economy, 61
    and Ronald Reagan, 56, 63, 66
    and tax increases, 91-92
        will not reduce, 75-79
        will reduce, 70-74
    and trade deficit, 125
    as declining, 78
    as exaggerated, 60
    as good, 58-61, 62-64
    as harmful, 54-57, 65-69
    costs of alternatives to, 63-64
    effects of, 59, 61, 63-64, 68,
        148
        are not harmful, 77
        are unknown, 71-72
    interest on, 55
deregulation
    airline, 38

banking, 38-39
harm of, 35-39
success of, 28, 30-34
telecommunications, 31, 38, 39
Dickinson, Dan, 228
Doig, Don, 187-190
dollar
falling, 66
overvaluation of, 206
rising, 79
strength of, 59-60, 124-125, 142-143, 198
and trade with Japan, 153

economic systems
freemarket
and farming, 190, 200
competition in, 128
defined, 27
in debtor countries, 230
need for, 228
private enterprise, 18, 19, 20-22, 48

farms
and trade restrictions, 126, 194
and big business, 185, 188
and the environment, 189, 194
and Third World technology, 184
crisis
as exaggerated, 177-182
as severe, 172-176, 200
solutions to, 176
government support for
harm of, 187-190
need for, 183-186
subsidies
harm of, 191-196
need for, 197-200
Faux, Jeff, 16-22
Fava, Athos, 223-240
Federal Reserve Bank, 64
actions of, 68
harm of, 79
monetary policy of, 63
federal revenue, 85, 86
federal spending
cuts in, 78

effects of deficit on, 72-73
growth of, 76
to reduce deficit, 75-79
Fischbein, Charles M., 183-186
Fowler, Mark, 30-34
Friedman, Milton, 19, 219

Gaydos, Joseph M., 138-144
government
rights of, 95
role in business
benefit of, 16-22
harm of, 23-29, 31, 195-196
trend toward greater, 17, 25
size of, 101-102
Gramm-Rudman-Hollings Act
basis for, 63
defined, 59
effects of, 64, 66, 184
Gunderson, Lee E., 25

Hall, Gus, 205-210
Hannon, Esther Wilson, 226-232
Hattori, Ichiro, 159-167
Heller, Walter, 72
Hudgins, Edward L., 226-232

Iacocca, Lee A., 54-57, 127-128
International Monetary Fund (IMF)
harm of, 225, 227, 244
practices of, 215
as exploitive, 206, 207
US domination of, 208, 236
imports
benefits of, 126
costs of, 140
effect on jobs of, 132, 140, 142-143, 147-148
need for, 122-123
quality of, 125
restriction of
case against, 145-150
case for, 138-144
see also trade, protectionism
income redistribution, 94-99, 100-106
inflation
and federal deficit, 59
and income tax, 85
causes of, 77

rate of, 79
interest rates
    affected by
        deficits, 59, 68
        tax increases, 76-77
    and farming, 173
Internal Revenue Code, 85, 90

Japan
    and trade restrictions
        as exaggerated, 159-167
        as harmful, 151-158
    and US, 18, 146, 157, 162,
        165-167
        dollar, 67
        jobs, 161
        trade, 135-136, 141
    economy of, 59, 166
        and US economy, 61
        goods in, 153
    investment of, 147
    markets of
        openness of, 160-161
        US desire for, 152
    products of
        bought by Americans, 164
        made in the US, 166
        quality of, 160
    research and development
        spending of, 113
    welfare in, 101
Johnson, Clifford M., 20

Kamber, Victor, 18
Kemp, Jack, 75-79, 92
Kennedy, Edward M., 172-176
Kirkland, Lane, 142

Laffer, Arthur B., 27
Lee, Susan, 114
Leonard, T.F., 177-182
Leviton, Sar A., 20

McEntee, Gerald W., 44-49
McIntyre, Robert S., 107-111
Marti, Eric, 145-150
Moore, Stephen, 40-43
Moorhouse, John C., 32
Morris, Charles R., 58-61

Nikolayev, Pyotr, 237

Office of Management and
    Budget (OMB)
    and deregulation, 37
    and privatization, 42
    predictions of, 68-69
    statistics from, 85
Olson, Mancur, 100-106
O'Neill, Thomas P. Jr., 102
Ortner, Robert, 60
Oswald, Rudolph A., 134

Pepper, Thomas, 165
Peterson, Peter G., 65-69
payment-in-kind (PIK), 188
poverty
    and trade restrictions, 123
    government aid for
        benefit of, 100-106
        harm of, 94-99
private sector
    and economic incentive, 41
    as less efficient than govern-
        ment, 44-49
    as more efficient than govern-
        ment, 40-43
privatization
    benefit of, 41-43
    harm of, 44-49
    in debtor countries
        need for, 228-229
The Progressive, 39, 64
protectionism, see trade

Reagan, Ronald, 149
    and farm subsidies, 193
    and the federal deficit, 56, 63,
        66
    and federal spending, 17
    policies of, 115-116
    loan, 222
    tax, 72, 109
    trade, 131, 133, 156
recession, potential for
    as imagined, 59
    as real, 68
Richman, Sheldon L., 125
Roche, George, 23-29
Rothbard, Murray N., 77

Schumer, Charles E., 245
Social Security
    need for, 63-64

Stein, Herbert, 70-74
subsidies, farm, *see* farm,
  subsidies
supply-side economice
  deficits in, 62, 66
  failure of, 74, 108-111

tariffs
  defined, 122
  harm of, 148
  need for, 144
taxation
  flat rate
    fairness of, 84-88
    unfairness of, 89-93
  incentives
    for research and develop-
      ment spending, 113-114
    unfairness of, 108-111
  increase in
    and politicians, 72
    as bad, 57, 73, 75-79
    as good, 56-57, 64, 70-74
  loopholes in
    harm of, 105-106, 111
  obligation to pay, 94-99
  of corporations
    less needed, 112-116
    more needed, 107-111
  of the wealthy
    fairness of, 100-106
    unfairness of, 94-99
  on gasoline
    need for, 69
    unpopularity of, 57
  personal deduction, 86
  reforms in
    and corporations, 113
    and federal deficit, 56
    predictions for, 92-93
  shelters, 87
taxpayers
  and farmers, 178, 180, 188,
    189
  as harmed by Ronald Reagan,
    43
  benefit from deregulation, 32
  burdened, 85-88
    by federal deficit, 55
    by private enterprise, 20-21
  effects of flat tax on, 90-91
Tolchin, Susan J., 35-39

trade
  and foreign debt, 242-243
  austerity programs
    harm of, 208, 210
  competition
    as bad, 139
    as good, 128
    Japanese, 152
  deficit
    and the dollar, 124-125
    and standard of living, 60
    effect on jobs of, 140, 148
    severity of
      exaggerated, 146-147
      real, 131-133, 139
  exports
    and farming, 194
    to Japan, 156
  free
    and US allies, 126, 134-135
    case against, 130-137
    case for, 121-129, 152
  Japan's restrictions on
    exaggeration of, 159-167
    harm of, 151-158
  protectionism
    against Japan, 155
    case against, 121-129, 145-
      150, 162, 166
    case for, 130-137, 138-144
    Congressional support for,
      141, 156
    costs of, 122
    effects of, 123, 136, 143,
      148, 149

US
  economy of
    and Japanese, 18, 67, 135-
      136, 141, 146, 157, 161,
      162, 165-167
    and jobs, 148
    and trade, 131
    international, 113
    competition in, 116, 128
    complexity of, 77
    decline of, 134
    deficits in
      harm, 65-69
      stimulate, 62-64
    effects of redistribution on,
      105

263

growth of, 128-129
health of, 59, 60, 125, 147,
   165
lending policies of, 227, 231
   harm of, 217-225
products
   bought by Japanese, 160,
      164
   made in Japan, 162
   quality of, 153-154, 155
banks
   as unjustly blamed for
      foreign debt, 212
   corruption of, 220
   inadequacy of, 244
   nationalization of, 20
   plight of, 221-222
   traps of, 237
   unfair profits of, 207
US Chamber of Commerce, 163
Utley, Jon Basil, 241-247

The Washington Times, 195
welfare
   elimination of, 96
   fairness of, 100-106
Wesson, Robert, 241-247
Wicker, Tom, 62-64
Wilson, Pete, 151-158
World Bank, 225
   mistakes of, 231
   practices of, 215

Zimmerlein, Eleanor, 197-200